The Port of Medieval Dublin

The Port of Medieval Dublin

Archaeological Excavations at the Civic Offices,
Winetavern Street, Dublin 1993

ANDREW HALPIN

WITH CONTRIBUTIONS BY

Aidan O'Sullivan, Mary Deevy, Cliona Papazian,
Peter Coxon, Daire O'Rourke, Linzi Simpson,
David Brown and Joanna Wren

FOUR COURTS PRESS

Typeset in 10.5 pt on 14 pt AGaramond by
Carrigboy Typesetting Services, County Cork for
FOUR COURTS PRESS LTD
Fumbally Court, Fumbally Lane, Dublin 8, Ireland
e-mail: info@four-courts-press.ie
http://www.four-courts-press.ie
and in North America for
FOUR COURTS PRESS
c/o ISBS, 5824 N.E. Hassalo Street, Portland, OR 97213.

ISBN 1–85182–584–3 hbk
1–85182–585–1 pbk

SPECIAL ACKNOWLEDGMENT

Dublin Corporation
Bardas Átha Cliath

This publication has received support from Dublin Corporation

Printed in Ireland
by ßetaprint, Dublin

Foreword

John Fitzgerald
Dublin City Manager

In 1993, due to the proposed building of a new carpark for the Civic Offices at Wood Quay, Dublin, it was necessary to undertake an archaeological excavation of the site. Dublin Corporation's then archaeologist, Dr Andrew Halpin, undertook this work.

The archaeological excavations on the site of the Civic Offices carpark revealed evidence of 13th century waterfront activity. It also confirmed the status of Winetavern Street as a major bustling routeway in the 12th and 13th centuries. Daily life was represented by the abundance of locally made pottery, as well as foreign imports of English, French and German origin. The numerous leather finds, wooden artefacts etc. unearthed during the excavations have provided more valuable information on life in Dublin in the medieval period.

One of the most exciting aspects of the excavations for Dublin Corporation was the location of the foundations of a large stone structure on the site. This is thought to be the Tholsel or Guildhall for the medieval town of Dublin. Historical evidence points to the Tholsel as being located in this approximate area. Thus, continuity of place sees the location of Dublin's Civic Authority on the same site. It is fitting that Dublin Corporation is associated with this publication in the same year as we have completed major restoration works to the City Hall, the probable successor to the Tholsel.

Today, Dublin Corporation is the largest Local Authority in the country, employing over 6,000 people and overseeing a wide range of services from its role as Planning Authority to its functions with development, traffic control, sanitary services, roads etc. ... In many of these areas archaeology has an important role to play. We are committed to the protection, research and publication of Dublin's archaeological heritage.

Once again, we are delighted to be associated with the publication of vital work on the archaeological heritage of the city

Contents

Abbreviations

Arch. J.	Archaeological Journal
B.A.R.	British Archaeological Reports
Bot. Jnl. Scotland	Botanical Journal of Scotland
J.C.H.A.S.	Journal of the Cork Historical and Archaeological Society
J.R.S.A.I.	Journal of the Royal Society of Antiquaries of Ireland
Med. Arch.	Medieval Archaeology
P.R.I.A.	Proceedings of the Royal Irish Academy
Rep. Dep. Keeper Pub. Rec. Ireland	Report of the Deputy Keeper of Public Records of Ireland
Trans. Bristol & Gloucs Arch. Soc.	Transactions of the Bristol and Gloucestershire Archaeological Society.

List of figures, illustrations and plates

FIGURES

ILLUSTRATIONS

PLATES

Plates appear between pages 96 and 97

Acknowledgments

The archaeological excavation which is the subject of this report was commissioned and funded by Dublin Corporation, and I wish to thank Mr Derek Brady, former Assistant City Manager, for invaluable assistance at all stages of the project. I must also thank David O'Connor, John O'Connor, Des Boyham, John Melvin and Tom Kerrigan (all of Dublin Corporation), and the staff of Pierse Contracting Services Ltd, for assistance during the on-site phase of the excavation. Particular thanks are due to the archaeological excavation team of James Eogan, Maria Fitzgerald, Ciara O'Donnell, Edmund O'Donovan and especially Cia McConway who, as site supervisor, was substantially responsible for the day-to-day running of the excavation and initial preparation of the site archive.

I must also acknowledge with gratitude the work of the contributors to this report: Cliona Papazian, Dr Peter Coxon, David Brown, Daire O'Rourke, Linzi Simpson, Joanna Wren, Ivor Harkin and Georgia Rennie, who prepared the illustrations. Dr David Ball and Dr John de Courcy made helpful suggestions on fluvial mechanics. Finally, special recognition is owed to Aidan O'Sullivan who (with the assistance of Mary Deevy) made an enormous contribution both to the on-site excavation and to this report, as will be seen in the following pages. The work of the various contributors appears under their respective names. Otherwise all material is the work of the author.

ANDREW HALPIN
Dublin, July 2000

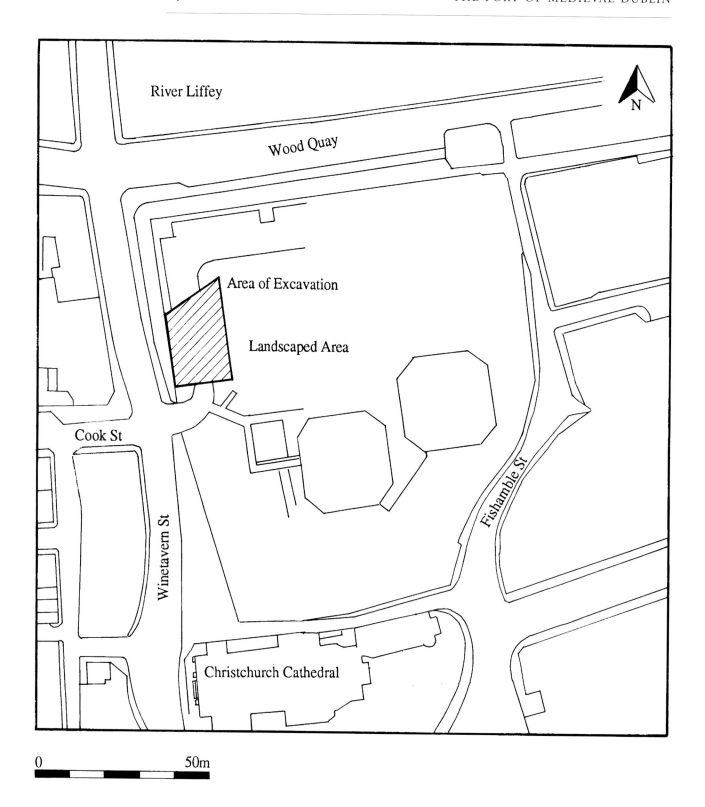

Fig. 1: Location map of site (scale 1:1000)

CHAPTER I

Introduction

In 1993 the writer conducted an archaeological excavation on part of the Civic Offices site at Winetavern St/Wood Quay, Dublin (excavation licence no. 93E 024; see Fig. 1), on behalf of Dublin Corporation. The purpose of the excavation was to record and remove undisturbed archaeological deposits in advance of the proposed second phase of construction of Civic Offices. These deposits were discovered by the writer in January 1993 in an area of the site where it was thought that all deposits had been removed during the original Civic Offices construction work of c.1973–85. This area adjoined (and partly included) the western edge of a raised landscaped area within the Civic Offices site, which was known to contain areas of undisturbed archaeology.

Archaeological background

The site lies within the area of 13th-century reclamation largely excavated by P.F. Wallace of the National Museum of Ireland (see especially Wallace 1981, 1985). Part of the area (immediately to the east of the present cutting) had previously been excavated by A.B. Ó Ríordáin, also for the National Museum of Ireland, and Mitchell (1987, 12–17) has discussed a complete cross-section running north from the city wall to the river, located in O'Riordain's cutting immediately to the east of the present excavation. The present report differs from Mitchell, however, in some aspects of interpretation of the stratigraphic sequence of features.

The area to be excavated (see Fig. 2 and Pl. I) lay north of (outside) the original city wall of c.1100 AD. It is an area of late 12th/13th century reclamation from the river Liffey, a process discussed by Wallace (1981), and it was assumed that the present site would produce a similar range of archaeological features to that uncovered further to the east by Ó Ríordáin and Wallace. The primary focus of excavation was likely to be the sequence of waterfront features erected north of the town wall between c.1200 and c.1300 AD. Wallace (1981) noted six waterfronts; of these, the three latest waterfronts, Revetments 2 and 3 and the stone quay wall of c.1300 AD, are known to have lain well to the north of the present site (that is, north of the current limit of survival of archaeological deposits) and, as expected, were not encountered in the present excavation. The waterfront immediately predating these, Revetment 1: Extension, seems to have been a localised extension in the eastern part of the site, which did not extend as far west as the present site. Thus only Wallace's two earliest waterfronts, Bank 4 and Revetment 1, were likely to be of direct concern on the present site.

Revetment 1, a large timber revetment dated c.1210 AD, clearly extended further west than the section excavated by Wallace. Ó Ríordáin exposed a similar revetment, undoubtedly the continuation of Revetment 1, c.44m north of the town wall on the western edge of the present site and it was assumed that Revetment 1 continued across the present site. Wallace felt that his earliest waterfront, Bank 4 (a post-and-wattle fence associated with a clay bank of c.1200 AD) did not

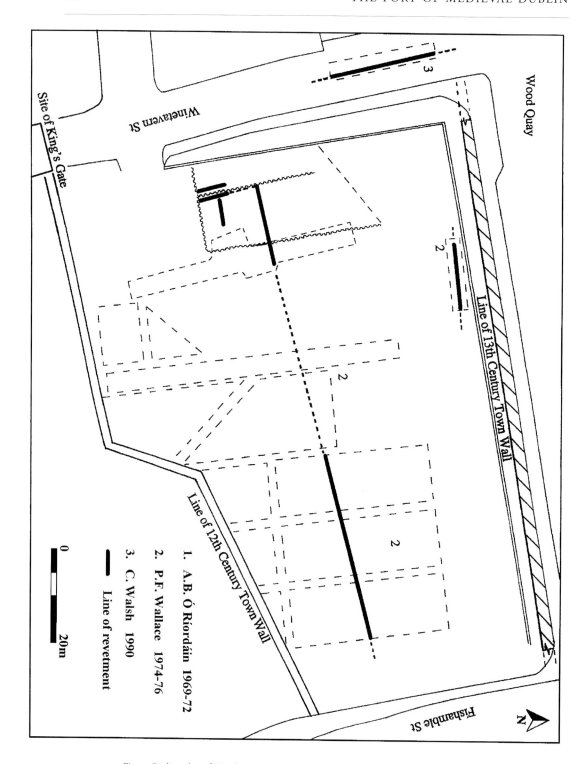

Fig. 2: Outline plan of Wood Quay area showing site in relation to previously excavated features

extend as far west as the present excavation area. Mitchell (1987, 15), however, saw a similar structure of two post-and-wattle fences with associated earthen bank in Ó Ríordáin's cutting as an extension of Wallace's Bank 4, although this was located too far south to be encountered in the present excavation.

Extent of archaeological deposits

Excavation procedure was constrained from the outset by the fact that much of the area to be excavated was occupied by the access road onto the new office construction site, an access route which had to be kept open at all times. In order to achieve this it was necessary to split the excavation area longitudinally (that is, along a north-south line) into two parts so that at any given time, one part of the site could be used as an access route while the other part was being excavated. A row of sheet piling was inserted on a line approximately 7m east of the main retaining wall on the west (Winetavern St) side of the Civic Offices site (see Fig. 2). This divided the excavation area into two parts, Area I to the west of the piles and Area II to the east. Sheet piling was also inserted around the southern and eastern edges of the excavation area (Fig. 3).

Area I, which was excavated first, proved to be by far the smaller area. A large trench, dug for the construction of the main site retaining wall in the 1970s, occupied the full width of Area I and had removed all archaeological deposits apart from a small area at the south (see Fig. 8). This area, measuring approximately 7m by 7m, was the only part of Area I which survived to be archaeologically excavated. In Area II, archaeological deposits survived across the full width of the cutting (c.12.5m), but towards the north, they had been truncated by the insertion of the access road. The depth of archaeological deposits surviving under the road decreased from a maximum of just under 2.0m (at c.6m north of the southern edge of Area II) to less than 0.2m at 23m north of the southern edge (see Fig. 4). Beyond this, no archaeological deposits survived under the line of the road.

Immediately east of the road was a raised, lanscaped area, within which archaeological deposits survived to a much higher level (up to 3.25m in total depth) and extended for up to c.36m north of the southern edge of Area II, ending abruptly at the east return of the access road (see Fig. 4 & 5). Even here, however, considerable truncation had been caused by the grading of the edges to an angle of roughly 45°. A strip of this raised area, up to c.5m in width, was included within Area II but most of this consisted of the graded western edge. Thus the archaeological deposits within Area II were severely truncated, both from south to north (by the access road) and from east to west (by the access road and the grading of the landscaped area), so that the amount of intact stratigraphy available for excavation was very small.

Scope of the report

The present Report is divided into two major sections, Part I dealing with the site's features and stratigraphy, and Part II dealing with the range of artefactual evidence recovered from the site. General conclusions are drawn together in Part III. Despite the considerable previous literature on Wood Quay, no comprehensive survey of contemporary documentary material has as yet been published; Chapter II, below, is intended as a first step toward the filling of this gap, setting the results of the excavations in their historical context. The most interesting features excavated on the site are, of course, the large timber revetment structures constructed as part of the initial reclamation. The morphology and carpentry of these structures has been discussed comprehensively by Wallace (1981, 115–16; 1982, 275–89) but in recent years new approaches to the analysis of ancient worked wood have developed. These approaches were applied, under the supervision of Aidan O'Sullivan, in the excavation and recording of all wooden structures on the site and the results are presented in Chapter IV, a study of the revetments which complements Wallace's work. The opportunity was also taken during the excavation to obtain a series of dendrochronological determinations for these

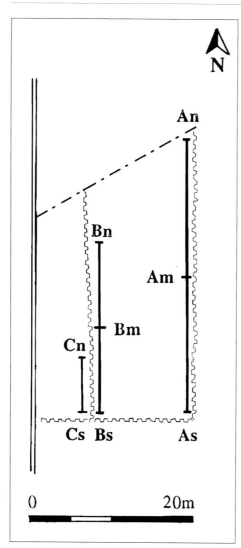

structures, the results of which are presented in Chapter V.

During the course of the excavation it became clear that an adequate interpretation of the stratigraphy of the site would demand specialist analysis of a series of layers within the overall reclamation deposit, including gravels, clays and silts with varying levels of organic inclusions. Of particular importance was the question of the origins and genesis of these layers, which at face value were open to interpretation either as of natural (riverine) or artificial genesis. Sedimentological analyses were carried out by Dr Peter Coxon on a range of samples and the results, presented in Chapter VI, enable a more definitive archaeological interpretation of the deposits concerned and ultimately, of the development of the site.

In view of the extensive prior excavation of the Wood Quay site, a rich range of artefactual and ecofactual material was anticipated. Indeed, precisely because of the extent of previous work, certain standard areas of analysis could be excluded as unnecessary duplication; the most important example is analysis of faunal remains, for which a comparable sample has been studied by Butler (1984). On the other hand, the previous excavations have produced a very large and important assemblage of medieval pottery but the very size of this assemblage has militated against comprehensive analysis. The pottery sample from the present excavation was readily manageable, probably representing less than 5% of the total Wood Quay assemblage, but large enough to be statistically meaningful. Cliona Papazian's report (Chapter VII) constitutes an invaluable analysis of a representative sample of the Wood Quay assemblage, taking account of the most recent developments in ceramic studies, both in Ireland and elsewhere.

The assemblage of medieval boat and ship timbers from the earlier Wood Quay excavations has recently been published by McGrail (1993), but these artefacts are so important and still so rare that a full study of the material recovered in the present excavation was considered essential. Aidan O'Sullivan's study (Chapter VIII) not merely provides a full record of this important new assemblage but already has made several important additions to the picture of medieval Dublin's shipbuilding traditions provided by McGrail. Another rich and important assemblage from the waterlogged levels of the site is the leather artefacts, of which a comprehensive study has been prepared by Daire O'Rourke (Chapter X). Ironically, the assemblage of more typical medieval artefacts (of metal, stone and organic materials) is, if anything, somewhat disappointing but does nevertheless make a useful contribution to filling out the picture of activity on the site, especially for the earliest post-reclamation occupation, in the later 13th century.

REFERENCES

Butler, V.G. 1984 *Cattle in thirteenth century Dublin: an osteological examination of its remains.* M.A. thesis Department of Archaeology, University College Dublin, unpublished.

McGrail, S. 1993 *Medieval boat and ship timbers from Dublin.* Medieval Dublin Excavations 1962–81, Ser. B, vol. 3. Dublin. Royal Irish Academy.

Mitchell, G.F. (ed.) 1987 *Archaeology and environment in early Dublin.* Medieval Dublin Excavations 1962–81, Ser. C, vol. 1. Dublin. Royal Irish Academy.

Wallace, P.F. 1981 Dublin's waterfront at Wood Quay, 900–1317. In G. Milne and B. Hobley (eds), *Waterfront archaeology in Britain and northern Europe*, 108–18. London. Council for British Archaeology Research Report **41**.

Wallace, P.F. 1982 Carpentry in Ireland AD 900–1300 – the Wood Quay evidence. In S. McGrail (ed.), *Woodworking techniques before AD 1500, 263–99.* Oxford. B.A.R. British Series 129.

Wallace, P.F. 1985 The archaeology of Anglo-Norman Dublin. In H.B. Clarke and A. Simms (eds), *The comparative history of urban origins in non-Roman Europe*, 379–410. Oxford. B.A.R. International Series, 255 (2).

PART I

The site

This section is concerned with the description and interpretation of the
stratigraphy, structures and other archaeological features encountered during
the excavation of the Winetavern St/Wood Quay site. For purposes of
recording during the excavation, each layer, structure or feature was given a
unique identifying number prefixed with F (for feature) – for example,
'revetment F166' or 'silt F233'. Individual elements within composite
structures were given suffixed numbers; thus 166.1, 166.2 and 166.3 were
upright posts within the revetment F166.

These numbers are retained and used in the present report as a means of
clear identification of individual features and for cross-reference between the
text and the illustrations. However, it should be clearly understood that the
numbers are of no archaeological significance in themselves, and were
assigned more or less randomly. Thus no importance should be attached,
either to the numbers themselves or to the order in which they appear.

CHAPTER II

Historical background

Linzi Simpson

The excavation site at Winetavern St/Wood Quay is in an important location between two phases of the mural defences of Dublin (see Fig. 2). The first wall, built during the 'Ostman' or Hiberno-Norse phase of Dublin's history, was built *c.*1100. In 1170, however, Dublin was taken by the Anglo-Normans, who were responsible for building a second wall in the mid-13th century. This second wall was an extension joined onto the original circuit on the northern side of the town, towards the river Liffey. The construction of this new wall was a response to the general expansion of the town outside of the old wall, and specifically to a major reclamation programme which reclaimed land between the old wall and the river front.

Ostman mural defences

The first mural fortification around the town of Dublin consisted of a limestone wall which has been dated to *c.*1100 and which replaced the earthen banks originally encircling the town (Wallace 1981, 113; Thomas 1992, 86). A section of this early wall still survives in a modified form in the modern landscape at Cook St, while the National Museum's excavations at Wood Quay exposed a substantial section of this wall as it extended east, running parallel with the river Liffey (Wallace 1981, 113). In addition, recent excavation at Ross Road/Christchurch Place exposed part of the southern continuation of this wall, orientated east-west and running parallel to a later Anglo-Norman wall (Walsh and Hayden 1994). When Anglo-Normans arrived at Dublin in 1170 the inhabitants took refuge within this wall but the Anglo-Normans took the city after a surprise attack (Scott and Martin 1978, 67–9) and soon began to strengthen the existing mural defences. By the late 12th century, the city's western gate had been rebuilt and renamed Newgate (Gilbert 1889, 100) and on the southern side of the town, a new city fosse had apparently been dug outside the wall near Patrick St, further strengthened by the rechannelling into it of the river Poddle to form a water-filled moat (Simpson 1997, 26–7; Walsh 1997, 78).

Anglo-Norman Dublin

The 13th century saw the development of the port of Dublin, with a rise in prosperity suggested by general expansion and an increase in building in stone. In 1204, for instance, the royal castle was under construction by order of the King while ten years later, permission was given to construct a new bridge across the Liffey (Sweetman 1875–86i, 81: no. 511; 89: no. 577). There was also an increase in the number of stone houses in the town and the streets were apparently paved, as in 1303 the King was informed that the pavements of the city were in a state of disrepair (Sweetman 1875–86v, 81: no. 239). In addition, in 1244, Dublin received a piped water-supply (Berry 1890–1, 557–8), catering for the stone houses of the wealthy merchants and various ecclesiastical houses.

The influx of new settlers to Dublin was presumably the driving force behind the expansion of the settled population outside the line of the walls, although it must be admitted that little is known of the degree of extra-mural expansion in pre-Norman Dublin. Many of the new extra-mural properties were granted to the ecclesiastical establishments which ringed the walled town and surviving registers and chartularies from some of these houses give details of new properties and plots. These indicate general expansion along Thomas St, Patrick St and Francis St and by 1228, for instance, New St, at the southern end of Patrick St, was well settled (Brooks 1936, 92:no. 127; 95:no.133; McNeill 1950, 78, 86). However, expansion of population outside the town walls was most marked on the northern side of the town towards the river Liffey, where extra-mural settlement began early in the Anglo-Norman period. By the early 13th century property was recorded as being located 'outside the King's Gate'; the Kings Gate, at the top of Winetavern St, was one of the gateways through the early wall, which gave access to the Liffey. It was used extensively as a topographical landmark in locating properties in the newly reclaimed area and was replaced by the street name Winetavern St (*Vicus tabernariorum vini*) in the early to mid-14th century (*23rd Rep. Dep. Keeper Pub. Rec. Ireland*, 98: no. 557).

The silting up of the Liffey

Reclamation of the land between the original city wall and the river was probably made possible by the silting up of the river Liffey. As is well known, by the later 14th century ships fully laden could no longer get into the port of Dublin and had to go further south to the small port of Dalkey, nine miles outside the city (Gilbert 1889, 19; McNeill 1950, 233). Although the major problem was most likely to have been sand-bars at the mouth of the Liffey, deep deposits of sand and silt were also being deposited along the banks of the river. This was particularly the case on the northern side of the river, but sand and silt were also being deposited on the southern side especially on the west side of Winetavern St towards Bridge St and the slight bend in the river at this point may have caused a gradual accumulation of material outside the early wall. The result was that by 1220 and probably earlier, this area was settled extensively with a network of property plots and laneways, some of which had stone houses (*23rd Rep. Dep. Keeper Pub. Rec. Ireland*, 77: no. 477; Gilbert 1889, 95).

The Wood Quay area

To the east of Winetavern St, in the modern Wood Quay area, the foreshore had to be more actively reclaimed, probably because of a natural inlet or harbour in this area. Thus archaeological excavation has produced evidence of substantial reclamation works dating from the late 12th century onwards. This pushed the river front further north, possibly in an attempt to increase the depth of water in the channel while reclaiming the land to the rear. Unfortunately there are no historical sources documenting this extensive reclamation work. The new land would have been under the control of the Mayor and Commonalty of Dublin and they were presumably responsible for developing it. A regularised street grid was laid out and the land was divided into specific plots. Towards the river, the quayside was developed with a 'King's highway', a main road, running parallel to river and quay. South of the quay, property was granted to prominent citizens for domestic habitation but religious houses also acquired property outside the line of the old wall. The hospital of St John the Baptist, which lay outside the Newgate, held a property on the east side of Fishamble St as did the abbey of St Mary de Hogges (Brooks 1936, 77: no. 105).

The Anglo-Norman extension wall

The reclamation and development of the area between the old city and the Liffey had one serious consequence, in that it pushed the quay front further north, beyond the protection of the city wall. The new stone houses and shops to the south of the quays were totally unprotected and vulnerable to attack and more importantly, the new quayside was open to the river with no protection from attack from land or by sea. This soon resulted in a decision to build a new city wall surrounding the reclaimed land. In effect, an extension wall was joined onto the existing circuit with the old city wall left *in situ*. Historical sources indicate that the new wall was under construction by the 1240s (Simpson 1994, 6–7). A possible quarry for the wall was recently located in an excavation on the north side of Essex St West, within the reclaimed area (ibid.). It appears that the north-east corner was the last section of the wall to be built, although it was completed by *c*.1260 (Gilbert 1889, 95).

The place-name 'Wood Quay'

Few 13th-century historical references can be identified as being specifically related to property in the Wood Quay area, mainly because the place-name does not appear in the documentary sources for this period. In the various sources the river front is referred to simply as 'the wall of the Liffey', 'the riverbank', 'towards the Liffey' or simply '*Kayum*' (quay; Brooks 1936, 32: no. 55). As late as 1303 a reference to property in the parish of St Olave, clearly within the Wood Quay area, did not record the place-name; instead the quay was referred to simply as the 'Quay of Dublin' (ibid., 356: no. 573), although the name 'Wood Quay' may well have been current at this date. This is not unusual, however, as grants of land when renewed often simply repeated topographical landmarks used in the original grant. Thus, a grant dated to 1338 uses the topographical landmarks 'outside the King's Gate' and 'the water of the Liffey' with no mention of the new wall (ibid., 59: no. 88).

The place-name *Wood Quay* may be descriptive of a quayside constructed primarily from wood, suggesting that it originated in the 13th century while timber revetments still formed the river front. This might also suggest that this wooden section differed and was distinguishable from the rest of the quay which was already constructed of stone. Thus the place-name may have been acquired in the period between the commencement of the new extension wall, *c*.1240, and its completion *c*.1260. The wooden revetments were definitely replaced by a stone quay wall since this wall, presumably part of the extension wall, was located in the National Museum's excavations at Wood Quay (Wallace 1981, 117). However, this derivation of the place-name has been queried by Wallace (1976, 23), who feels it is more likely to reflect the shipping of wood through the port in the Middle Ages. In the final analysis the derivation of the name cannot be definitively resolved because of the lack of documentary evidence.

Wood Quay, as a place-name, first appears in documentary records in the 15th century. In 1451 the prior and convent of Holy Trinity (Christchurch) granted a garden to Philip Bellewe, described as being 'on the *Wodkey* of Dublin, near Newchambers and situated between the way leading to Isoldtour (Isolde's Tower) on the east, the land of Richard ... on the west, Prestons land on the south and the key aforesaid on the north' (*23rd Rep. Dep. Keeper Pub. Rec. Ireland*, 150: no. 951). This is an interesting reference for several reasons. The garden mentioned in the grant can be identified as the garden belonging to Isolde's Tower, the north-east corner tower on the city wall. The boundaries of this garden are well documented and its location is known, on the east side of Fishamble St, immediately west of the tower (Simpson 1994, 8). This indicates that the medieval Wood Quay extended as far east as Isolde's Tower and was not confined to the quay west of Fishamble St. In addition the garden, which is described as being 'on the Wodkey' is actually on the other side of the 'King's highway' which ran along southern the side of the quay. Thus, by the 15th century, the placename Wood Quay included land on the other side of the street.

Stone houses in Dublin

Archaeological evidence supports the documentary sources' indications of expansion from the late 12th century onwards, outside the line of the old Viking wall. The area closest to the old wall was settled first and as early as 1220 the hospital of St John the Baptist received a grant of two stone houses outside the King's Gate (Brooks 1936, 55: no. 84), with a third in 1238 (ibid., 55:no. 83). These houses were on the western side of Winetavern St, towards Cook St, which was settled first, but similar developments were probably occurring on the eastern side of the street towards Wood Quay.

A description of a house received by the priory of the Holy Trinity from Gilbert de Lyvet in 1234 is probably representative of the type of stone houses current in Dublin at this date; it is described as a stone hall with a loft and cellar and a portico on the northern side, and was beside a second stone house which had a kitchen and an oven (*20th Rep. Dep. Keeper Pub. Rec. Ireland,* 43: no. 47). A later description of a second stone dwelling, dating to 1355, mentions a cellar with a stone vault with a lease to build a room 30ft long and 10ft broad (*23rd Rep. Dep. Keeper Pub. Rec. Ireland,* 111: no. 657). The house was described as roofed with stone, possibly referring to the use of slates or shingles of stone, which is known from the 13th century onwards. Probable fragments of sandstone slates found during the present excavation, together possibly with a number of architectural fragments (see Chapter IX, below), may be derived from medieval stone buildings on the site.

The Tholsel/Guildhall at Winetavern St

The Tholsel or guildhall of Dublin was originally located outside the old city wall, on the east side of Winetavern St, in the newly reclaimed area (Gilbert 1889, 106). It was a municipal building where the mayor of Dublin was elected and was also the merchants' headquarters and the town's main courthouse (Gilbert 1854–59 i, 162). By 1305, however, it had been moved to the more prestigious location of Werburgh St, in the core of the medieval city (Gilbert 1889, 110, 223). A later reference, dated to 1311, preserves a grant in which the Mayor and Commonalty granted the 'old Guildhall and all their tenements in Taverners St' to Robert de Bristol (Webb 1929, 13); the old guildhall is described as having two cellars with a garden to the east. The new tholsel in Werburgh St was probably a much larger building, containing two jails, an upper one and a lower one, in the late 14th century (Gilbert 1854–59 i, 162).

REFERENCES

Berry, H.F. 1890–91 The water supply of ancient Dublin. *J.R.S.A.I.* **21**, 557–73.

Brooks, E. St John (ed.) 1936 *Register of the hospital of St John the Baptist, Dublin.* Dublin. Irish Manuscripts Commission.

Gilbert, J.T. 1854–59 *A history of the city of Dublin,* 3 vols. Dublin. McGlashan and Gill.

Gilbert, J.T. (ed.) 1889 *Calendar of ancient records of Dublin,* vol.i. Dublin. Joseph Dollard.

McNeill, C. (ed.) 1950 *Calendar of Archbishop Alen's register, c.1172–1534.* Dublin. Royal Society of Antiquaries of Ireland.

Scott, A.B. and Martin, F.X. (eds) 1978 *Giraldus Cambrensis: Expugnatio Hibernica.* Dublin. Royal Irish Academy.

Simpson, L. 1991 Historical background to the Patrick St excavation. In Walsh 1997, 17–33.

Simpson, L. 1994 *Excavations at Isolde's Tower, Dublin.* Dublin. Temple Bar Properties.

Sweetman, H.S. (ed.) 1875–86 *Calendar of documents relating to Ireland 1171–1307,* 5 vols. London. Public Record Office.

Thomas, A. 1992 *The walled towns of Ireland,* 2 vols. Dublin. Irish Academic Press.

Wallace, P.F. 1976 Wood Quay: the growth of thirteenth-century Dublin. *Dublin Arts Festival Handbook 1976,* 22–4. Dublin.

Wallace, P.F. 1981 Dublin's waterfront at Wood Quay, 900–1317. In G. Milne and B. Hobley (eds), *Waterfront archaeology in Britain and northern Europe,* 108–18. London. Council for British Archaeology Research Report **41**.

Walsh, C. 1997 *Archaeological excavations at Patrick, Nicholas and Winetavern Streets, Dublin.* Dingle. Brandon Books/Dublin Corporation.

Walsh, C. and Hayden, A. 1994 Christchurch Place, Dublin. In I. Bennett (ed.), *Excavations 1993: Summary accounts of archaeological excavations in Ireland*, 16–17. Dublin. Organisation of Irish Archaeologists/ Wordwell.

Webb, J.J. 1929 *The guilds of Dublin*. Dublin. Sign of the Three Candles.

White, N.B. 1943 *Extents of Irish monastic possessions 1540–1541, from manuscripts in the Public Record Office, London*. Dublin. Irish Manuscripts Commission.

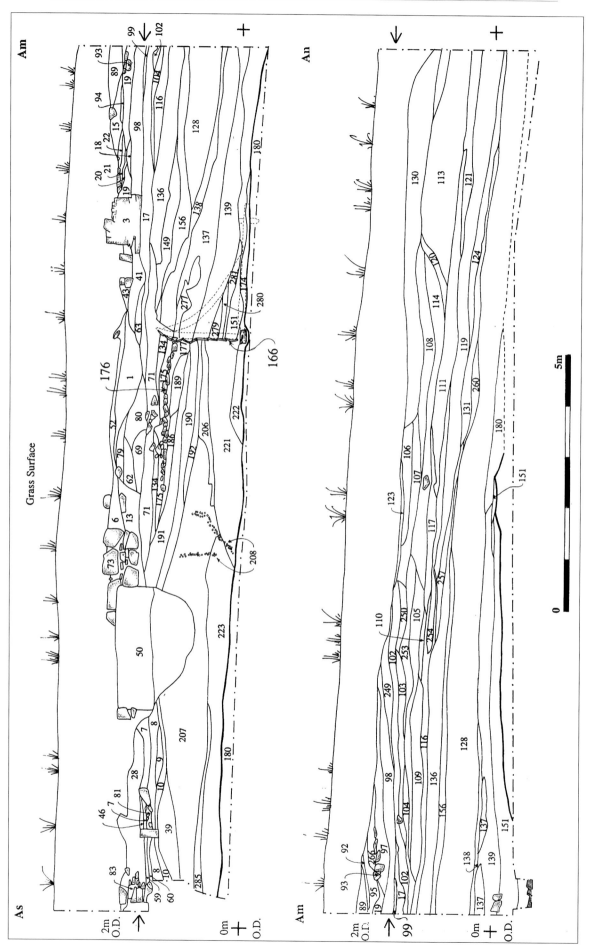

Fig. 4: Composite cross-section along eastern edge of Area II; As-Am above, Am-An below

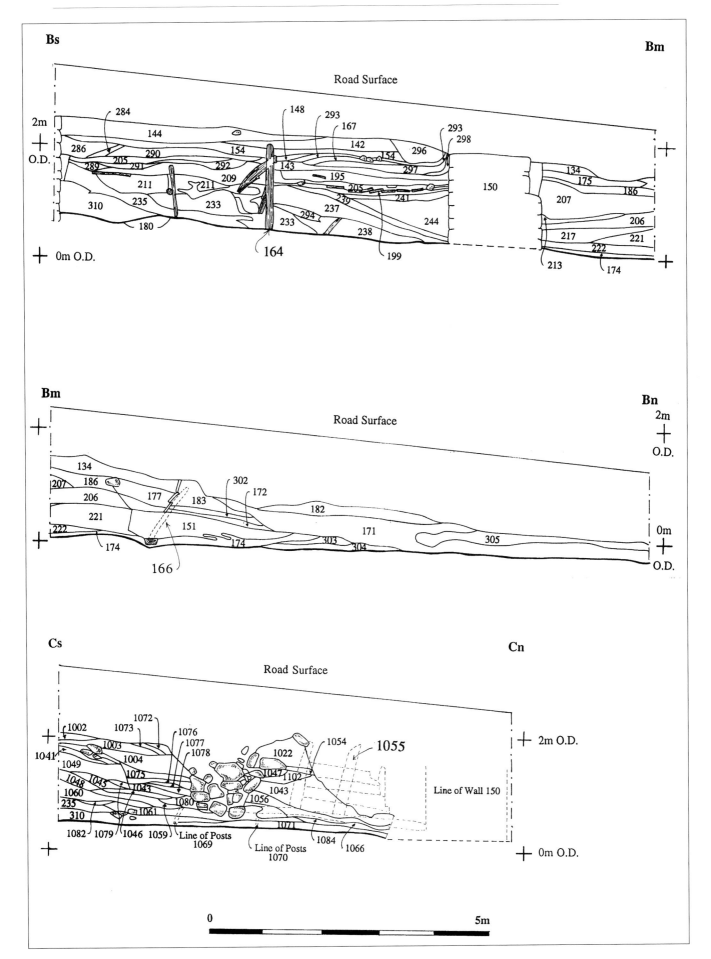

Fig. 5: Composite cross-sections along western edge of Area II (Bs-Bm above, Bm-Bn centre) and eastern edge of Area I (Cs-Cn below)

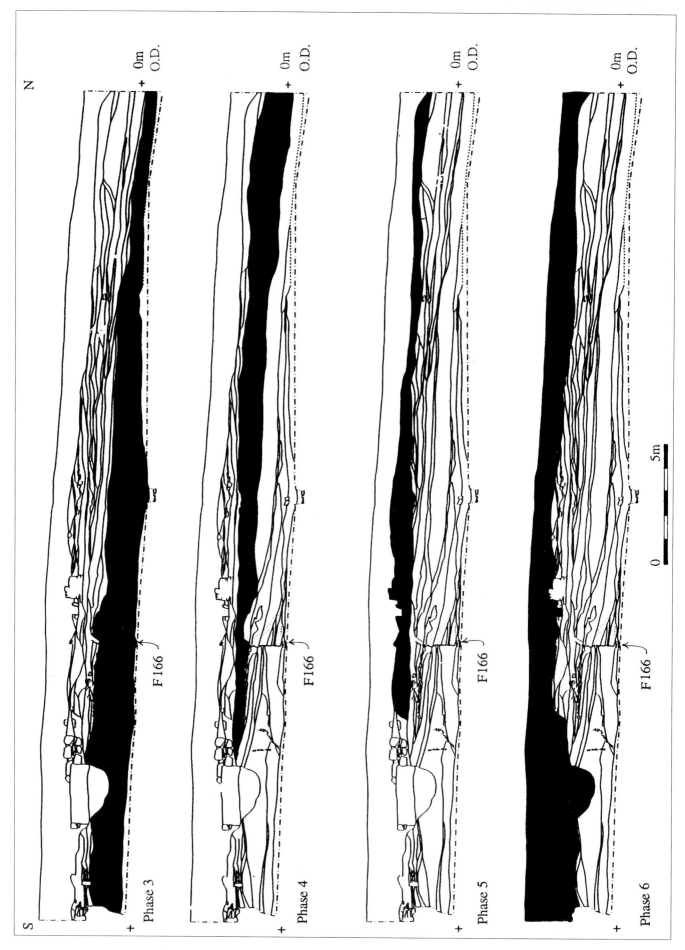

Fig. 6: Composite cross-section along eastern edge of Area II (As-An), showing distribution of deposits by phases

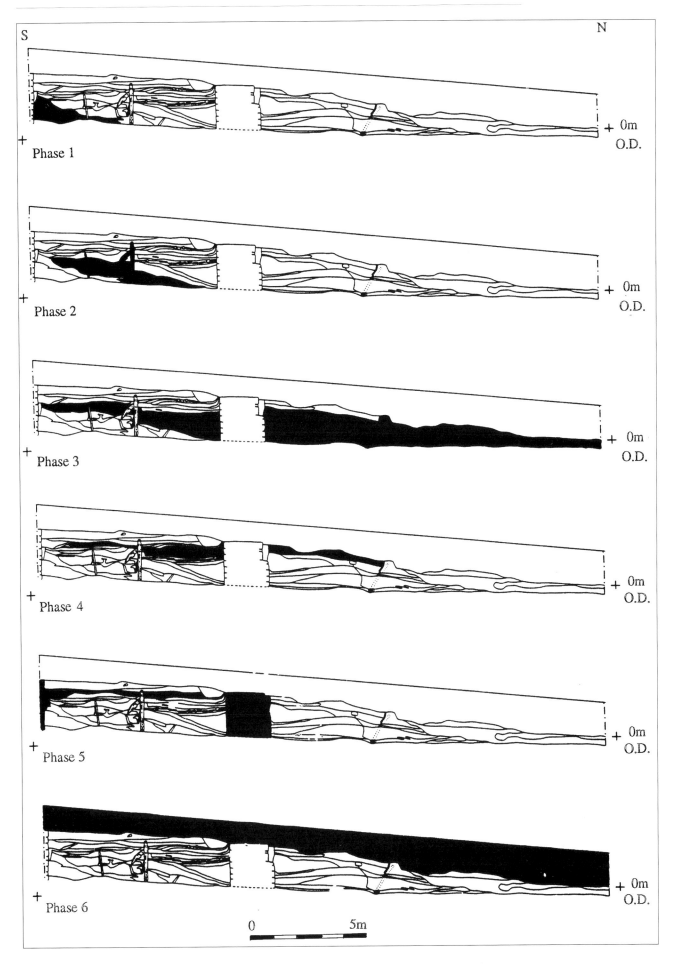

Fig. 7: Composite cross-section along western edge of Area II (Bs-Bn), showing distribution of deposits by phases

CHAPTER III

The stratigraphy of the site

As anticipated, the material recovered in the excavation related largely to episodes of land reclamation centering mainly on the 13th century. Stratigraphically, six main phases could be distinguished (see Figs 6 and 7), as follows:

Phase 1: Pre-reclamation phase (to late 12th century).

Phase 2: First reclamation phase (late 12th century)

Phase 3: Second reclamation phase (early 13th century)

Phase 4: Third reclamation phase (early to mid-13th century)

Phase 5: Medieval occupation phase (later 13th century)

Phase 6: Late/post-medieval activity.

PHASE 1: PRE-RECLAMATION PHASE (FIG. 8)

The entire site at its lowest level was covered by poorly sorted sandy gravels with abundant quartz and mica platelets (F180). This foreshore deposit was not entirely sterile, containing small quantities of animal bone and twigs and one small area of brushwood (F1087) but there is little doubt that it was deposited by natural rather than human agency (that is by the river Liffey). A trench cut at one point revealed the underlying calp bedrock directly below these gravels, which at this point were no more than 50cm thick. Residues of black boulder clay in the uneven surface of the calp bedrock indicated a wave-cut platform, with the original boulder clay having been washed out and replaced by gravels through the action of the river. The underlying natural contours definitely sloped downwards from south to north but the incline was quite gradual, with no evidence of the more pronounced slopes described by Mitchell (1987, 16) and Walsh (1997, 105). It must be noted, however, that because of the naturally dynamic and changing nature of the foreshore, identification of the 'original' surface was sometimes difficult.

In the south-western part of the site the gravels were overlain by layers of enriched gravels (F310) and organic silts (F235) containing patches of brushwood, reeds and occupation debris such as animal bone, pottery and leather. Near the northern limit of F310 a relatively substantial row of posts (F1069) ran east-west. It contained at least 21 posts (average length 37cm, average diameter 7cm) at an average spacing of c.14cm and angled at c.45° to the north (Ill. 1). The posts had been driven into gravel F180, apparently to retain the material to the south (F310, F235). 1.8m to the south, an east-west run of wattling (F1068) was noted, its posts driven into F310 and the wattle covered by F235 (Ill. 1). F1068 survived for a length of 3.4m, having been truncated at either end by later walls. These results confirm that the excavation area was originally an open foreshore,

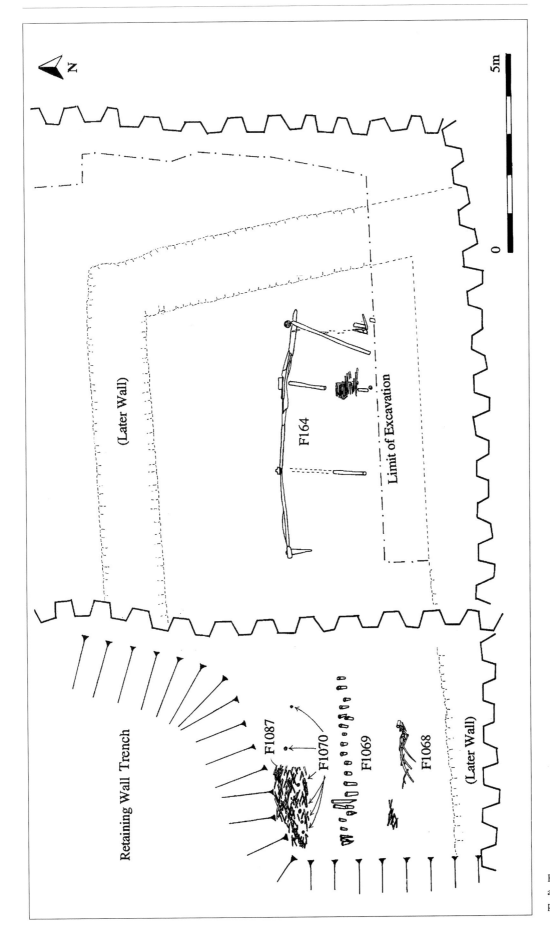

Fig. 8: Phases 1
and 2: general
plan of features

Ill. 1: Area I from south, showing F1068 (foreground) and F1069 (background)

inundated by river tides, at least periodically. The organic silts overlying the gravels may result from intermittent human activity along the foreshore, but the retaining line of posts F1069 and wattling F1068 suggest that they may relate to earlier reclamation episodes located further south or west than the present excavation.

PHASES 2–4: THE RECLAMATION PHASES

By far the most substantial and significant material recovered during the excavation relates to the initial reclamation of the site, for which a date from the late 12th to mid-13th century is indicated. Evidence was noted for three distinct episodes of reclamation and at least four separate wooden revetments were discovered, two of them with an east-west orientation and the other two with a north-south orientation.

During the excavation of the two areas, unexcavated baulks c.1 metre wide were left against the central row of sheet piles, for recording purposes, and were only excavated after the remainder of the areas had been fully excavated. As misfortune would have it, the line chosen for the central row of sheet piles ran almost precisely between the two unsuspected north-south timber revetments (see Fig. 10 and Ill.5, Pl. VI), which were subsequently incorporated within unexcavated baulks to either side of the piles. Thus not only was the stratigraphic link between the revetments disrupted by the piles but the revetments themselves were only discovered in the final removal of the baulks and had to be hurriedly excavated, out of sequence. Unfortunately, this has caused inevitable difficulties in interpreting the stratigraphical sequence of these revetments and the layers surrounding them.

Further difficulties in interpretation were caused by the nature of the earliest layers, most closely associated with the revetments, which were almost entirely composed of estuarine muds and organic silts. It was often unclear whether these layers were naturally deposited *in situ* or had been redeposited. Furthermore, it is likely that they would have been in a fluid or semi-fluid state when the revetments were being erected. Cuts made in such layers for the insertion of revetment baseplates may not necessarily have left any trace, as the layers may simply have flowed back to fill such voids. In consequence, the relationship between revetments and the earliest surrounding layers was often difficult to establish and differing interpretations were possible. However, the most likely interpretation, presented here, envisages three separate episodes of reclamation.

PHASE 2: FIRST RECLAMATION PHASE (FIG. 8)

This episode involved the reclamation of a small area in the south-western part of the site, behind a crude timber revetment. This episode cannot be precisely dated, as no dendrochronological dates could be obtained from the revetment, but it is clearly earlier than the second reclamation phase, which can be dated *c.*1200 AD. The evidence of associated ceramic material indicates a late 12th century date.

Revetment F164

The first revetment feature (F164; see Fig. 9 and Pl. II) was found running roughly on an east-west line near the southern end of Area II. F164 was unlike the other timber revetments, consisting of a wall of planking, mainly reused ships' planking, placed against four uprights embedded into backfilled silt (F233). At least three of the uprights were clearly reused timbers while by contrast the easternmost upright showed little sign of working at all and was merely the bole of a tree or large branch. The entire structure was *c.*6.4m long and 1.6m in surviving height.

In preparation for the erection of the revetment, a thick deposit of estuarine silt (F233/F238) was laid down over the pre-existing deposits (F310, F235) and four uprights driven into it. A shallow slot was cut into F233 alongside the uprights, into which the planking wall of the revetment was placed and the trench then backfilled with soft organic material. To the front of the revetment, silt F233 was embedded with large stones, presumably to lessen the eroding action of the river. Insofar as the revetment was braced at all, it was rear-braced but not with conventional raking braces. A row of vertical posts were driven into silt F233 *c.*1.5m south of and directly aligned on the four uprights, and horizontal timbers were laid on F233, jammed between the uprights and facing posts. This arrangement was presumably intended to counterbalance the natural southward thrust of the planking in the revetment. Once the structure of the revetment had been erected the area behind it was backfilled with estuarine silt (F211, essentially the same as F233 below it).

The outer uprights were further supported with crude raking rear braces (both reused timbers). At the west end of the revetment a short raking timber was mortised into the upright and set into silt F233, with the prepared cut again filled with organic material. The east end of the revetment had unfortunately been disturbed by pre-excavation trial trenching but its main features were recorded both in the trial trenching and excavation phases. A row of upright timber boards, 15–20cm wide, ran between the upright and an additional rear post and served to retain the silt within the revetment. In addition, a longer raking brace was placed between upright and rear post. It may have been mortised into the upright but because of the poor condition of the top of the upright, this could not definitely be established.

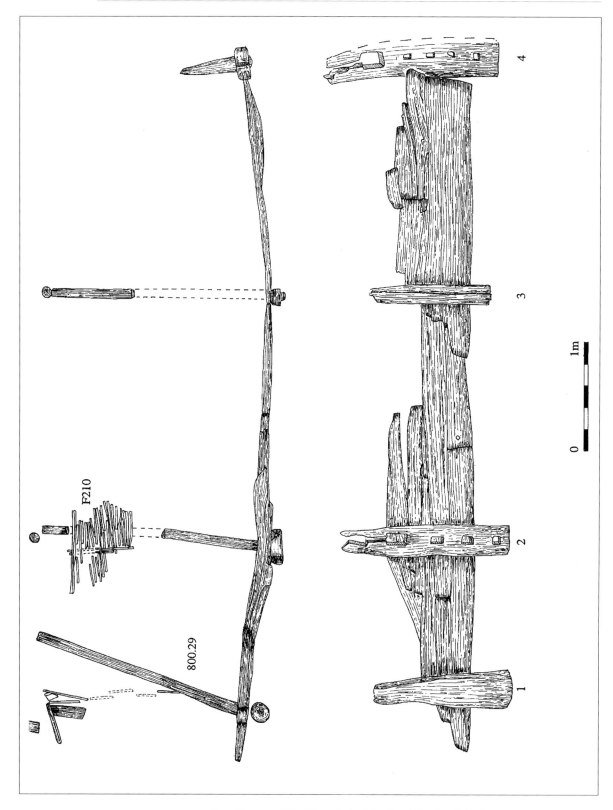

Fig. 9: Revetment F164 (Phase 2): plan (above) and elevation (below)

Posts F1070

In Area I a poorly surviving row of five posts (F1070) was found running east-west roughly in line with revetment F164. The posts (21.5cm in average length and 4cm in average diameter) were set at irregular intervals and leaned at an angle of *c.*75° towards the north. They were driven into gravel (F1071) which had accumulated outside posts F1069 (Fig. 5). Posts F1070 seemed to be associated with the deposition to the south of a series of layers, mainly of organic refuse or organic silts (F1061, F1082, F1060, F1059, F1048, F1045, F1049) but including some gravels (F1080, F1046, F1079, F1084). This material was deposited directly over organic silt F235 which, along with the alignment of F1070 with F164, suggests that it is part of the same reclamation episode as F164.

PHASE 3: SECOND RECLAMATION PHASE (FIG. 10)

A much larger area was reclaimed in this episode and at least three separate timber revetments constructed, resting on organic silts or gravels (F174, F238, F1071) containing brushwood, reeds and occupation debris such as animal bone, pottery and leather, which had accumulated subsequent to the erection of revetment F164. The main revetment exposed (F166) was a large, front-braced revetment running east-west across the site, which was clearly the continuation of Wallace's Revetment I (see Fig. 2). What was of particular interest was the fact that the other two revetments (F246 and F1055) had north-south orientations, suggesting that they may have acted as terminal features for the entire reclamation works associated with Revetment I along Wood Quay.

Revetment I has previously been assigned a date of *c.*1210 AD (for example, Wallace 1981, 115; Mitchell 1987, 15), but the actual basis for this date has never been published and it would now appear to be slightly too late. Dendrochronological dates have been obtained for timbers from each of the three revetments associated with this phase in the current excavation (see Chapter V below). The relevant felling dates (see Fig. 11 and more detailed discussion below) are:

Revetment F166 :   1190–1208 AD
Revetment F246 :   1194–1201 AD
                   1194–1212 AD
Revetment F1055: 1195–1213 AD

The congruence of these dates and the stratigraphic evidence for the contemporaneity of the revetments, clearly indicate that the timbers for all three revetments were felled within a decade either side of 1200 AD. Further refinement of the dendrochronological dating evidence is possible if the contemporaneous construction of the revetments is accepted. This suggests a best estimated felling date not earlier than 1195 AD (based on revetment F1055) and not later than 1201 AD (based on revetment F246). None of the principal timbers show evidence of reuse (apart from some possible evidence for re-use in the case of F1055; see below) and there is no other reason to suppose a significant time lag between the felling of the timbers and construction of the revetments; indeed, such a time lag is unlikely on woodworking grounds (see Chapter IV). Revetment F246, therefore, must have been constructed by 1201 AD at the latest, and it is unlikely that it would have been constructed before the main revetment (F166) was in position. It therefore seems reasonable to suggest that the major reclamation phase at Wood Quay associated with Wallace's Revetment I commenced with the construction of the revetments in the period 1195–1201 AD.

Revetment F166

F166 was a large, front-braced revetment, up to 1.8m in surviving height, which was exposed for a length of approximately 12.5m (see Figs 12–15 and Pl. I). It clearly continued further to the east,

Fig. 10: Phase 3: general plan of features

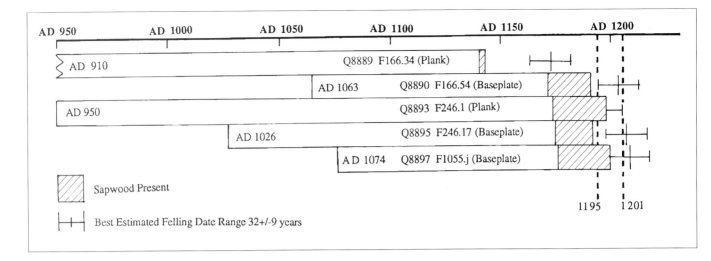

AD 950   AD 1000   AD 1050   AD 1100   AD 1150   AD 1200

AD 910   Q8889 F166.34 (Plank)

AD 1063   Q8890 F166.54 (Baseplate)

AD 950   Q8893 F246.1 (Plank)

AD 1026   Q8895 F246.17 (Baseplate)

AD 1074   Q8897 F1055.j (Baseplate)

Sapwood Present

Best Estimated Felling Date Range 32+/-9 years

1195   1201

beyond the limits of the excavation, but the original western termination may have been present. In preparation for the construction of the revetment a shallow slot was cut on an east-west line though organic silt F174 into the underlying gravel F180. Into this slot the main horizontal baseplate of the revetment was placed, in three separate sections; the scarf joints suggest that the sections of the baseplate were laid down from east to west. Six subsidiary baseplates extended northwards at right angles to the main baseplate, resting on F174 and tenoned into the northern edge of the principal baseplate (Pl. III). Apparently no slot was cut for these baseplates. A certain amount of silt F174 seems subsequently to have flowed back or been packed around and over the principal and subsidiary baseplates. A deposit of compact estuarine silt (F222) was also deposited immediately behind (south of) the principal baseplate, presumably to prevent it from moving during construction of the revetment.

Once the baseplates were in position, a total of 13 mortises were cut through the top of the principal baseplate at an average spacing of *c.*95cm; every alternate mortise was located opposite a subsidiary baseplate. It was noted that in at least two (and possibly four) cases these mortises cut through the tenons of the subsidiary baseplates (Ill. 2). Clearly the mortises were cut after the subsidiary baseplates had been tenoned into the principal baseplate, indicating that at least some of the carpentry for the revetment was carried out *in situ*. Large upright posts were then tenoned into these mortises (although one mortise was empty) and raking front braces were inserted between the subsidiary baseplates and the opposing uprights (see Figs 13–14 and Ill. 3). The revetment was now ready to accept the horizontal boards which actually retained the dumped infill behind the revetment.

The insertion of the horizontal boards appears to be inextricably linked to the deposition of the organic silts (F221) immediately behind it. The almost complete absence of nails in the revetment structure indicates that the boards could only be placed in position according as F221 was being deposited, as it was only the pressure of the build up of F221 which held the boards in place; as the level of F221 rose, each ascending, overlapping board could be placed in position. Thus the deposition of F221 must be contemporary with the construction of revetment F166. The deposit of silt F221 was, in turn, revetted to the south by a well made post-and-wattle fence, F208 (see below), clearly indicating that it was not a haphazard dumping but rather a carefully planned operation.

A puzzling feature of the revetment was that horizontal boards only extended to the base of the revetment over the length of the easternmost baseplate (Ill. 3). Over the remainder of the revetment boards were absent for *c.*70cm above the baseplate, with the result that F221 had been eroded away for *c.*50cm to the rear of the revetment and replaced by river-deposited sand and gravel (Pl. IV). At first glance the most likely explanation for this is that the boards themselves had been washed away by river action, but it is difficult to envisage how this could have happened when the uprights and braces remained in position and boards remained in place at a higher level

Fig. 11: Diagrammatic representation of dendrochronological dates for timber revetments (Phase 3)

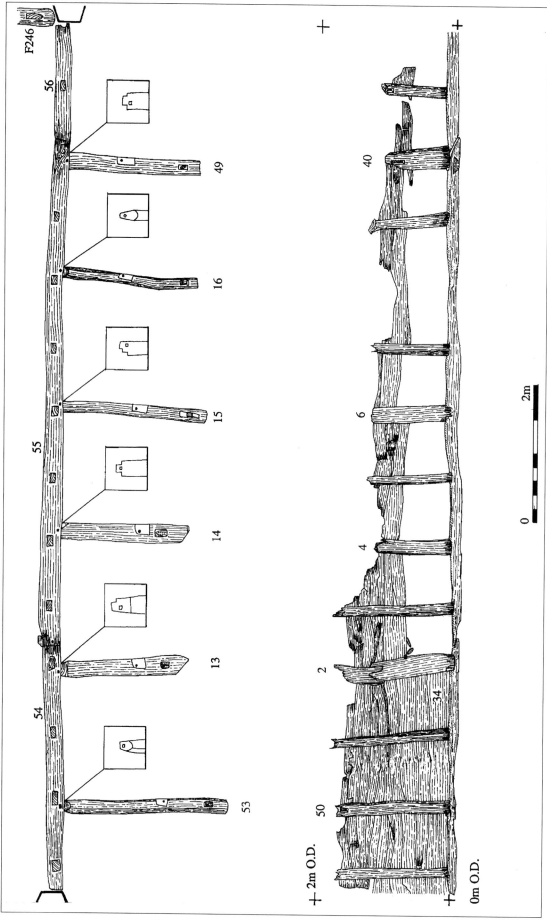

Fig. 12: Revetment F166 (Phase 3): plan (above) and elevation (below)

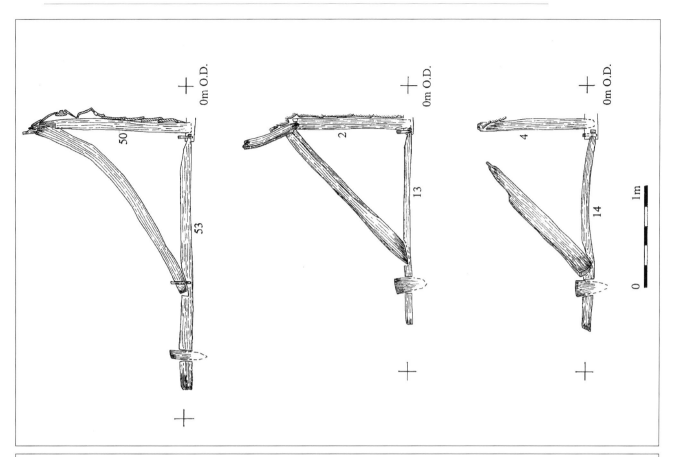

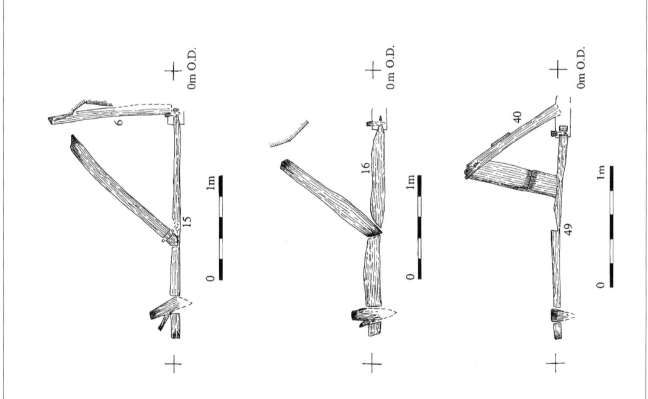

Fig. 13 (above): Revetment F166: cross-sections through revetment F166 at subsidiary baseplates 166.53, 166.13 and 166.14
Fig. 14: Revetment F166: cross-sections through revetment F166 at subsidiary baseplates 166.15, 166.16 and 166.49

Ill. 2: Revetment F166: detail of tenon of subsidiary baseplate 166.15. The right-angled cut at the tip of the tenon has been caused by the cutting of the upper mortise in the principal baseplate, after the subsidiary baseplate had been tenoned into position.

(although, of course, these could be replacements). It is significant that the distinction between the area of full boarding down to base and the area of no boarding at base coincides exactly with the junction of two of the principal baseplates (Ill. 3). Furthermore the area of no boarding at base is approximately in line with the location of revetment F164, *c*.8m to the south. This suggests that the gap at the base of the western section was an original feature of the revetment as first built and may be related to the presence of revetment F164. Nevertheless, it is still not clear why the builders should choose to leave such a gap.

Dendrochronological dates were obtained from two samples of oak wood from revetment F166 (see Chapter V, below). A sample from one of the horizontal boards (Q8889; F166.34) indicated a best estimated felling date of 1160–78 AD which, in view of the overall dating evidence for this phase, indicates that this board was reused in the context in which it was found. A sample from one of the baseplates (Q8890; F166.54) indicated a best estimated felling date of 1190–1208 AD which seems a more reliable indicator of the date of construction of the revetment.

Wattle fence F208

Approximately 4m to the south of the revetment, at the eastern edge of Area II, a post-and-wattle structure (F208) was discovered. It consisted of two diverging rows of post-and-wattle walling, both apparently originating from a single post at the west end, from which one row ran roughly eastwards and the other roughly north-eastwards. Unfortunately everything to the west of the shared 'origin' post had been destroyed by the insertion of a later stone wall (F30/150). A

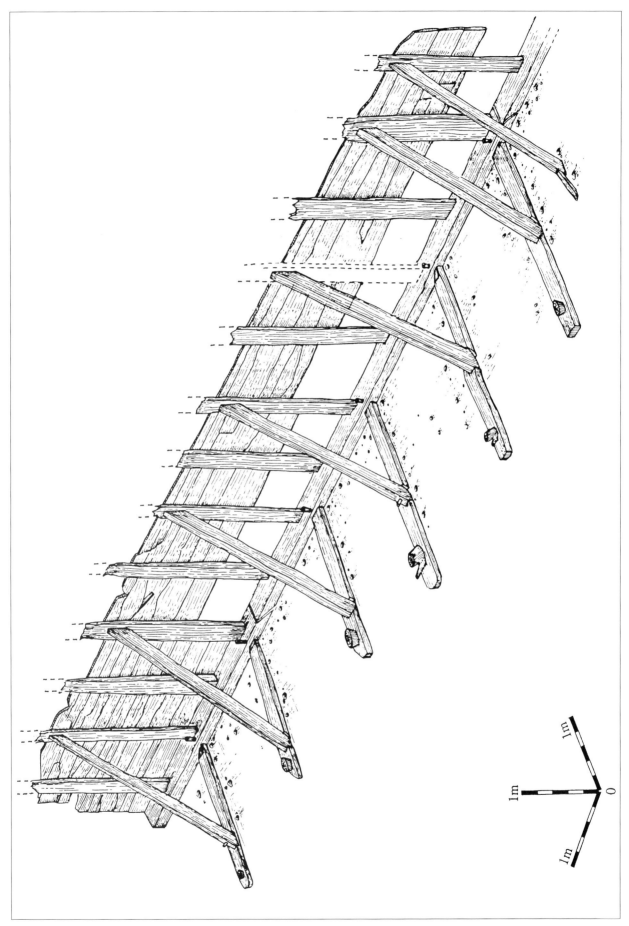

Fig. 15: Axonometric reconstruction of revetment F166 (Phase 3), viewed from north-west

Ill. 3: Revetment F166: detail showing raking brace at upright 166.2 and subsidiary baseplate 166.13. Note full boarding to east of upright 166.2 and partial boarding to west.

maximum height of 1.0–1.2m of wattling survived (Ill. 4). The structure was packed around with silts F221 (to the north) and F223 (to the south), while significant amounts of straw/moss were noticed within the wattle. F208 is clearly earlier than silts F221 and F223, since not only the posts but even the lowest courses of wattling were set into river gravel F180, but it is likely that the silts were deposited immediately after F208 was erected.

The form and position of F208 are so similar to the post-and-wattle structure in Wallace's Bank 4 that it seems very likely that it represents a continuation of that structure. Wallace (1981, 114) interpreted the latter as forming 'a stabilizing core or retaining fence' for an embankment erected slightly earlier than the main timber revetment, but in the present excavation F208 was interpreted as a fence designed to retain the silts (F221) deposited in conjunction with the erection of revetment F166. It is, therefore, contemporary with and directly related to revetment F166.

It can hardly be coincidental that the 'origin' post shared by the two diverging parts of F208 was directly in line with (that is, due south of) the scarf joint between the two easternmost baseplates of revetment F166, which as noted above also marked the junction between the area of complete planking to the base of the revetment and that of partial planking, further west. Unfortunately everything to the west of the 'origin' post in F208 had been destroyed but it seems clear that the 'origin' post/scarf joint alignment represents a significant break in the construction both of the revetment and of the post-and-wattle fence F208.

Revetment F246

Apparently at the same time as F166 was being erected, a second revetment was constructed running south from the west end of F166; unfortunately, the surviving evidence for this revetment

Ill. 4: Post-and-wattle fence F208, from north

was fragmentary. At the west end of F166, a short (*c.*60cm) fragment of a baseplate with one mortise was noted, running southwards (Pl. V). It is not certain that the surviving west end of F166 represents the original termination of the revetment, as everything west of this had been removed by the excavation of the retaining wall trench in the 1970s. Indeed the surviving west end had been damaged by the insertion of the retaining wall trench and/or the sheet piles (which coincide at this point) but the conjunction with another revetment raises at least the possibility that this was the original termination. Almost 5m south of the fragmentary baseplate was another, much more complete section of revetment (F246) which is probably part of the same structure. The remainder of this revetment, between the two fragments, could have been destroyed by any of a series of events: the irruption of a flood channel in the 13th century, the construction of a large medieval wall (F150), or the excavation of the retaining wall trench in the 1970s.

The main section of revetment F246 (Fig. 16 and Ill. 5) survived for a maximum length of 4.3m, although the southern 1.1m had been damaged by a wall foundation or stone-filled pit F1024 and was possibly rebuilt (Ill. 6). The baseplates were apparently laid from south to north on silt F238 (equivalent to F174), although without a bedding slot being cut into the underlying gravels. The construction of F246 differed from F166, the major difference being that F246 was apparently not braced. Horizontal boards roughly 2m long were placed on the east side of the uprights; five survived in all. Each board spanned three uprights, the midspan supporting the centre of the board, while two uprights supported the ends. There was a small vertical overlap in the bottom row of boards, which indicated that this lower row was positioned from north to south. As with F166, further boards were added above as the level of infilled silts (F237, F239, F244) rose. While these boards overlapped those below, they did not overlap those on either side and were inserted in a staggered formation to those below and above, so that the midspan uprights of one row became the principal uprights of the row above.

Dendrochronological dates were obtained from two samples of oak wood from F246 (see Chapter V below). A sample from one of the horizontal boards (Q8893; F246.1) indicated a best estimated felling date of 1194–1201 AD, while a sample from one of the baseplates (Q8895; F246.17) indicated a best estimated felling date of 1194–1212 AD. Taken together, these samples seem to indicate a date of 1194–1201 AD for the construction of the revetment.

At some point in the construction of revetments F166 and F246 a much larger area to their rear was filled with silts essentially similar to F221 (F223, F237, F239, F285 and F215) and organic refuse

Ill. 5: Revetment F246 from east, as exposed during removal of baulk

Ill. 6: Revetment F246 from east, during excavation. Note how southern two uprights stand in seperate
baseplate sections, indicating possible rebuilding.

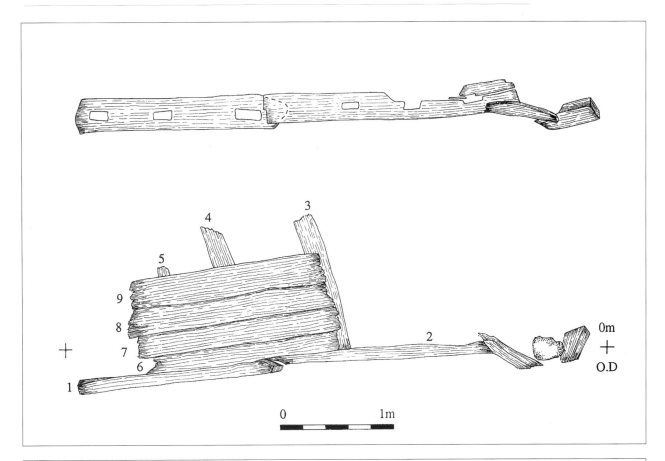

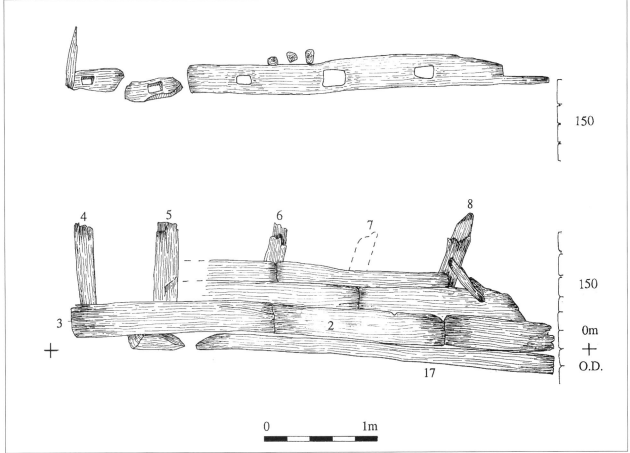

Fig. 16: Phase 3: Plans and elevations of revetments F1055 (above) and F246 (below)

Ill. 7: Revetment F1055
from west, as exposed
during removal of baulk

(F217, F241, F213). The banked deposit of F221 against revetment F166 was also topped with a
compact silt layer (F206). A collapsed post-and-wattle wall (F240) found running south from
F208, in and under silt F223, may have been part of a division such as those noted by Wallace
(1981, 114) between Bank 4 and the city wall. Like them it probably served to facilitate reclamation,
or as a property boundary, or both. This reclamation may well have occurred at the same time as
embankment F1057 was being constructed further west (see below).

Revetment F1055

Approximately 0.8m west of revetment F246 (but unfortunately separated from it by the sheet
piling) a second, parallel revetment (F1055) was discovered (Ill. 7). Its location and form suggest
that it may have been practically contemporary in construction with F246. Indeed, it is possible
that F246 and F1055 should be viewed as parts of a single structure rather than as two separate,
parallel revetments but unfortunately the circumstances under which they were excavated makes
it impossible to be certain of this. In revetment F1055, two baseplates with a total length of c.4.6m
were laid on gravel F1071, with a scarf joint indicating that the northern baseplate was laid down
first (Ill. 8), in contrast to revetment F246. The revetment was truncated at the north end by the
same medieval wall (F150) as truncated F246, but the southern end of the revetment (although
damaged by the sheet piling) seemed to represent an original termination (Ill. 9).

Like F246, revetment F1055 (Fig. 16 and Pl. VI) was unbraced; it is possible that both
revetments may have been back-braced with horizontal tiebacks at a high level, such as Walsh
(1997, 79–80; Fig. 38) suggest for revetments at Patrick St, but no evidence for this survived. The
baseplate contained at least six mortises but only three contained uprights and boarding was
confined to a relatively short span of c.1.8m between these uprights. The superstructure of the
revetment had almost certainly been removed to the north of this span by the insertion of the
retaining wall trench in the 1970s. It may also have been destroyed by a wall foundation or stone-
filled pit F1024 to the south but this is less certain because no trace of damaged uprights or boards
was found. This raises the possibility that, at least at the southern end, the form of the revetment
as it survived may have been close to the original and the superfluous mortises may indicate that
the baseplates were reused. The boarding was placed on the west side of the uprights, indicating

Ill. 8: Revetment F1055: detail of scarf joint in baseplate. Note how southern section overlies (and thus was laid down later than) northern section.

that F1055 (unlike F246) was intended to revet material deposited to its west, rather than east. This almost certainly links F1055 with an embankment-like feature (F1057) found running east-west across Area I.

One dendrochronological date was obtained from a sample of oak wood from F1055 (see Chapter V, below). A sample from one of the baseplates (Q8897; F1055.1) indicated a best estimated felling date of 1195–1213 AD, which seems a reliable indicator of the date of construction of the revetment. The fact that only three of six mortises were occupied by posts may indicate re-use of the baseplate, but because of the fragmentary condition of the revetment, this is by no means certain. Even if re-use is accepted it is at least as likely to reflect reconstruction of the revetment in its original position as the construction of a new structure with elements re-used from elsewhere.

Embankment F1057

F1057 consisted of a build-up of mixed layers of organic refuse (F1056, F1102, F1023) and silt/estuarine mud (F1103, F1043, F1047, F1054, F1022) into which a heavy concentration of large timbers, brushwood and upright posts had been incorporated (Ills. 10–12). A group of six closely-spaced posts (F1052) was also driven through F1043 at one point (Ill. 10). Their purpose is uncertain but is presumably related to the embankment F1057. F1057 was truncated both to north (by the retaining wall trench) and south (by post-medieval wall foundations F1024 and F1029), creating the misleading impression of a narrow, steep bank. F1057 should probably be seen as part of a larger deposition of mixed silt (F1103, F1043, F1078, F1041, F1101) and organic (F1077, F1076, F1056, F1074, F1004) layers to the south. Nevertheless, the estuarine silt layers F1043 and F1022 seemed to have been banked up in a manner not visible in the stratigraphy south of walls F1024/F1029 and the striking concentration of timbers was clearly not accidental.

F1057 was roughly aligned with the boarded section of revetment F1055. This suggests that revetment F1055 may have been erected specifically to retain and support F1057 and that the impression of F1057 as an embankment was not entirely misleading. Although it no doubt spread further north originally, F1057 may have always been a relatively narrow linear feature, running westwards for an unknown distance from revetment F1055. It can best be interpreted as a crude embankment, restraining the river outside of the area enclosed by the timber revetments. Unlike the other

Ill. 10: Embankment F1057: timbers at upper level, from east (note post cluster F1052 at upper centre)

Ill. 9: Revetment F1055: baseplate, from south, after excavation. Note northern end truncated by later wall F150 and straight, cut edge of southern end.

Ill. 11: Embankment F1057: timbers at middle level, from west (note two ships' knees)

Ill. 12: Embankment F1057: timbers at lower level, from north, with brushwood F1058 in foreground

revetments, the estuarine silt (F1043) behind F1055 was not packed directly against the boards, but was separated by a thin film of soft organic fill (F1088); the reason for this intervening fill is unclear.

Sand/gravel bank F207

At this point, apparently, the reclamation process was interrupted by the irruption of a channel of water into the area enclosed by the revetments. A large deposit of clean gravel and coarse sand up to 1 metre thick (F207), directly overlying infill layers F206 and F223, was interpreted as a bar deposited by a channel of water, possibly a flood channel. The sand/gravel occurred in a fan-shaped spread across Area II, widening markedly toward the east (Fig. 17); indeed the section published by Mitchell (1987, Fig. 4) shows the bar running right up against Revetment 1. This distribution indicates that the channel which deposited the bar flowed across the site from the west, widening as it moved eastwards. Mitchell (1987, 15) noted the presence in this bar of micaceous debris from the Dublin mountains and interpreted the bar as the result of a flash flood on the Liffey. The same conclusion is reached in Dr Peter Coxon's analysis of samples from this deposit (see Chapter VI below), which also suggests that the predominant flow of this irruption was towards the east-south-east.

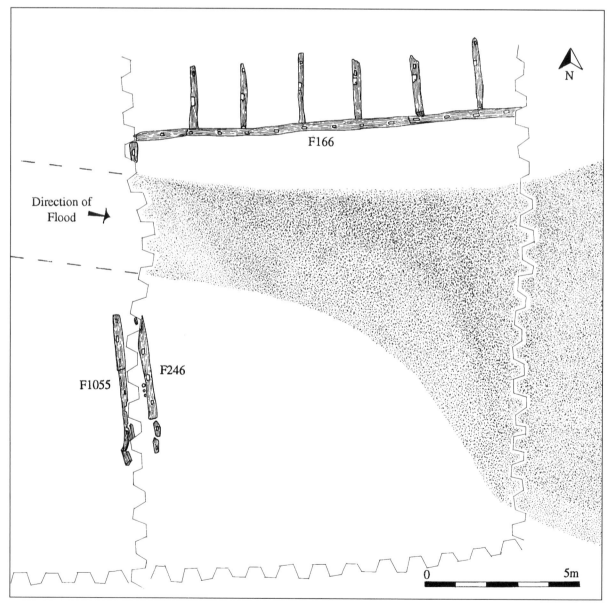

Fig. 17: Plan of gravel bar F207 in relation to Phase 3 revetments

Ill. 13: Revetment F166 from north: detail of eastern end, showing section of ship's keel and planking incorporated at upper level

The impact of this event on the reclamation process cannot fully be assessed, but it is possible that the gap between the two surviving sections of revetment F246 was at least partly due to this ingression of water. At the east end of revetment F166, moreover, it was notable that the orderly erection of overlapping boards ceased at the level at which this irruption took place (that is, just above sod layer F206). Thereafter a single piece of ship's hull was placed on its side against the uprights to bring the revetment to full height (Ill. 13). Stratigraphically, the ingression occurs at the same level as the latest surviving overlapping board of the revetment. Thus it is likely that further boards and associated silt backfill were washed away by the ingression, with the ship's hull being thrown up in the aftermath of the ingression as a replacement.

Cobbled Surface F176

The gravel bar F207 was in turn covered by a series of layers of organic refuse (F39, F190, F177, F199, F209) over an extensive area and by deposits of gravels (F192, F191, F189 and F186) over a more limited area inside the east end of revetment F166. This was probably done in conjunction with the erection of the ship's hull on the upper part of revetment F166 and in this area, at least, the purpose may have been to form a level surface behind the revetment. A small area of cobbling (F185) had been placed on a thin lens of organic refuse F177 and then covered in a thick deposit of F177, on which a much larger area of cobbling (F176) was placed. This extended for up to 4m across the site from the east baulk, with a further small patch of cobbling (F179) c.2.7m further west. The western limit of the main cobbled area roughly coincided with the junction of the first two baseplates; thus the cobbling was effectively confined to the area of full boarding down to the base of the revetment, which can hardly be coincidental.

The cobbled surface dipped both to the north (toward revetment F166) and to the west and was, for the most part, some 30–40cm below the level of the surviving top of the revetment (Ill. 14). However, the silts and organic deposits beneath the cobbling would have been particularly

Ill. 14: Area inside revetment F166, from west, showing cobbled surface F176

prone to compression and subsidence and it is quite likely that the cobbled surface was more level, and lay closer to the top of the revetment, originally. The cobbling must represent an attempt to form a working surface at the level of the top of the revetment. In between the two areas of cobbling (F176 and F179) a number of timber boards or planks were noted lying horizontally on the same surface as the cobbling (F178) but their relationship to the cobbling is unclear. A second spread of boards or planks and brushwood (F214) was noted c.2.5m to the south but it was not possible to establish whether the two spreads of timbers were contemporary. F214 was, however, clearly contemporary with a wooden trackway (F205) to the west.

Trackway F205

Immediately north of revetment F164 a timber trackway (F205) ran north-south just east of revetment F246 (Ill. 15). It was of crude corduroy construction with a series of overlapping planks (many of them clearly reused) on roughly parallel runners, lying on the same woody organic deposit (F199/F209) as timbers F214. This section of trackway was up to 2.0m wide and its total surviving length was c.2.7m, but it had been destroyed on the north by the large later wall F150. Another apparent section of trackway, but in much poorer condition, was uncovered to the south of revetment F164. This was not quite aligned with the trackway north of F164 and was physically at a slightly higher level (up to 30–40cm higher). Nevertheless it rested on the same organic base (F209, although in this case a thin deposit of gravels, F292 and F291 was laid down between the organic refuse and the trackway) and was judged most likely to be a continuation of the northern trackway F205. The presence of revetment F164 may account for the differences in level and alignment.

Trackway F205 must be closely related to revetment F246. It is almost certainly closely contemporary with it and ran on the same north-south line, immediately inside (east of) the revetment, which would, presumably, have been visible while the trackway was in use. Probably,

therefore, the primary purpose of the trackway was to provide access along the revetment. This
suggests a link with cobbled area F176, which has a similar relationship to revetment F166.
However, the stratigraphical relationship between trackway F205 and cobbled area F176 could not
be established with certainty. If anything, the indications were that F205 was slightly earlier than
F176 but it is quite possible that they were contemporary.

Ill. 15: Area inside revetment F166, from east,
showing trackway F205
and associated timbers
(toward top of plate).
Note top of revetment
F164, running vertically
to the left.

A further, apparently related feature in this post-irruption phase was two groups of posts (F162
and F158) located roughly on the same north-south line and c.4.5m apart. Both consisted of
clusters (c.1.0–1.5m in diameter) of closely spaced, relatively thin posts driven into the underlying
layers and associated with (sometimes driven through) several horizontal timber boards. The
boards were stratigraphically equivalent to trackway F205 (in the case of F162) and cobbled area
F176 (in the case of F158), suggesting that all these features may indeed be contemporary. The
function of the posts was not clear.

PHASE 4: THIRD RECLAMATION PHASE

On the outer (northern) face of revetment F166 a deep wedge-shaped deposit of gravels (F151,
F172, F279, F302, F277), organic silts (F280, F139, F278, F138) and estuarine mud (F281, F137) was
banked up (Pl. VII; see Figs 4–7). This represents the accumulation, mainly by natural processes,
of debris during the functioning lifetime of the revetment. This material was largely overlain by
another massive sand/gravel deposit (F128), up to 0.7m thick and extending for at least 14m north
of the revetment, at which point it became indistinguishable from the underlying river gravels.
F128 must have been deposited by another sudden flood on the river and seems to mark a definite
break in the deposition of material on this part of the site.

F128 was overlain by a series of layers of organic refuse (F156, F149, F136, F120, F119, F116, F110, ff)
with some sand/gravels (F109, F105, F111) and silts (F260, F257, F254, F124, F253, F117, F104). At the

northern end of the excavated area, this organic refuse was overlain by another massive sand/gravel
bank (F113), against which further layers of organic refuse (F120, F114, F108) were laid. To the south
of revetment F166, cobbled area F176 was overlaid by organic refuse (F175) and gravels (F283, F134)
before another organic refuse layer (F71/273) was deposited over the top of revetment F166 and
extending to the north. The area south of wall F150 was overlain by layers of organic refuse (F195,
F143, F297) which are probably equivalent to F175 overlying cobbled area F176.

The fact that this series of mainly organic layers overlies revetment F166, together with the
presence of the intervening sand/gravel deposit F128, indicates that it relates to a separate and later
phase of activity superseding the reclamation episode associated with revetment F166. Given the
nature of the material, the most likely explanation is that it represents a third reclamation episode,
presumably associated with one or more further revetments which lay to the north of the present
excavation area. Traces of such revetments were noted by Wallace (1981, 116–17; Revetments 2
and 3) who suggested a later 13th century date, but the ceramic material associated with this third
reclamation episode suggests a date not later than the middle of the 13th century. By this date,
clearly, the area enclosed by revetments F166, F246 and F1055 was well and truly dry land, with
the waterfront a considerable distance to the north.

PHASE 5: MEDIEVAL OCCUPATION PHASE (FIG. 18)

A new phase of activity on the site, characterised for the first time by actual habitation rather than
riverside or reclamation-related activity, is signalled by the construction of at least two substantial
masonry structures (Structures A and B), apparently in the later 13th century.

Ill. 16: Phase 5: north wall of Structure A (F150), from north

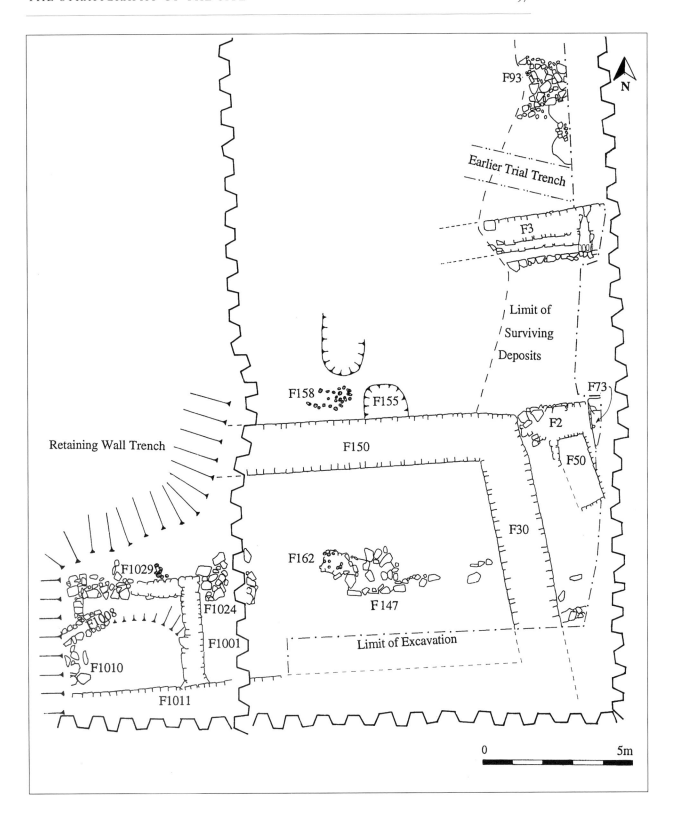

Structure A

Fig. 18: Phases 5 and 6: general plan of features

This was a large rectangular building which probably fronted onto Winetavern St, and was represented by the substantial foundations of its south, east and north walls (F1011, F30 and F150 respectively). The external dimensions of the structure were *c.*10m (north-south) by at least 17m (east-west) and its wall foundations were very substantial, *c.*1.6m thick on average, of roughly coursed limestone rubble with a rubble core and surviving up to 2.0m in height (Pl.VIII). The walls were founded directly on river gravels, trenches having been dug through all the overlying reclamation deposits. These trenches were then completely filled with mortared rubble masonry of much poorer quality than the upper levels, which were relatively carefully faced and coursed (Ill. 16).

This method of 'trench fill' construction has left no cut marks by which the correct place of the construction of the wall in the stratigraphic sequence could be established. Apparent foundation cuts bordering the walls were noted at relatively high levels but these seem to relate to rebuildings of the walls and cannot be used to date the primary construction. Furthermore, no floor surface or occupation layers which could be associated with the building had survived. This makes it extremely difficult to assign a date to the construction of the building, although it is clearly later than the various reclamation episodes. However, the ceramic material from layers (F154, F167) which are stratigraphically later than wall F150 is indicative of a later 13th-century date. Some caution must be exercised here, because the amount of pottery involved is quite small, but it can be said that the available evidence indicates a later 13th-century date for Structure A.

Structure B

The second masonry structure was represented by a single wall (F3) roughly parallel to the north wall of Structure A and located *c.*6.2m north of it (Ill. 17). A total length of 4.4m was exposed, although the wall continued further east beyond the limits of the excavation area. The wall was of roughly coursed limestone rubble with a loose rubble core and had a maximum width of 0.82m and a surviving height of 0.8m, including a basal plinth 0.26m in height. Unlike Structure A, F3 was not founded on natural gravels, but on redeposited gravels (F17/F33) which had been laid down on top of the latest reclamation organics (F71). On the south side of the wall was a stone-built drain, apparently a later addition of uncertain date, with an even more recent addition built of red brick at its east end. A horizontal wooden plank, probably of relatively recent date, lined the base of the drain. Interpretation of F3 is hindered by the lack of other walls relating to it but it is most likely to be the south wall of a building, as immediately north of it a series of habitation layers and an associated area of rough stone paving were found. The east wall should lie outside the excavated area and the west wall would have been removed in the construction of the access road but the absence of a north wall is puzzling.

The paving north of the wall (F93) extended over an area of *c.*2.5m (north-south) by *c.*1.5m (east-west), although it continued further east beyond the limits of the excavation area and had been truncated by modern disturbance on the west. It was a consistent spread of large and relatively flat stones, although there was no evidence of any stones having been dressed flat for the purpose; fragments of stone mortars were included. It could have been a floor surface or alternatively a form of hearth, as several layers of ash and burnt material (F94, F95, F20, F21, F22, F89, F88/90) occurred immediately above and adjacent to it. Further layers of burnt material (F97, F99) occurred beneath the paving. Further north, F123 seemed to represent a thin spread (probably truncated) of similar burnt material, while the other layers at the top of the surviving stratigraphy, F106 and F130, may also relate to this phase of activity. Associated ceramic material indicates a later 13th century date.

To the south, the area between the two walls F3 (Structure B) and F30/150 (Structure A) was built up further with deposits of gravel (F17/68/72/78, F62, F63) and gritty loam (F80). Clearly gravels were laid down on the reclamation material in order to establish a relatively firm and dry surface for occupation. At some point the drain (F4) on the south side of wall F3 was inserted on a bed of gravel (F41). Further deposits of gritty loam (F1, F52, F79) occurred in an apparent depression in the gravels, possibly a wide, shallow pit of unknown function.

Ill. 17: Phase 5: south (?) wall of Structure B (F3), from east, with drain F4 to south, after removal of red brick additions

PHASE 6: POST-MEDIEVAL ACTIVITY (FIG. 18)

The site had largely been stripped of its overburden of recent deposits prior to excavation; indeed Mitchell (1987, 5–6) commented on the reduction of the site to 13th century levels even before the first archaeological excavations commenced in 1969. Nevertheless, some evidence for post-medieval activity survived. The most substantial remains were foundations of probable cellar walls, occurring mainly in two locations. The first of these was immediately east of the north-east angle of Structure A. Here the north-west angle of a wall of mortared limestone masonry (F73) was exposed for 1.6m at the eastern edge of Area II (see Fig. 4). Unfortunately, because most of the wall lay beyond the area of excavation, its orientation and dimensions could not be determined. It is even possible that the wall is actually contemporary with Structure A, with which it is effectively aligned. Whatever its date, F73 was clearly earlier than a narrow, rectangular cellar or pit (F50)

Ill. 18: Phase 6: wall F2 from north. Note butt joint with north-eastern corner of Structure A (right)
and stones of F73 protruding from baulk (left).

formed of mortared limestone masonry with plastered inner faces, which was built onto F73 on
the west. Finally a short, shallow wall of limestone masonry (F2) was built on a roughly east-west
line, linking the northern ends of F30/150 and F73 (Ill. 18). F2 was stratigraphically later than cellar
F50 but may have been effectively contemporary with it.

The second main focus of cellar wall construction was actually within Structure A, at the
southern end of Area I. A small structure (c.3.0 x 3.2m internally) had been built against the inside
of the southern wall of the larger structure (F1011). The walls of the later structure were largely
of mortared limestone rubble construction, 60–75cm thick but many bricks were noted in the
upper courses. The north wall of the structure (F1029) is stratigraphically earlier than the east and
west walls (F1001 and F1010 respectively) but presumably all are broadly contemporary. A stone-
lined drain (F1008), crudely built of unshaped limestone blocks, cut obliquely through the west
wall (F1010) for a surviving length of 1.8m.

At the north-east corner of this structure a linear dump of loose stones (F1024) occurred,
continuing the line of the north wall, F1029, to the east. This stone dump, possibly from a dismantled
wall, ran across the southern ends of revetments F1055 and F246 and indeed, was retained to the west
by upright timbers set in short sections of baseplates, probably reused from revetment F246 (see Fig.
16, Ill. 6). The date and function of this stone dump are unknown but it may be related to a large
pit (F147) filled with stones, mortar and red brick located 2.6m east of revetment F246 on the
same east-west line as F1029 and F1024 (Ill. 19). This pit cut through the horizontal support beams
to the south of revetment F164. It in turn may be related to another late stone-lined pit (F155)
located 4.5m to the north against wall the north face of wall F150. This pit was cut through to the
natural river gravels and filled with a rubble of stone, mortar and red brick (F152).

Ill. 19: Phase 6: stone-filled pit F147, from south. Note tips of 164.2, upright timber of revetment F164, protruding on right.

REFERENCES

Mitchell, G.F. (ed.) 1987 *Archaeology and environment in early Dublin.* Medieval Dublin Excavations 1962–81,
 Ser. C, vol. 1. Dublin. Royal Irish Academy.

Wallace, P.F. 1981 Dublin's waterfront at Wood Quay, 900–1317. In G. Milne and B. Hobley (eds), *Waterfront
 archaeology in Britain and northern Europe,* 108–18. London. Council for British Archaeology Research
 Report **41**.

Wallace, P.F. 1985 The archaeology of Anglo-Norman Dublin. In H.B. Clarke and A. Simms (eds), *The
 comparative history of urban origins in non-Roman Europe,* 379–410. Oxford. B.A.R. Int. Series

Walsh, C. 1997 *Archaeological excavations at Patrick, Nicholas and Winetavern Sts, Dublin.* Dingle. Brandon
 Books/Dublin Corporation.

CHAPTER IV

The wooden waterfronts: a study of their construction, carpentry and use of trees and woodlands

Aidan O'Sullivan

INTRODUCTION

The excavation revealed a series of timber revetments and related features on the medieval foreshore of the river Liffey. There were four contemporary revetments, including one back-braced, one front-braced and two unbraced types, dated to the late 12th and early 13th centuries. These represented a continuation of the waterfronts known from previous excavations at Wood Quay, but the intensity of structural activity at this site indicates that it was a location of some significance. This report describes firstly, the methodology of the study and the techniques of the excavation; the revetments are then described and discussed in detail, with reference to stratigraphy and chronology. The character of the trees and woodlands that supplied the timbers are reconstructed. The woodworking techniques employed and the carpentry joints used are discussed, followed by an account of the waterfront assembly and reconstruction. Finally, the medieval Dublin urban waterfronts are assessed in relation to medieval water levels to ascertain their harbour function.

In the first and second reclamation phases (Phases 2 and 3) a range of different types of waterfront structures were built, including post-and-wattle and roundwood post fences and a number of variously unbraced, back-braced and front-braced timber waterfronts. Detailed examination of the timbers during excavation and in post-excavation analysis included recording of species, age, rate-of-growth, knottiness and grain. With this information it is possible to attempt a reconstruction of the woodland source and parent trees of the timbers used. The woodworking techniques employed in the waterfronts were also closely recorded on Wood Record Sheets, allowing a discussion of the carpentry and assembly of the structures. Recent research on former water levels in the Liffey estuary enables an interpretation of the nautical function of the waterfronts.

DESCRIPTION OF THE WATERFRONT STRUCTURES

PHASE I (PRE-RECLAMATION)

The River Liffey foreshore

In the late 12th century AD, the area investigated by the excavation was an open tidal foreshore, diurnally inundated by the River Liffey, whose tidal reach stretched at least 3km further upstream to Islandbridge. The evidence suggests (see above) that at some point in time, a channel shift or major flood caused erosion of the riverbank, washing away the boulder clay and gradually replacing it by a deposit of gravels. The shoreline in this area inclined only gently down to the river to the north, suggesting that it had become an area of either only gentle erosion or backwater deposition. The shore to the north-west was in contrast more steeply sloping. Such local changes in erosion and deposition patterns are common in complex upper estuary channels.

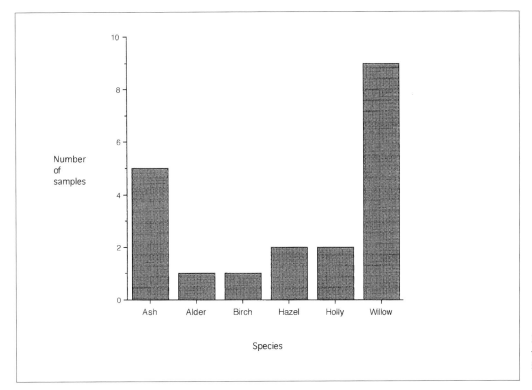

Fig. 19: F1069: wood species in posts

Wooden post structures F1069 and F1068

F1069 (Fig. 8; Ill. 1) was a relatively substantial row of 21 roundwood posts running east-west, driven into the river gravel F180, apparently to retain material to the south (F310, F235). The posts measured in average length 37cm and ranged in diameter from 4.5cm to 9.0cm, were spaced at 14cm intervals and were angled 45o toward the north. The structure was predominantly of strong willow and ash, with lesser amounts of holly, alder, birch and hazel (Fig. 19). The posts were of fairly uniform age, typically between 20 and 25 years (Fig. 20). The section of vertical wattling F1068, situated 1.8m to the south of F1069, was made solely of immature ash and hazel rods, 1.2–2.3cm in diameter, the ash typically aged between 6 and 10 years, the hazel typically 3–4 years (Fig. 21).

Contemporary foreshore structures

The post structure F1069 and post-and-wattle F1068 were deliberate foreshore constructions, sealed by organic silts. They may have served as simple boat jetties or may be the remains of structures related to fishing activities, but it is more likely that they relate to an early episode of foreshore reclamation further to the south or west, outside the excavated area. Similar structures have been found elsewhere on the Liffey foreshore. Mitchell (1987, 15) noted a 'light post-and-wattle palisade erected on thinly stratified foreshore deposits' retaining a thick deposit of sods, 20m north of the town wall, with a further post structure 2m north of that again; there was also an apparently natural bank of river gravel which was topped with wattle mats for use as a causeway. Recent excavations further to the north-west on Winetavern St also uncovered the remains of a possible late-12th century timber jetty or boardwalk on this shore (Walsh 1997, 95–8).

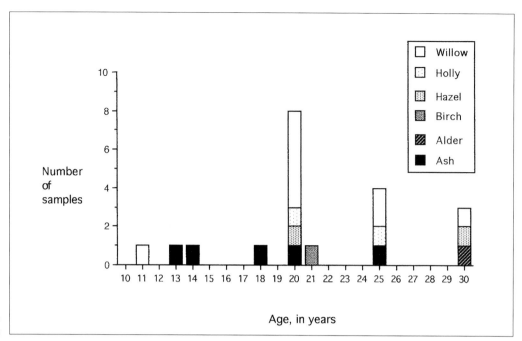

Fig. 20: F1069:
ages of posts

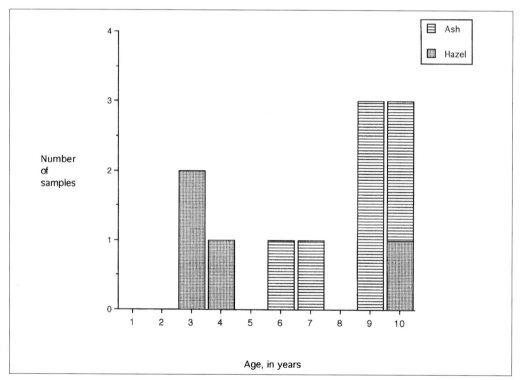

Fig. 21: F1068: age of
hazel and ash rods

PHASE 2 (FIRST RECLAMATION)

Revetment F164

F164 (Fig. 9; Pl. II) was a crude back-braced post and plank revetment, oriented east-west, measuring 6.4m in length and 1.6m in surviving height. It was of simple construction, comprising four large earthfast posts (164.1–4) driven vertically into redeposited silt at 1.0–2.2m intervals, behind (south of) which was placed a wall of reused ships' planking. Horizontal beams were laid behind the revetment in the manner of tie-backs or rear braces, jammed against a series of small vertical posts driven into silt F233, c.1.5m south of and directly aligned on the four main uprights. This was presumably intended to prevent the revetment falling back to the south, while the insertion of the planking into a prepared slot may also have helped to hold the structure upright.

Once this structure was erected, the area behind it was backfilled with estuarine silt (F211) and it seems that raking braces were added at either end of the revetment, to the rear. At the west end a single, short timber block was mortised into the main upright (164.4) and set into silt F233, with the prepared slot again backfilled with soft organic material. At the east end of the revetment a row of upright timber planks, 15–20cm wide, ran between the main upright (164.1) and an additional rear post and retained silt within the revetment. A longer diagonal raking brace was placed between the upright and rear post, possibly originally mortised into the top of the upright.

The timbers employed in the structure were predominantly re-used. The main earthfast posts were substantial and varied in form, and all but one were obviously re-used structural or ships' timbers. The exception was the easternmost upright (164.1), a substantial and barely modified roundwood trunk, 40cm in diameter and aged 62 years, simply hewn to a roughly squared surface, although much sapwood was retained as waney edges. This tree was a fast-grown, straight-grained oak, quite likely to have grown as a standard oak within a managed woodland system. 164.2 had five through-mortises up its length, spaced at 20cms intervals; the lower mortises were square and had no apparent function in this structure, although the upper mortise was larger, rectangular and roughly level with the top of the structure. 164.3 was an unusual piece, of thick T-shaped cross-section, which has been tentatively identified as part of a cross-beam from a small ship (see Chapter VIII). The westernmost upright (164.4) was a rectangular oak beam, 31cm wide and 13cm thick, which also had five through-mortises spaced along its length, one being a single large rectangular through-mortise (20cm x 13cm) near the top; it too may possibly have been a ship's timber originally (see Chapter VIII). The plank cladding of the revetment comprised at least six runs of planks, four of which appeared to be originally boat timbers (see Chapter VIII).

Brushwood structure F210

F210 was a brushwood spread set on silt F211 packed behind revetment F164. The posts and rods were predominantly of hazel, tightly grouped in age between 3 and 6 years, with lesser amounts of alder and ash (Figs 22–23). The wood measured between 1.1 and 2.1cms in diameter (Fig. 24).

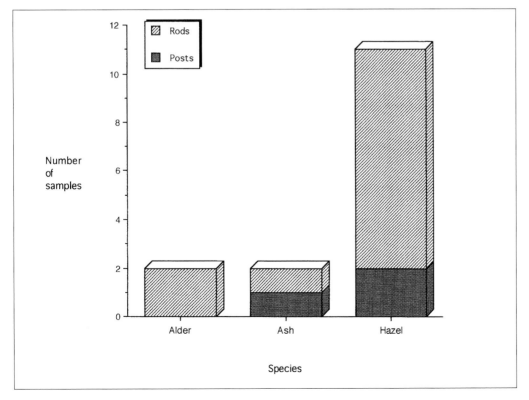

Fig. 22: F210: wood species in post-and-wattle

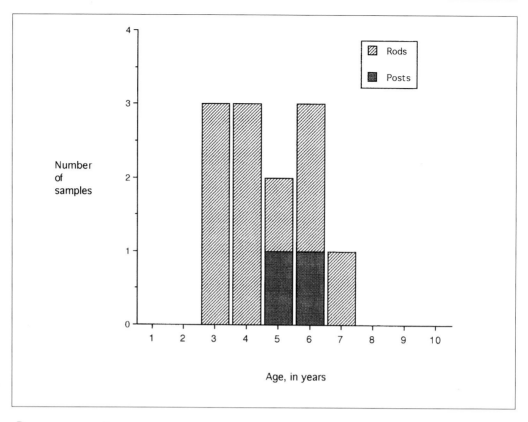

Fig. 23: F210:
hazel – ages of
posts and rods

Post structure F1070

F1070 was a row of five posts running east-west roughly in line with revetment F164 in Area I. The posts averaged 21.5cm in surviving length and 5cm in diameter and were entirely of mature ash roundwood, aged between 15–23 years.

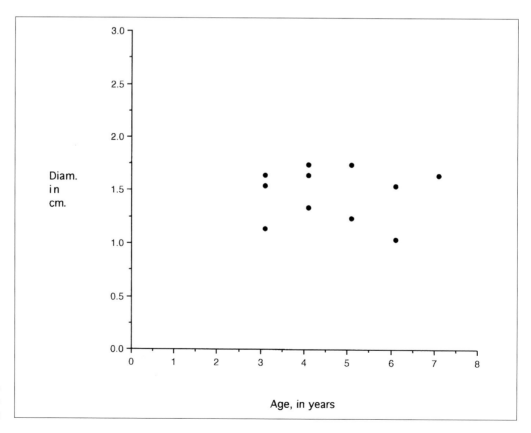

Fig. 24: F210:
hazel – age / size
relationships

PHASE 3: (SECOND RECLAMATION)

Revetment F166

F166 (Figs 12–15), a large front-braced revetment, was the most elaborate of the four waterfronts revealed and had over fifty separate timbers which were almost entirely of oak, although there was occasional use of ash and alder. It was constructed of a series of principal baseplates, subsidiary baseplates and diagonal braces supporting a wall of planks and uprights. It measured at least 1.8m in original height and a length of c.12.5m was revealed in excavation.

Baseplates

Construction of the revetment began with the laying of the principal baseplate in a slot dug through silt F174 into the underlying gravel F180. The baseplate was made up of three separate substantial timbers (166.54, 55, 56) joined together by means of simple pegged through-splayed scarfs. The placing of the scarf joints suggests that the baseplate was laid down from east to west. Six subsidiary baseplates (166.13–16, 49, 53) were added, extending northwards at right angles to the main baseplate (Pl. III), laid on silt F174 and tenoned into mortises cut into the northern edge of the main baseplate (Fig. 12; Ills. 2, 3). A spread of compact estuarine silt (F222) was also deposited immediately behind (south of) the principal baseplate, presumably to prevent it from moving during construction of the revetment. The subsidiary baseplates measured between 1.7m and 2.0m in length, 15–20cms in width and 10cms thick. They were tenoned into the main baseplate by a range of pegged joints, comprising barefaced and double-shouldered tenons or by means of ends simply hewn to a tapered shape (Fig. 12). The subsidiary baseplates were pinned to the foreshore silts by heavy cleft-wood pegs driven through rectangular mortises at their northern ends (Pl. III, Ill. 20).

The complete principal baseplate had 13 rectangular through-mortises, spaced at average intervals of c.95cm, cut entirely through its thickness from top to bottom. In at least two cases these mortises were also cut through the ends of the nearest housed subsidiary baseplates, suggesting that the mortises were cut after the insertion of the subsidiary baseplates (Ill. 2). This in turn suggests construction of the revetment on site, rather than prefabrication off site. These mortises held twelve (one mortise was empty) vertical posts by means of shouldered and pegged tenons. The posts were generally hewn to a rectangular section (boxed-heart and boxed-halved type) and measured between 15cm and 25cm in width and 5–10cm in thickness. Every alternate post was held in position by a raking front brace (see Figs 13–14), the remaining mid-span posts being unsupported. The front braces were of radially-cleft timber, typically measuring c.1.50m in length, c.15cm in width and c.10cm in thickness. The only raking brace to remain attached to its upright post (166.50) was housed in a probable chase-mortise in the upright (Ill. 13). The lower ends of the raking braces were pegged into position in notched-lap joints in the subsidiary baseplates (Ill. 20).

The revetment by this stage was a framework of principal baseplates, subsidiary baseplates, vertical uprights and front braces and was ready to accept the horizontal planks which actually retained the dumped infill behind the revetment. The planking was made up of at least nine runs of overlapping radially-cleft planks, which typically measured c.2m long, c.25cm wide and c.1cm thick. The absence of nails in the revetment structure indicates that the planks could only be placed in position as silt F221 was being deposited to the rear, as only the pressure of this deposit would keep the planks in place. One separate, discrete area of planking could be recognised, at the east end where part of the keel and planking of a clinker-built boat was incorporated into the structure (Ill. 13; see Chapter VIII).

Ill. 20: Revetment F166: detail of subsidiary baseplate 166.14, showing raking brace seated in notched-lap joint, and peg in mortise at northern end, pinning baseplate to foreshore silts

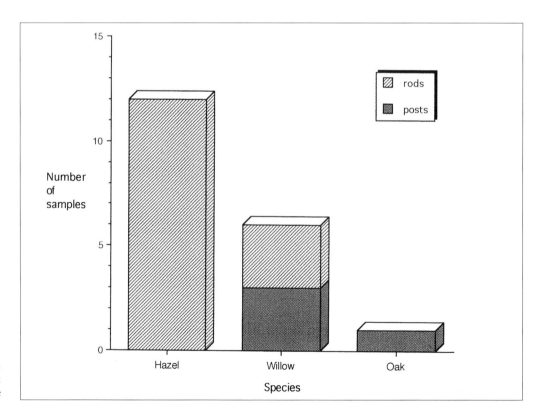

Fig. 25: F208: wood species in post-and-wattle

Wattle fence F208/F240

F208, a post-and-wattle structure constructed *c*.4m south of revetment F166, was interpreted as a fence designed to retain the silts (F221) deposited in conjunction with the erection of revetment F166. It consisted of two diverging rows of post-and-wattle fences, both apparently originating from a single post at the west end, from which one row ran roughly eastwards and the other north-eastwards. A maximum height of 1.0–1.2m of wattling survived. The vertical posts were predominantly of willow roundwood (Fig. 25) and typically measured 4–5cm in diameter but a single oak post measured 14cm in diameter. The wood species used in the interwoven wattles was almost entirely immature hazel, which measured 1.0–3.1cm diameter (Fig. 26), with small amounts of willow (Fig. 25). The hazel rods were aged between 4 and 10 years and the distribution of ages indicates a range of managed coppice rotations, on a rotation of 4, 7 and 10 years of age (Figs 27–28).

A post-and-wattle structure F240 was found running north-south in silts F223, south of F208. The alder, ash, hazel and willow posts (Fig. 29) measured 4–5 cm, and the hazel rods 1.7–2.0cm, in diameter (Fig. 30). The hazel wood ranged broadly in age from 1 to 11 years, with peaks at 4 and 7 years (Fig. 31).

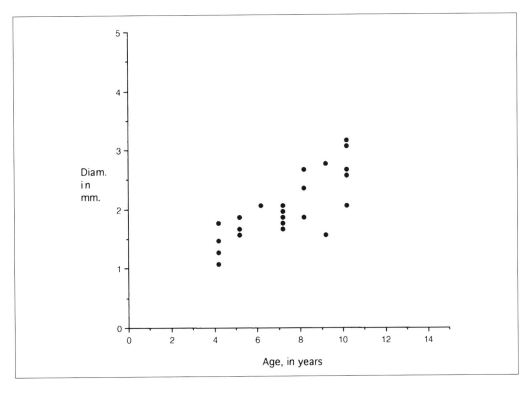

Fig. 26: F208: hazel – age / size relationships

Revetment F246

F246 (Fig. 16; Ill. 5–6) was an unbraced post and plank revetment with a horizontal baseplate, which appears to have been erected contemporaneously with F166, running southwards from the western end of the more substantial structure. The horizontal baseplate (246.17) was laid in a south to north direction on silt (F238, equivalent to F174), although without a cut bedding slot, and measured 3.20m in length, 26cm wide and 18cm thick; it had been damaged for 1.1m from the southern end by a later wall foundation or stone-filled pit (F1024). It was splayed at the southern end, possibly representing the remains of a scarf joint, and had three rectangular stopped-mortises, not fully cut through the baseplate, spaced at 60cm intervals.

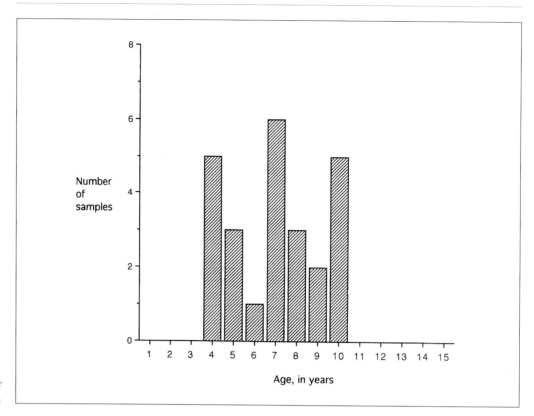

Fig. 27: F208:
hazel – age of
wattles

These mortises held three vertical posts (246.6–8), *c*.1.0m in average length, 20cm wide and 10cm thick. A wall of planking, comprising three horizontally laid planks (246.1–3), was placed on the east side of the posts. These planks measured on average 1.77m in length, 26cm in width and 2cm in thickness. Each plank spanned three uprights, the midspan supporting its centre and the end posts supporting the plank ends. A small vertical overlap in the lowest row of planks indicates

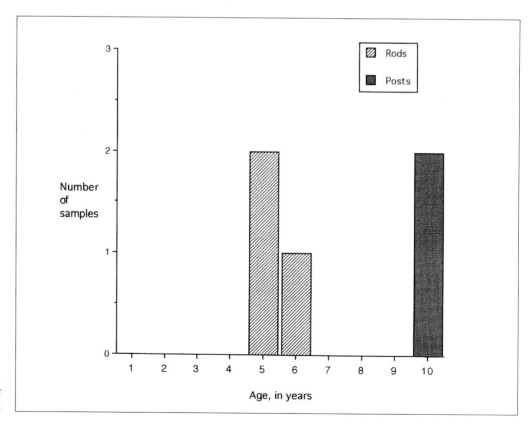

Fig. 28: F208:
willow – ages of
posts and rods

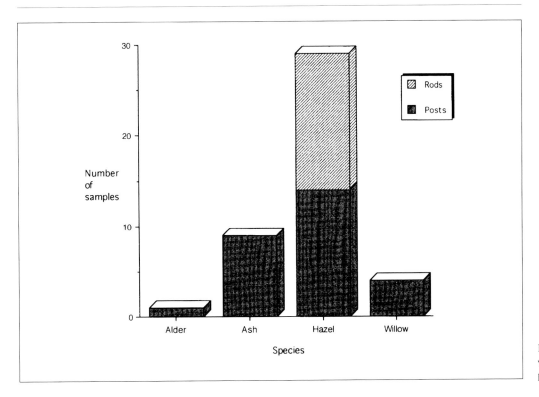

Fig. 29: F240:
wood species in
posts and rodsr

that the planks were laid out from north to south. As with F166, further planks were added above
the lower planks as the level of infilled silts (F0237, F0239, F0244) rose. Two further vertical posts
(246.4, 5), inserted in two blocks of timber measuring 50cm in length, 20cm in width and 10cm
in thickness, stood at the southern end of the revetment but had probably been re-erected or
added later.

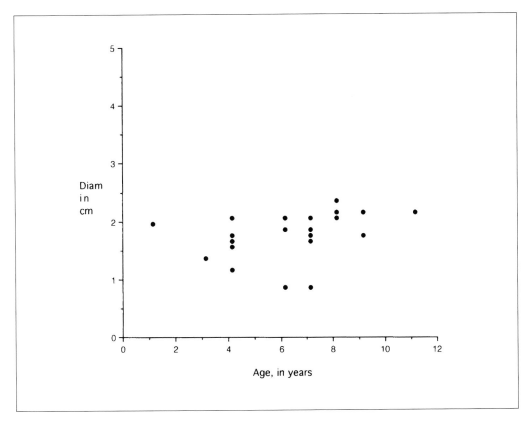

Fig. 30: F240:
hazel – age / size
relationships

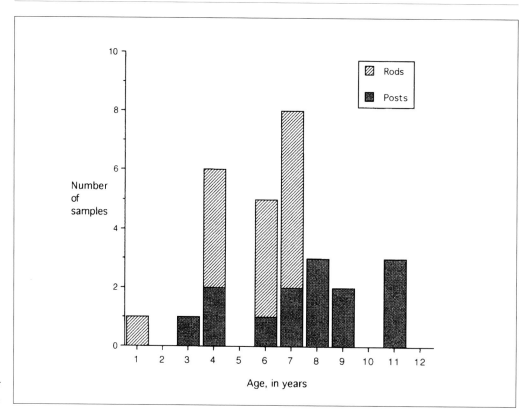

Fig. 31: F240: hazel – ages of posts and rods

Revetment F1055

F1055 (Fig. 16; Ills 7–9, Pl. VI) was another unbraced post and plank revetment measuring 4.70m in length and 1.30m in present height, located 0.8m west of F246. Its location and form suggest that it was contemporary in construction with F246 and it is possible that revetments F246 and F1055 should be viewed as parts of a double-walled structure rather than two separate parallel waterfronts. Like F246, the revetment was truncated at the north end by the later medieval wall F150, but the southern end of the revetment (although damaged by sheet piling) seemed to represent an original termination. In F1055, the baseplate consisted of two separate hewn timbers (1055.1, 2) laid on gravel F1071 and jointed together by a pegged, through-splayed scarf joint (Ill. 8), which indicated that the northern baseplate was laid first. The baseplate had six rectangular through-mortises at c.40cm intervals.

Three of these mortises held vertical posts (1055.3, 4, 5), measuring on average 1.50m in length, 20cm in width and 12cm in thickness. The cladding of planks was confined to a relatively short span of c.1.8m between the uprights and comprised four horizontally laid planks (1055.6–9) placed on the west side of the posts. These planks measured on average 1.7m in length, 22cm in width and 1cm in thickness. In one example (1055.8) the plank was attached to the vertical post by an iron nail. The upper part of the revetment had almost been destroyed by the insertion of a modern wall trench and a stone-filled pit (F1024) to the south. The form of the revetment as it survived may be close to the original construction, with a re-use of the baseplate possibly indicated by the superfluous mortises.

Embankment F1057

F1057 consisted of a build-up of mixed layers of organic refuse (F1956, F1102, F1023) and silt/estuarine mud (F1103, F1043, F1047, F1054, F1022) into which a heavy concentration of large timbers, brushwood and upright posts (F1052) was also driven through F1043 at one point (Ills. 10–12). Their purpose is uncertain but is presumably related to the embankment F1057. An area

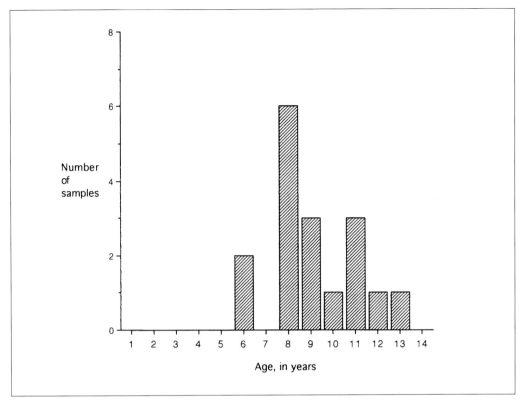

Fig. 32: F1058: age of rods

of hazel brushwood, F1058, was found in the silts F1056 (Ills. 12). The rods measured 1.7–2.3cms in diameter and were aged between 6 and 13 years (Fig. 32); a peak at 8 years may indicate a coppice rotation.

Timber pathway F205

F205 (Fig. 10; Ill. 15) was constructed by laying a series of overlapping planks (many of them re-used) on a foundation substructure of roughly parallel runners. A wide range of wood species was used, including oak, ash, alder, holly, birch, elm and dogwood (Fig. 33). The oak was entirely of radially cleft planks and beams, 10–24cm in width, taken from trunks aged 60–100 years. The remaining wood species were of mature roundwood, 6–9cm in diameter and typically aged between 20 and 40 years.

Post clusters F162 and F158

F162 and F158 consisted of clusters (c.1.0–1.5m in diameter) of loosely spaced, relatively narrow posts driven into the underlying layers and associated with several horizontal planks. Post cluster F162 was possibly stratigraphically equivalent to trackway F205. The wood used was oak roundwood and planks, 7.5–9.5cm in diameter and 26–35 years in age.

THE WATERFRONT TIMBERS, TREES AND WOODLAND

RECONSTRUCTING MEDIEVAL TREES AND WOODLANDS

An important innovation in the study of medieval urban wooden structures is the recent recognition that archaeological timbers provide a unique archive for the reconstruction of contemporary rural woodlands (Goodburn 1991; 1994). This is because every timber, in its tree-rings, size and shape, documents the history of the parent tree's growth, selection and conversion to a structural

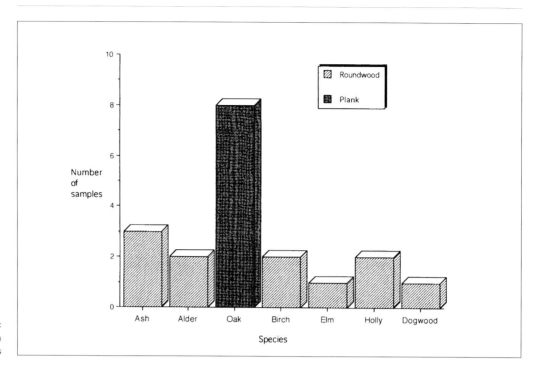

Fig. 33: F205:
wood species in
planks and posts

timber. It is possible, through detailed recording, to reconstruct the logs and thence the trees from which the timbers were cut and ultimately the type of woodland in which they grew.

A Wood Record Sheet was employed during the Winetavern St/Wood Quay excavation to enable close examination of each individual waterfront timber. In the post-excavation phase, a series of these timbers were re-drawn at 1:10 scale, recording in detail the natural features of the timbers. The elements recorded include the grain, location and size of knots, the cross-section of the timber showing the location of the pith, sapwood and orientation of the tree-rings. The natural 'wane' or bark edge if present on the timber was recorded. A number of timbers were also sampled for dendrochronological dating, which when allied to the regularity and rate of growth of the tree-rings noted on the drawings provides an impression of the growth history of each tree.

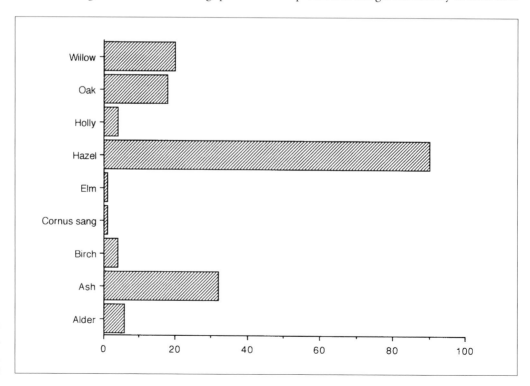

Fig. 34: Winetavern St/
Wood Quay, smaller
structures: total
wood species

A sampling strategy for the smaller roundwood was employed during excavation to enable a reconstruction of the age and size patterns of contemporary medieval underwood.

THE WINETAVERN ST/WOOD QUAY WOOD; SPECIES AND WOODLANDS ENVIRONMENT

The range of native Irish wood species identified in the Winetavern St/Wood Quay structures included oak (*Quercus sp.*), hazel (*Corylus avellana*), willow (*Salix sp.*), alder (*Alnus sp.*), ash (*Fraxinus excelsior*), holly (*Ilex sp.*), birch (*Betula sp.*), and dogwood (*Cornus sanguinea*). Oak completely dominated in the larger timber structures (revetments F164, F166, F246 and F1055), providing the raw material for the baseplates, vertical elements and braces, although on infrequent occasion mature hazel, alder and ash trunks were also used. The predominance of oak in the heavier timbers is understandable given the large girth of its trunk, its strength, load-bearing properties and relative resistance to rot. A much wider range of mixed woodland species was used

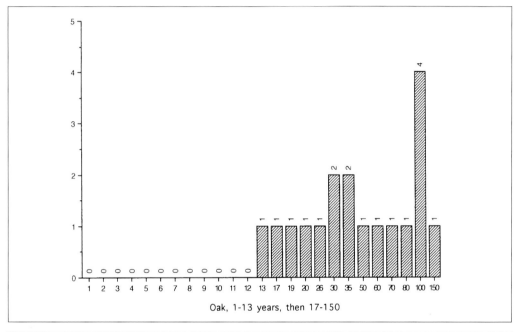

Fig. 35: Winetavern St/ Wood Quay, smaller structures: oak – age in years

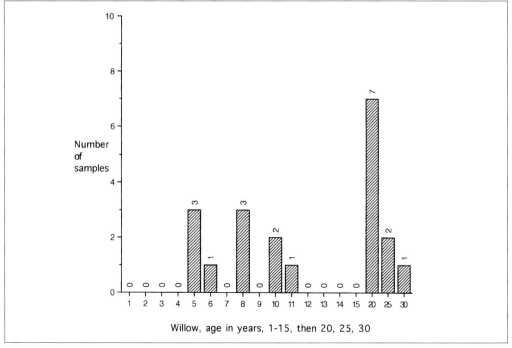

Fig. 36: Winetavern St/Wood Quay, smaller structures: willow – age in years

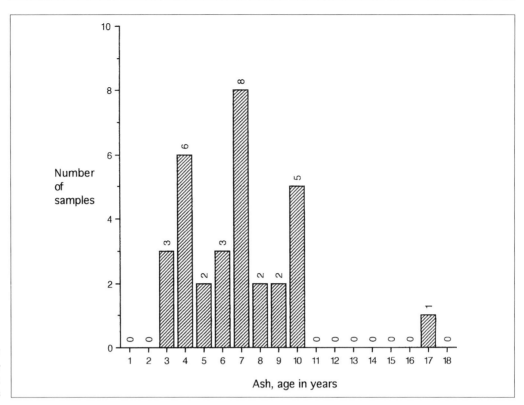

Fig. 37: Winetavern St/
Wood Quay, smaller
structures: ash
– age in years

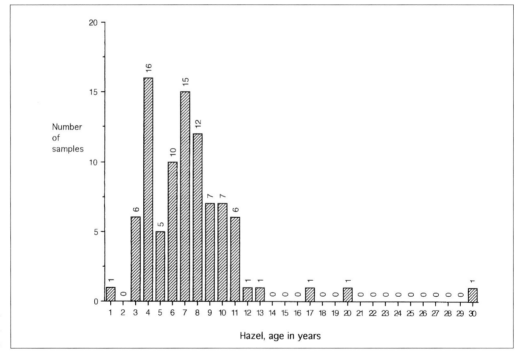

Fig. 38: Winetavern St/
Wood Quay, smaller
structures: hazel –
age in years

for the foreshore post alignments, F1069, F1068 and F1070, post-and-wattle fence F208 and
timber pathway F205.

The graphed results (Fig. 34) indicate that hazel was easily the most common species used in
these structures (51.14%), while the other predominant species were ash (18.1%), willow (11.36%)
and oak (10.23%). Lesser amounts of alder, holly, birch, oak and dogwood were also used. The
four main species have also been analysed in terms of age. The oak wood was typically taken from
mature trunks. The large timbers from the revetments ranged widely from c.30–250 years, while
the smaller structural oak aged between 15 and 100 years (Fig. 35). The willow indicates little
patterning, ranging between 5 and 30 years, although a large proportion of the willow roundwood

was aged 20 years (Fig. 36). By contrast, the ash and hazel roundwood indicate tighter age ranges. The ash roundwood was tightly clustered between 3 and 10 years, with peaks at 4, 7 and 10 years (Fig. 37). The hazel roundwood was also tightly clustered between 3 and 11 years, with peaks at about 4 and 8 years (Fig. 38). The implications of this analysis are that both large oak trunks and immature hazel and ash roundwood of restricted age were being deliberately obtained for the waterfronts, with a range of other species also incidentally employed in the structures.

The Winetavern St/Wood Quay wood assemblage confirms that a range of woodland environments was being exploited by the settlement of medieval Dublin. The fast-grown hazel and ash would probably have grown best on dry, lime-rich soils, although occasional hazel and willow trunks that were longer lived but with narrower growth rate indicate that stressed or scrubby trunks were also exploited. The alder and willow would have thrived best on waterlogged mineral soils, perhaps adjacent to the River Liffey wetlands. More acidic, upland soils may be indicated by the oak, holly and birch. However it is also possible that the predominant woodland used was of hazel/ash with additional stands of holly, willow, elm and dogwood growing on its fringes (Rackham 1980). Increased demands on local woodland in the vicinity of medieval Dublin, from at least the 10th century onwards, must have lead to organised and controlled woodland management strategies. By the time of the arrival of the Anglo-Normans in the late 12th century it is likely that these managed woodlands had evolved to have certain characteristics which may possibly be reconstructed through archaeological and historical investigation.

THE WINETAVERN ST/WOOD QUAY STRUCTURES, SPECIES, AGE AND SIZE

Hazel and ash underwood

The overall patterns in the Winetavern St/Wood Quay wood indicate that a range of species, sizes and ages were utilised but when the hazel and ash, the most commonly used species, are analysed more complex patterns emerge. Several structures have posts and rods that are tightly clustered in age. In contrast, other structures display broad patterns of underwood extraction, with the wood ranging widely in age. This would suggest that a combination of quality managed woodland and poorer scrub woodland was being exploited (Fig. 39).

The brushwood structure F1068 was comprised solely of ash and hazel rods. Although the sample was small the hazel was typically aged 3–4 years; the ash was older, but similarly tightly clustered in age between 9 and 10 years (Fig. 21). Two other structures illustrate a slightly clearer distribution. The post and wattle fence F208 was comprised of hazel, willow and oak with hazel dominant in the both posts and rods (Fig. 25). This hazel was exclusively aged between 4 and 10 years, with slight peaks noted at three year intervals of 4, 7 and 10 years (Fig. 27). The hazel age/size relationships indicate an even increase in diameter with age (Fig. 26), which might suggest a common source for the wood. The post and wattle structure F210 was mostly of hazel, with a small amount of alder and ash (Fig. 22). The hazel was quite tightly clustered in age, between 3 and 7 years (Fig. 23). However the age/size relationships of this hazel (Fig. 24) indicate that an evenly sized crop of rods was also a requirement in the structure. Hazel was the only species used in the structure F1058. This hazel tended to be older than that used in other structures, between 6 and 14 years, although a distinct peak was noticeable at 8 years (Fig. 32).

Several Winetavern St/Wood Quay structures, however, show more irregular tree-ring and age/size patterns. The post and wattle structure F240 was comprised mostly of hazel, with some ash and a few pieces of willow and alder (Fig. 29). The rods were typically aged between 4 and 7 years, while the larger posts ranged more widely from 4 to 11 years; slight peaks in ages are visible at 4 and 7 years (Fig. 31). The widest variability in species and ages was displayed by the post

Fig. 39: Suggested parent trees and woodland for waterfront post-and-wattle and small roundwood structures

structure F1069 and the timber pathway F205. F1069 was composed mostly of willow and ash, with lesser amounts of alder, birch, hazel and holly (Fig. 19). The wood was fairly mature, given its size, typically aged about 20 years (Fig. 20). F205 had oak, ash, alder, holly, birch, elm and dogwood (Fig. 33). The oak was entirely of radially cleft planks and beams taken from trunks aged 60–100 years. The ash, alder, birch, elm, holly and dogwood was mostly mature roundwood and typically aged between 20 and 40 years.

This distinction between some post and wattle and brushwood structures and some of the larger roundwood post rows is partly due to different sizes of wood used, but it is also likely that post and wattle requires more evenly aged rods. Furthermore, the location and form of the waterfront structures would probably mean that high quality craftsmanship or fine raw materials were not required. Nevertheless, there is possible evidence for the extraction of wood at defined intervals, typically at about 4, 7–8 and 10–11 years. Recent analysis (by the present writer and Mary Deevy) of wood from 13th century house structures, pathways and boundary fences at Back Lane, Dublin indicates that at that site, wood was coppiced at 4–8 year intervals.

Immature oak

There are also patterns to be discerned in the types of trees used for the larger timber structures, F166, F164, F246 and F1055. The smaller elements – the vertical posts and subsidiary baseplates – were taken from a combination of fast-grown, immature oak trunks and slightly older trees (Fig. 40). One vertical post in revetment F166 (166.50) was taken from a very straight-grained trunk, c.15cm in diameter and aged c.35 years. Its growth rate was initially very fast but slowed thereafter. Two subsidiary baseplates were taken from fast-grown, straight-grained oak trunks measuring 10–15cm diameter, while a third subsidiary baseplate was taken from a half-split oak trunk aged c.40 years. Another subsidiary baseplate (166.16) was a worked roundwood oak trunk, c.25–30 years of age, with both bark and sapwood retained. These smaller oaks were probably taken from either fast-grown young oak saplings or coppiced mature oak-wood. Trees of this type are best found in periodically felled woodland.

Fig. 40: Suggested parent trees for waterfront timber baseplates, uprights, planking and ships' timbers

Medium-aged oak trunks

The main revetment F166 provides the best information about tree selection. The principal baseplate was formed of three sections, of which only one (166.55) was recovered complete in the excavation. This section was formed from a beam at least 7.25m long, of boxed-heart conversion with pith at the centre of the beam and the sapwood retained along one side edge. The grain was slightly wavy, with a few side-branches. The original trunk diameter can be estimated as *c.*30cm. The tree was aged *c.*100 years and the tree-rings seemed to indicate a fast early growth, with a later gradual slowing in rate of growth. Another baseplate section, 166.54, was of similar dimensions and appearance and was found through dendrochronology to be aged 125 years. Revetment F164 also produced extremely fast-grown oak trunks, notably the upright post 164.1, a barely modified roundwood oak trunk which measured *c.*40cm in diameter and was aged 62 years. Most of the planks and beams from the wooden pathway F205 were taken from medium aged trunks, *c.*70–100 years in age and 30–50cm diameter.

   The impression gained from these timbers is of straight-grained, relatively branch-free trunks grown in close competition with both trees and an understorey of lower vegetation (Fig. 40). These were either growing in regenerated secondary woodland or were taken from mature managed oaks. This picture of fast-grown, branch-free trunks being used for baseplates, beams and stakes is supported by the evidence from Walsh's (1997, 99–103) excavations on Winetavern St. One massive baseplate (F719b) from the revetment at Site K was hewn from a straight-grained, relatively branch-free oak trunk with a bole which measured in excess of 10.6m in length, yet was aged only *c.*130 years. This provided a best-estimated felling date of 1204 +/–9 AD (ibid., 188) and is clearly very close – if not identical – in date to the revetments on the present site. A second baseplate from this revetment, in excess of 7.35m in length, was aged 102 years. Again, there are two possible origins for these oak trunks, either that they were taken from secondary growth in a wild woodland or that they were grown in a managed mature woodland. Given the historical evidence for woodland curation and use, the latter explanation seems more likely.

Ancient oak trunks

Notwithstanding the evidence for woodland management, there is also strong evidence to suggest that much more substantial trunks were available for use. The planks from revetment F166 in particular were taken from quite distinctive trees, long-lived oak trunks of substantial girth. The ships' timbers discovered during the excavation were also taken from long-lived oak trunks (Fig. 40). Stems and knees were taken from curved and forked branch wood; heavy side branches were used. Such trees are typically found in hedgerows or in open land.

THE CRAFT OF MEDIEVAL WOODMANSHIP

The Winetavern St/Wood Quay wood indicates a range of species, age and size of wood used. Although the patterns are variable, with clear evidence for the use of poorer quality underwood, there is also evidence for the exploitation of managed underwood and timber. Woodmanship is the craft of producing a renewable and constant supply of wood from wild trees in woodlands or hedgerows. It derives from the ability of most trees to produce a new spring growth of branches from a recently felled stump. Although most deciduous tree species will produce a coppice growth, hazel, ash and willow are particularly vigorous (Rackham 1982, 1990). The coppice stool produces a large number of spring shoots, providing rods, poles or logs depending on the cropping interval (Rackham 1980, 1990). Hazel stools can produce rods 1.5m in length in a single season's growth, while ash can produce rods up 2.1m and willow rods as much as 3m in length. The first 2 or 3 years growth are very fast, producing wide growth rings. A coppice stool will not produce rods precisely similar in size or age; younger shoots tend to be shadowed and thus restricted in growth by taller, older shoots. Furthermore, throughout the growth cycle, new and therefore younger shoots will be produced with every successive year. Large trunks can also be produced as timber trees, with certain poles being left to age and thicken. Single tree saplings may also be managed and protected for decades. It is also possible that mature oak woodland would be managed by selective cropping and restrictive access.

Underwood provided the narrow rods (*virge*) and slightly stouter poles for weaving wattle panels (*claie*), for fuel wood or for smaller structural timbers. It must be emphasised that the quality and quantity of rods produced by natural coppice in scrub woodland or as a result of animal grazing is insufficient to supply a constant demand. Unmanaged branches are knotty, with frequent side twigs and irregularities. Topwood branches were, however, used as general infill in pathways, for fuel wood and probably for domestic wood crafts. Even small areas of coppice could have produced a useful crop. The amount of rods produced from an area of coppice-wood depends on a variety of factors, including wood species present, the number of stools per acre and drainage and soil conditions. However, a well-tended hazel coppice with 600 stools per acre can produce as much 12,000 rods every seven years (Tabor 1994). Trees can also be pollarded to produce a crop of rods from a bolling, whereby a trunk is regularly cropped at a height of several metres. The pollarding of trees has the advantage that the woodland floor can still be used for animal grazing. Trees can also be pollarded in hedgerows.

Timber

Timber trees provided the raw material for baseplates, vertical supports, roof beams, planks and boards, preferably being larger trunks over 2 feet (60cm) in girth with a branch-free bole.

Hedgerow trees are thick and knotty, slow-grown with low, heavy side branches, but trunks grown in competition in secondary woodland are in contrast straight, fast-grown and relatively free of branches. Timber trees can be grown in a variety of situations but the best means of controlling the quality of timber trees is to grow them as standards within a managed system. The trunks grow straight and tall, but are free of lower branches because of the surrounding underwood cover (Goodburn 1991, 1994). The economic value of a timber tree was typically reckoned according to the maximum size of timber possible to obtain from it. In medieval England this was reckoned in terms of a unit of value known as a load, typically being 40–50 cubic feet (Rackham 1980).

THE COPPICE MANAGEMENT OF MEDIEVAL DUBLIN WOODLANDS

There was a fundamental distinction in Anglo-Norman Ireland between *silva*, *boscus* and *bruaria* woodland (O'Sullivan 1992, 1994a, 1994b). In medieval Latin, *silva* was a timber wood exploited for construction timber and wood pasture, *boscus* woodland provided the underwood for fuel and wattles and *bruaria* is derived from the Latin *brucaria*, similar to the 12th-century French term *bruyere*, and may have referred to an area of poor quality, scrubby brushwood (Jäger 1983). It is possible that *bruaria* underwood would have been cheaper to obtain than fine quality *boscus* underwood and could have been used for rough brushwood structures such as cruder waterfront fences.

The available information on land use in the manors around Dublin for 1326 indicates that 8% of land was held in woodland as against 65% for arable and 16% for pasture (Jäger 1983). Although this is relatively low by English standards, it would have provided sufficient supplies of underwood (Rackham 1990). It has also been pointed out that seemingly small areas of woodland often provided a more substantial income than larger areas of arable land. Dissolution extents of the properties of the Dublin monasteries clearly indicate that most still controlled several acres of boscus woodland in the 16th century (White 1943, 212). *Mellyfaunte Woode* was 60 acres of coppice (*boscum*) which provided the raw material for *howsebota* (use of woodland in the repair of houses) and *haybote* (use of woodland for making enclosures, hedges and fences) to the Cistercian monastery of Mellifont, Co. Louth (Jager 1983, 58). The 13th-century Tristernagh, Co. Westmeath documents describe rights of 'hosbots' and 'heybots' and distinguish between *bosca* (underwood) and *ligna* (which was like *silva*, a timber wood) in the phrase 'boscum et omnia ligna crescencia' (Jager 1983, 56; Clarke 1941). Timber and underwood could be produced from the same woodlands. An inquisition for the manor of Callan, Co. Kilkenny, taken on 19 April 1307, states that 'there are there a park of oaks whereof none may be sold without waste, and a wood, the underwood of which may be sold without waste to the value of half-a-mark a year' (Le Fanu 1893, 275).

Woodlands such as these would have been managed and exploited in a rotational fashion. The Winetavern St/Wood Quay wood suggests cropping at about 4, 8 and 10 years, although this was not inflexible, a pattern which can be compared with Irish historical evidence. The rental of the manor of Lisronagh, Co. Tipperary, states that a brushwood could be cut in its eighth year (Curtis 1934, 45). Short coppice rotations were the norm in the early medieval period; in south-east England, early medieval coppiced woodlands were cropped between 4 and 8 years; the longer rotations of 15–20 years, familiar in more recent management practices, were introduced in the later medieval period (Rackham 1980, 1982). Woodland was divided into compartments, with rotation systems for periodically cropping the underwood in each area (Rackham 1982) and supplies of rods could have been stored in piles before haulage into the town. Alternatively underwood could have been cropped whenever needed for specific tasks. Oak was more likely to have been transported quickly to the construction site, as seasoned oak is almost impossible to work with hand tools (Darrah 1982).

THE EXPLOITATION OF TIMBER AND UNDERWOOD IN
MEDIEVAL DUBLIN WOODLANDS

There is a range of early 14th century historical evidence for the organised cropping and valuation of underwood for Dublin. The *Account Roll of the Priory of the Holy Trinity* details the payment '*in hire of two men cutting underwood in the wood of Clonken for 14 days in Autumn at board ... to each by the day , 1d*' (Mills 1891, 60). In the same document, a load of rods was priced at 3*d.* and a number of hurdles for roofing cost 3*d.* (ibid.). There are even early 14th century references to the deliberate creation of new woodland at Finglas, Co. Dublin, whereby an area of land formerly under tillage was enclosed so that by 1528 it could be described as woodland (boscum domini; Jager 1983, 61).

A more detailed account of the procurement of underwood in 1302 is described in the account of William de Moenes, who was keeper and manager of the Glencree royal forest (O'Connor 1952; Lydon 1981). This text provides a valuable insight into the supply of underwood products into Anglo-Norman Dublin. The account details the wages, loads and man-hours involved in cropping rods for making hurdles for a military expedition. The task cost about £7 and involved a workforce of up to 33 men with two overseers, cutting 420 separate loads of rods for six days at various woodland locations in the vicinity of Dublin (including Clonken, Carybrenan and Rathgarf in south Dublin, Conlock, Kinsale, Sauntriff, Balygriffyn and Glassagh in north Dublin and Glencree and Newcastle MacKynegan in Wicklow). The rods were transported into Dublin by cartload, on horse back and also by boat. The location of these named woods can be traced (that is modern Clonkeen, Rathgar, Coolock, Kinsealy, Santry) and confirm that a number of discrete areas of woodland were deliberately maintained in the immediate neighbourhood of medieval Dublin. In medieval Dublin then, the trade in woodland products was variously in the hands of the native Irish, the monasteries, secular landlords and Dublin inhabitants.

Timber

The selection of larger timber trees for the waterfront structures at Winetavern St/Wood Quay, their felling and the subsequent transport of the rough timber from source to the town would also most likely have been the task of specialised woodmen, the first link in a chain of timber trade, involving vehicles, boats and draught animals to transport roughly prepared planks and beams to a construction site. Indeed there is historical evidence for just such a 'woodcutter' living in Oxmantown in the 15th century (Emer Purcell, pers. comm.). The *Account Roll of the Priory of Holy Trinity* records the purchase in 1340 for 20*d.* of nine couples of oak for building a barn including nails, wattles and the hiring of a carpenter (Mills 1891, 38).

Oak timber was undoubtedly a high-status raw material and would have been an expensive product, particularly when supplies would have been occasionally reduced. Although timber was also on occasion bought from the Irish (Mills 1891, 57), it is likely that control of timber woodlands quickly fell into Anglo-Norman hands. It may well have been transported large distances, and certainly from the relatively close north Wicklow woodlands, such as those at Glencree and Newcastle. A range of entries in the *Account Roll of the Priory of Holy Trinity* indicate that timber was graded according to size and price. A single unmodified tree (*arbore*) cost 1*d.*, while twenty-six beams of timber (*meremio*) cost 2*s.* 2*d.* Clearly certain types of board were more expensive, with 100 draughtboard costing 5*s.* as against a price of 14*d.* for 100 '*Wykinglowe bordis*' (Mills 1891, *passim*).

Wicklow, in fact, seems to have been an important source of timber oaks for Dublin in the medieval period. At Glencree, a large area of land fell under Forest Law after the Anglo-Norman invasion (Le Fanu 1893, 269). In 1280, seven oaks were given to John de Wallop from the park at 'Glincry' and in 1282 the same person petitioned for rights of 'inbote' and 'housebote' (see above) from

Glencree for house building (ibid., 274). In 1283, William le Devenais, keeper of the King's demesne lands, received twelve oaks from the King's wood in Glencree (ibid.). In June 1285 the Dominican friars of Dublin procured thirty Wicklow oaks for church-building, fifteen from Glencree and fifteen from Newcastle MacKinegan (ibid., 275). In 1289 the abbot and convent of St. Thomas, Dublin were granted twenty oaks fit for timber from the King's wood in Glencree to reconstruct certain buildings which had burnt down (ibid.) and in the same year William Burnell, constable of Dublin castle was granted twelve oak trees from the King's forest of Glencree to build his house (ibid.).

Interestingly, although oak timber seems to have been the main product from the royal forest at Glencree, there is also evidence for underwood management, pannage and wood-pasture. In 1285, 1286 and 1288 there are references to the sale of rods from the copsewood of Glencree by Thomas Godfrey, with prices ranging from 33s. to 58s. (ibid., 275). In 1304 much of the timber oaks at Newcastle MacKinegan had been cropped, but the sale of wood and herbage was providing an income of 60s. per annum (ibid., 276). There are also references to the winter foddering of pigs in the oakwoods, the 'pannage of the wood of Glencree' which provided an income in 1288 of 5s. 4d. (Kelly Quinn 1994; Le Fanu 1893, 276).

CARPENTRY AND ASSEMBLY

The carpentry of Anglo-Norman Dublin is at once the best studied and the least known of subjects. Wallace's (1982) seminal paper outlined the evidence for the carpentry of the waterfronts, presenting an image of increasing use of heavy structural beams, the selection of a limited number of joints and a general picture of hurried assembly. Other evidence for Anglo-Norman carpentry in Dublin includes the other waterfronts to the north-west on Winetavern St and Ushers Quay (see below) and a timber-lined well or pit at High St (Ó Ríordáin 1971, 77, Fig. 26). House construction evidence includes timber-framed 'warehouses' at Wood Quay (Wallace 1982, 277–78; 1985, 387–90), early timber-framed houses at High St and Back Lane (C. Walsh pers. comm.) and a mill structure employing re-used roof-timbers at Patrick St (Walsh 1997, 50–59, 81–89). In addition, McGrail's (1993) recent publication of ships' timbers testifies to the potential high quality of woodworking skills available in Dublin. The purpose of the following section is to examine the evidence for carpentry at the Winetavern St/Wood Quay revetments.

Tree-felling

The trees would have been felled with axes, probably the narrow-bladed type which permits a deeper kerf to be cut in the trunk (O' Sullivan 1994b). The archaeological evidence for tree-felling techniques is often difficult to trace, as the tool marks tend to be removed by subsequent woodworking. Nevertheless the subsidiary baseplates from revetment F166 had important evidence for such felling techniques. The northern ends of three subsidiary baseplates (166.53, 13, 14) were wedge-shaped with tool marks indicating the use of narrow bladed axes (Pl. III). There was a difference in the amount of woodworking on either side of the worked end; one side was typically cut at angles of c.40°, deep into the wood, while on the opposite side a shallower cut had been made at a steeper angle. This form of worked end results from the practice of felling trees by opposing kerfs. Most of the heartwood is cut from one side of the trunk, then a second kerf is cut on the opposing side, slightly higher up the trunk. The tree then falls in the direction the wider kerf – a safer technique which enables the woodmen to predict where the tree will fall. It is also useful for placing a trunk in an already cleared area, making its removal from the woodland easier. Smaller poles and rods were felled by means of billhooks, simply by slashing downwards at shallow angles.

Conversion of timber

The felled trunks would then have their branches removed, this topwood being used for a variety of infill or fuel wood functions. The logs were 'bucked', cross-cut to usable lengths, by means of narrow bladed axes, leaving straight, worked ends. The log was then converted to various timber sizes. Examinations of the end-grain of the Winetavern St/Wood Quay waterfront timbers are informative both about the type and method of conversion. Smaller underwood and (less often) larger trunks were left in the round. The baseplate beams were typically of boxed-heart section and the vertical posts were of boxed-halved conversion, whereby two timbers were extracted from a medium sized tree. Posts were also taken from radial and boxed-quartered section timber. Planking was predominantly radial in section. Cleft planks may also have been trimmed with axes.

The method of conversion involves the various tools and techniques used to reduce the parent log to a finished timber. Medieval timbers were typically prepared either by cleaving with wedges and mallets or by hewing with axes. To prevent waste, the medieval carpenter aimed to extract the largest possible structural element from the smallest possible trunk. In this way, bark and sapwood was left on the corners or edges. It seems to have been of little concern that this reduces the useful life-span of a timber, leaving it more open to insect attack and rot.

Hewing

Most of the timbers from the revetments were worked to their form by means of axes. The main baseplates and some front braces and posts from each revetment had all been worked by axes. The surviving tool marks were wide and slightly concave in section, suggesting the use of fairly broad-bladed axes. The general lack of woodworking debris indicates that this hewing was not carried out on the foreshore itself. Only in a small number of examples were unworked trunks incorporated into the structures. In revetment F164, the upright post 164.1 was simply a barely modified roundwood trunk. In revetment F166, one subsidiary baseplate (166.16) had been roughly squared leaving most of the original round surfaces, sapwood and bark, still intact. Indeed, in general the subsidiary baseplates typically had the least amount of woodworking carried out on them.

Cleft and possible sawn timbers

Some of the timbers used in the revetments were in contrast cleft by means of mallets and wedges; wooden wedges and heavy mallets are known from excavated medieval sites in Dublin. Half-split logs were common, as were radial-cleft posts. The front braces were typically simple radial-cleft timbers. The rough planks and timbers used in trackway F205 were almost entirely radially cleft. In contrast, the planks used in revetments F166, F246 and F1055 were often of quite narrow scantlings, taken from substantial long-lived trees and would have required very skilful cleaving techniques. The possibility must be allowed that these planks were actually sawn. In addition, a few timbers seemed to have cut ends that were so flat as to suggest sawing but unfortunately these timbers were not sufficiently well preserved to ascertain this.

The question of the introduction of the saw for the production of large timbers remains vexed in an Irish context. A saw used on a single trestle for ripping planks produces a distinctive type of tool mark of closely parallel, straight ridges across the width of the timber. Saw-marks of early date are known from 13th-century waterfronts from the Thames Exchange, London (Goodburn 1992, 123) but there has to date been little conclusive excavated evidence in Dublin for the use of the saws prior to the 16th century (saw marks occur on timber-framed house beams of this period recovered in the Dublin Castle excavations). The only actual medieval saws known from Ireland are small and suitable only for working bone or small pieces of wood. There are, however, some documentary references to the export of sawn boards ('borde of Irland') from Dublin to England in the 14th century (O' Neill 1987, 101) but it is important to note that the popular idea of large-scale exportation of medieval Irish oaks for use in English cathedrals and municipal buildings is an erroneous one, conflicting with the published historical evidence (Nelson and Walsh 1993, 118).

JOINTS AND CARPENTRY

The joints used in the revetments are of a limited range, including pegged rectangular and square through-mortises, stopped-mortises, a possible chase-mortise, through-splayed scarf joints and notched lap joints.

Mortise and tenon joints

The baseplates were mortised at various intervals to hold the vertical posts and subsidiary baseplates. These were typically through-mortises, although F246 employed stopped-mortises. These mortises were rectangular in plan, although some re-used timbers from revetment F164 did display square through-mortises. The subsidiary baseplates of revetment F166 each had a single simple through-mortise at their northern end to hold the substantial timber pegs that pinned them onto the foreshore. A single upright post from revetment F166 had a possible chase-mortise to hold the upper end of the front brace, which was, however, poorly preserved (Ill. 13). The mortises were made firstly by drilling the timber with narrow augurs, defining the corners and ends of the mortise; the waste wood was then chopped and prised out by means of narrow axes and possibly chisels. The mortises were usually pegged to hold the tenons and in a number of cases a wedge was also drive in to tighten the fit.

The tenons housed in these mortises varied in form. The crudest means of inserting the subsidiary baseplate or vertical posts into the main baseplate was simply by trimming the timber to a tapered end. Other tenons, such as the barefaced and two-shouldered tenons were simply cut with axes. An interesting feature of revetment F166 was the manner in which several of the main upright posts (for example 166.2, 4, and 6) cut through the tenons of subsidiary baseplates, thus weakening them (Ill. 2). In these cases the front through-surface was situated too close to the upper mortise, and it is clear that the insertion of the vertical post post-dated the insertion of the subsidiary baseplate. This in turn suggests that the fabrication of the revetment was in two stages, firstly the assembly of the baseplate element, followed at a later stage (perhaps at the next low tide) by the construction of the vertical wall.

Notched lap joints

A peculiar feature of the joining of the lower ends of the braces to the subsidiary baseplates of revetment F166 was the use of pegged notched lap joints (Ill. 20). These were not entirely successful in holding the braces, which in a number of cases slipped out to the west. Elsewhere on the Wood Quay site, in Wallace's Revetment 1, section D, the braces were inserted in chase-mortises on the subsidiary baseplates (Wallace 1981, Fig. 111; 1982, 283–5, Fig. 15.6). This suggests that F166, which represents the western end of Wallace's Revetment 1, was completed either by a separate team of carpenters or perhaps at a slightly later stage. There are interesting parallels to be traced with developments in English medieval carpentry at this point. Notched laps joints first appear in roof timbers in Herefordshire and Worcestershire after 1150 AD (Milne 1992, 85; Currie 1990). There also seems to be a transition from the use of notched lap joints to chase mortises at the foot of the front braces in the London waterfronts in the early 13th century (Milne 1992, 85). Other evidence from the Dublin carpentry indicates closely similar developments contemporary to the south-east England and West Country carpentry traditions (see below).

Scarf joints

Ill. 21: Revetment F166:
detail of joint between
baseplate sections 166.54
(left) and 166.55 (right),
showing possible edge-
halved scarf joint

There were five scarf joints, three on revetment F166 and a single example each on F246 and F1055 (Ill. 8). All were of the simple through-splayed scarf variety, typically pegged in position by a number of dowels of oak, ash and willow. The only possible exception to this is the joint between baseplate sections 166.54 and 166.55 in revetment F166 (Ill. 21), which may have been an edge-halved scarf, but unfortunately damage caused by crushing of the baseplate made it impossible to be certain about this. The alignment of the scarfs can be used to suggest the sequence of assembly of the waterfronts. Wallace (1982, 278) has noted that these scarf-joints would not have been very resistant to lateral or axial shear pressure – a likely outcome of river currents. However, the fact that almost all of the scarf-joints from these revetments were still intact during the excavation (so much so that the dowels had to be broken to disassemble the baseplates) indicates some measure of success. The pinning of the subsidiary baseplates to the foreshore (Ill. 20) may have provided some degree of protection against timber movement. The predominance of this simple type of scarf joint is paralleled elsewhere in the Wood Quay revetments, but the presence of a complex splayed tongue-and-grooved pegged scarf joint on a re-used roof timber from the Patrick St mill is an indication that other forms were in use in 12th-century Dublin (Walsh 1997, 195).

THE DUBLIN MEDIEVAL WATERFRONTS AND REGIONAL CARPENTRY TRADITIONS

Modern study of medieval carpentry in Ireland is primarily based on Wallace's (1982) analysis of the joints and woodworking techniques exhibited in the Dublin waterfronts. In that paper several separate traditions of carpentry were identified. In early medieval rural Ireland a native class of carpenters, accorded high status in early Irish laws and developing a complex, indigenous tradition, was employed in such structures as horizontal mills. Carpentry techniques in 10th-century Dublin were comparatively restricted, houses being of post-and-wattle with occasional squared and grooved jambs, notch-and-tenon joints and pegged tie-backs. In the late 11th and early 12th centuries heavier timbers were occasionally used as grooved sill-beams for fences and stave-built houses. These techniques have been taken to reflect the introduction of native carpentry styles, although mortise and tenon joints remained absent (Wallace 1982, 1992a, 1992b).

Mortise and tenon joints appear in the 13th-century waterfronts, often cut through heavier baseplates with grooved uprights. These techniques were recognised as being absent in pre-Norman Dublin. However, there were also some contrasts with the Irish tradition, notably the absence of edge-halved scarfs against the use of through-splayed scarfs and the lack of grooves in the waterfront baseplates for the horizontal planks. The 13th-century revetment carpentry was taken to represent a conservative Dublin-based tradition. The seemingly irrational use of through-splayed scarfs, misplaced mortise and tenon joints and use of timbers of unequal scantlings seemed to indicate rapid construction, employing prefabricated elements. Finally, it was felt that the waterfronts must have been built by carpenters working in the Dublin style, which was itself derived from earlier, native Irish and Viking styles (Wallace 1982, 294–6).

Dublin and London; a contemporary transition from earthfast to timber-framed carpentry

Since the appearance of Wallace's pioneering publication, further detailed study and excavation of medieval waterfront structures in London has enabled a new chronological model of English waterfront carpentry to be proposed recently (Milne 1992, 82–5). This model proposes a transition between earthfast and timber-framed revetments occurring in the late 12th/early 13th century, a transition that can also be traced in the carpentry used in contemporary houses, barns and bridges. The earlier earthfast tradition employed only roundwood and roughly squared timbers driven into the ground, few joints and rare use of sill-beams. The timber-framed carpentry tradition in contrast employed heavy, squared oak beams and baseplates and a wider range of complex joinery.

The Winetavern St/Wood Quay waterfronts can be shown to reflect closely this transition, implying a common source of innovation. At Winetavern St/Wood Quay, the late 12th-century-revetment F164 (Pl. II), with its use of barely modified roundwood timbers, the insertion of the uprights directly into the ground (earthfast posts) and the presence of low ratio (square mortises), would be typical of late 12th-century London waterfronts (for example, the Old Custom House 73 site; Milne 1992, Fig. 82). In contrast, the late 12th/early 13th century revetments F166, F246 and F1055 demonstrate the introduction of heavy baseplates, squared timbers, high-ratio (rectangular mortises) and generally more complex joinery. This is precisely the period when the transition in London waterfronts from earthfast to timber-framed structures is reckoned to have taken place (Milne 1992, 82–5). The introduction of timber-framed buildings in London also involved the use of more complex mortise and tenon joints, notably the introduction of two-shouldered tenons and the use of chase mortises and notched-lap joints. These joints saw their first use in London and Dublin at about the same time.

The 'great transition' in English carpentry from Norman to Early English traditions

The theory of a late 12th-/early 13th-century transition between earthfast and timber-framed wooden structures is also supported by Hewett's (1980) analysis of contemporary rural English house and church carpentry in Essex. He suggests from evidence at the Barley Barn, Cressing and other high-status structures that the crucial transition from earthfast post to timber-framed house building techniques occurred in England between the mid/late 12th century and the early 13th century (Hewett 1980, 59–73). These new timber-framed techniques seem to be a fusion of the independent techniques developed in the earlier 11th century earthfast and stave-building traditions. A recent study of medieval roofs in Herefordshire and Worcestershire indicates the introduction of notched lap joints after 1150 AD, a type of joint that also first appears on the Dublin waterfronts after this period (Milne 1992, 85; Currie 1990). A similar transition to boxed and timber-framed structures can also be traced in English bridge carpentry at this time (D. Goodburn pers. comm.). Incidentally, the use of square mortises and barely dressed timbers at the Cashen Bridge, Co. Kerry (O'Kelly 1961) may therefore indicate a pre-12th century date for this structure.

The chronological link in this transition between woodworking techniques in the Dublin and London/Essex/West Country carpentry styles suggests close contacts and common influences. The Winetavern St/Wood Quay structures seem to indicate that a significant change in carpentry techniques was occurring amongst the Dublin craftsmen at precisely the same time as their English contemporaries. This might suggest that the craftsmen responsible for this technological innovation were actually trained in the English carpentry tradition. However, it is also possible that certain Irish modifications were being made to imported carpentry techniques.

Medieval waterfronts in Bristol and on the Severn estuary

Such contacts might have been communicated via the medieval port of Bristol which, as is well known, had very close links with Dublin at the period of the Anglo-Norman invasion of Ireland. There is archaeological evidence for similar carpentry techniques in Bristol and Dublin at this period, including late 12th-/early 13th-century waterfronts, 13th-century fishweirs employing pegged and tenon mortise joints (O'Sullivan 1995) and a recently discovered 13th-century Scandinavian-type ship on the Severn estuary (Nigel Nayling pers. comm.). A medieval quay has recently been excavated on the Severn estuary intertidal zone at Woolaston Grange, Gloucestershire (Fulford et al. 1992). This waterfront employed heavy oak beams with long-ratio mortises and front-braced supports. Incidentally, the structure also utilises grooved vertical timbers, similar to a technique used in a timber-sluice gate at Inns Quay, Dublin (McMahon 1988, 281–5). The earliest Woolaston Quay structures have been dated to between the mid-12th and early 13th century AD (Fulford et al. 1992).

Medieval timber waterfronts are also known from Dundas Wharf, in the Redcliffe district of Bristol, on the east bank of the River Avon (Ponsford 1981). The waterfronts date from the late 12th/early 13th century to the late 14th century. In phases 3 and 4 at least, substantial timber baseplates had rectangular mortises to receive vertical elements. Incidentally, the types of trees (a combination of narrow, medium-aged trunks and ancient oak trunks) chosen for the Dundas Wharf structure (Nicholson and Hillam 1987) mirror closely the pattern observed in the Winetavern St/Wood Quay waterfronts. Thus the combined historical and archaeological evidence suggests that the tradition of waterfront construction on the upper Severn estuary may have influenced the construction of the Dublin medieval waterfronts. Indeed, this influence may have extended to Bristol carpenters actually being present and active in medieval Dublin.

THE WINETAVERN ST/WOOD QUAY EXCAVATIONS AND THE ROLE OF WATERFRONTS IN MEDIEVAL DUBLIN

Previous excavations of medieval Dublin waterfronts

There have been several important excavations of the medieval Dublin waterfront, of which the best-known are the series carried out by Wallace at Wood Quay, revealing a sequence of Hiberno-Norse and Anglo-Norman foreshore reclamation (Wallace 1981). The earliest waterfronts were a series of earthen banks built from *c.*900–1000 AD (Banks 1–3). A more substantial consolidation of this reclamation occurred *c.*1100 AD, when a stone wall was constructed to the north. By the late 12th/early 13th century reclamation was taking the form of the construction of a series of major timber revetments (Revetments 1, 2 and 3), succeeded finally by the construction of a stone quay wall around the middle of the 13th century. At the north-west corner of the walled town, excavations at Ushers Quay also uncovered a short length of front-braced timber revetment (Swan 1992). More recent excavations along Patrick St and on Winetavern St uncovered wooden boardwalks and substantial timber revetments (Walsh 1997, 95–103) and medieval reclamation structures and waterfronts have also been found on the north bank of the river Liffey (McMahon 1988; Hayden 1991).

The river Liffey and the function of the waterfronts

Medieval Dublin was situated on the south bank of a broad, tidally influenced river, overlooking large areas of estuarine mudflats, gravels and salt marshes. The wooden revetments excavated at Winetavern St/Wood Quay were placed out on this dynamic landscape, with diurnal tides flooding and ebbing up to the structures. An understanding of the nature of contemporary sea-levels, through a study of relative sea-level changes on the Irish Sea coast, is crucial to our interpretation of the function of these revetments. Although parts of the Irish coast (in particular the north-east and south-west coasts) have seen significant post-glacial changes in relative sea level, eustatic and isostatic studies suggest that the medieval mean sea level on the east coast and the Liffey estuary, although it may have been slightly higher, was not dissimilar to that of today (Devoy 1983, 1990, 1991; Synge 1985).

In this context, John de Courcy's (1984 and pers. comm.) detailed research on modern tide-levels has interesting implications for the function of the waterfronts. Assuming that the vertical posts and planking of revetment F166 were originally *c.*30–50cm higher than the incomplete surviving remains excavated in 1993, and that early 13th-century tide levels were essentially similar to modern levels, high spring tides at an average maximum level of *c.*2.0m Ordnance Datum (Malin) would have flooded to just below the top of the revetment. At a Mean Low Water level of approximately –2.3m Ordnance Datum (Malin), the foreshore and subsidiary baseplates would have been exposed. Thus it seems that the waterfronts were placed at a point on the foreshore where tides would have created a reasonable depth of water. The ships excavated at Wood Quay, judging by their displacement and size (McGrail 1993, 95–98; Table 30), could have berthed against these waterfronts (see Fig. 41). The front-braces would have served to shift the settling boats away from the planking as the tide ebbed, leaving the vessel to settle on the foreshore. A gang-plank could have provided access for the ships to the cobbled surface behind the waterfront. At optimum tide levels (as with all harbour and waterfronts) the Winetavern St/Wood Quay waterfronts could have provided excellent dock facilities for trading vessels.

REFERENCES

Clarke, M.V. 1941 *Register of the priory of … Tristernagh*. Dublin. Irish Manuscripts Commission.

Currie, C. 1990 Gazetteer of archaic roofs in Herefordshire and Worcestershire churches. *Vernacular Architecture* **21**, 18–23.

Curtis, E. 1934 Rental of the manor of Lisronagh, 1333, and notes on 'betagh' tenure in medieval Ireland. *P.R.I.A.* **43C**, 41–76.

Darrah R. 1982 Working unseasoned oak. In McGrail 1982, 219–230.

De Courcy, J. 1984 Medieval banks of the Liffey estuary. In J. Bradley (ed.), *Viking Dublin exposed: The Wood Quay saga*, 164–6. Dublin. O'Brien Press.

Devoy, R. 1983 Late Quaternary shorelines in Ireland: an assessment of their implications for isostatic movement and relative sea-level changes. In Smith, D.E. and Dawson, A.G. (eds), *Shorelines and Isostasy*, 227–54. Institute of British Geographers Special Publication no. 16. London. Academic Press.

Devoy, R. 1990 Controls on coastal and sea-level changes and the application of archaeological-historical records to understanding recent patterns of sea-level movement. In S. McGrail (ed.), *Maritime Celts, Frisians and Saxons*, 17–27. Council for British Archaeology Research Report **71**. Nottingham.

Devoy, R. 1991 *Sea level changes and Ireland*. Enfo Briefing Sheet 27, Dublin. The Environmental Information Service.

Fulford, M.G., Rippon, S., Allen, J.R.L. and Hillam, J. 1992 The medieval quay at Woolaston Grange. *Trans. Bristol & Gloucs Arch. Soc.* **110**, 101–27.

Goodburn, D. 1991 Waterlogged wood and timber as archives of ancient landscapes. In J. Coles and D. Goodburn (eds), *Wet site excavation and survey*, 51–3. Exeter. Wetland Archaeology Research Project.

Goodburn, D. 1992 Woods and woodland: carpenters and carpentry. In Milne 1992, 106–130.

Goodburn, D. 1994 Trees underground: new insights into trees and woodmanship in south-east England c.AD 800–1300. *Bot. Jnl. Scotland* **46**, 658–62.

Hayden, A. 1991 9–12 Arran Quay, Dublin. In I. Bennett (ed.), *Excavations 1990: Summary accounts of archaeological excavations in Ireland*, 27–8. Dublin. Organisation of Irish Archaeologists/Wordwell.

Hewett, C.A. 1980 *English historic carpentry*. London. Philimore.

Jäger, H. 1983 Land use in medieval Ireland: a review of the documentary evidence. *Irish Economic and Social History* **10**, 51–65.

Kelly Quinn, M. 1994 The evolution of forestry in County Wicklow from prehistory to the present. In K. Hannigan and W. Nolan (eds), *Wicklow history and society*, 823–54. Dublin. Geography Publications.

Le Fanu, T.P. 1893 The royal forest of Glencree. *J.R.S.A.I.* **23**, 268–80.

Lydon, J.F. 1981 Edward I, Ireland and the war in Scotland, 1303–1304. In J.F. Lydon (ed.), *England and Ireland in the later Middle Ages: essays in honour of Jocelyn Otway-Ruthven*, 43–61. Dublin. Irish Academic Press.

McGrail, S. (ed.) 1982 *Woodworking techniques before AD 1500*. Oxford. B.A.R. International Series 129.

McGrail, S. 1993 *Medieval boat and ship timbers from Dublin*. Medieval Dublin Excavations 1962–81, Ser. B, vol. 3. Dublin. Royal Irish Academy.

McMahon, M. 1988 Archaeological excavations at the site of the Four Courts extension, Inns Quay, Dublin. *P.R.I.A.* **88C**, 271–319.

Mills, J. 1891 *Account Rolls of the Priory of the Holy Trinity, Dublin 1337–1346*. Dublin. Royal Society of Antiquaries of Ireland. Reprinted Dublin, 1994.

Milne, G. (ed.) 1992 *Timber building techniques in London c.900–1400*. London. London and Middlesex Archaeological Society Special Paper 15.

Milne, G. and Hobley, B. (eds) 1981 *Waterfront archaeology in Britain and northern Europe*. London. Council for British Archaeology Research Report **41.**

Mitchell, G.F. (ed.) 1987 *Archaeology and environment in early Dublin*. Medieval Dublin Excavations 1962–81, Ser. C, vol. 1. Dublin. Royal Irish Academy.

Nelson, E.C. and Walsh, W.F. 1993 *Trees of Ireland; native and naturalised*. Dublin. Liliput Press.

Nicholson, R.A. and Hillam, J. 1987 A dendrochronological analysis of oak timbers from the early medieval site at Dundas Wharf, Bristol. *Trans. Bristol & Gloucs Arch. Soc.* **105**, 133–45.

O'Connor, P. 1952 Hurdle making in Dublin 1302–3. *Dublin Historical Record* **13 (1)**, 18–21.

O'Kelly, M.J. 1961 A wooden bridge on the Cashen river, Co. Kerry. *J.R.S.A.I.* **91**, 135–52.

O' Neill, T.P. 1987 *Merchants and mariners in medieval Ireland*. Dublin. Irish Academic Press.

Ó Ríordáin, A. B. 1971 Excavations at High St and Winetavern St, Dublin. *Med. Arch.* **15**, 73–85.

O'Sullivan, A. 1992 Trees and woodland in early medieval Ireland: an ethnohistorical approach. *NewsWARP* **11**, 3–7. Exeter. Wetland Archaeology Research Project.

O'Sullivan, A. 1994a Trees, woodland and woodmanship in early medieval Ireland. *Bot. Jnl. Scotland* **46 (4)**, 674–681.

O'Sullivan, A. 1994b The craft of the carpenter in medieval Ireland; some hints from book illuminations. *Irish Association of Professional Archaeologists Newsletter* **19**, 18–22.

O'Sullivan, A. 1995 Wood technology and the use of raw materials. In S. Godbold and R.C. Turner, Fishtraps on the Severn estuary, *Med. Arch.* **38**, 19–54.

Ponsford, M.W. 1981 Bristol. In Milne and Hobley 1981, 103–4.

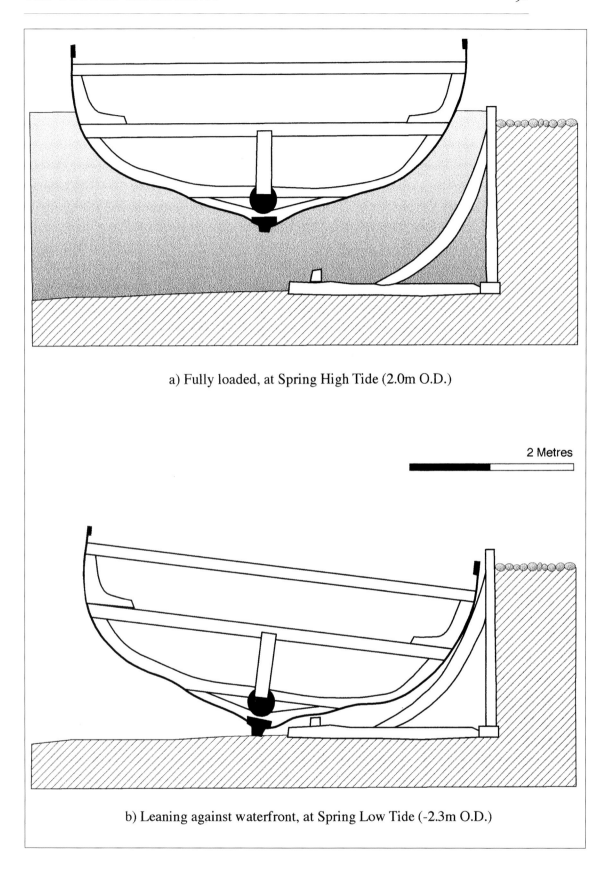

a) Fully loaded, at Spring High Tide (2.0m O.D.)

2 Metres

b) Leaning against waterfront, at Spring Low Tide (-2.3m O.D.)

Fig. 41: Diagrammatic representation of a small ship (Skuldelev 1, after Mc Grail 1993) berthed against revetment F166 at high spring tide (above) and at low tide (below)

Rackham, O. 1980 *Ancient woodland; its history, vegetation and uses in England.* London. Edward Arnold.

Rackham, O. 1982 The growing and transport of timber and underwood. In McGrail 1982, 199–218.

Rackham, O. 1990 *Trees and woodland in the British landscape.* London. Dent.

Swan, D.L. 1992 6–8 Usher's Quay, Dublin. In I. Bennett (ed.), *Excavations 1991: Summary accounts of archaeological excavations in Ireland,* 15. Dublin. Organisation of Irish Archaeologists/Wordwell.

Synge, F.M. 1985 Coastal evolution. In K.J. Edwards and W.A. Warren (eds), *The Quaternary history of Ireland,* 115–131. London. Academic Press.

Tabor, R. 1994 *Traditional woodland crafts.* London. Batsford.

Wallace, P.F. 1981 Dublin's waterfront at Wood Quay, 900–1317. In Milne and Hobley 1981, 108–18.

Wallace, P.F. 1982 Carpentry in Ireland AD 900–1300 – the Wood Quay evidence. In McGrail 1982, 263–99.

Wallace, P.F. 1985 The archaeology of Anglo-Norman Dublin. In H.B. Clarke and A. Simms (eds), *The comparative history of urban origins in non-Roman Europe,* 39–410. Oxford. B.A.R. International Series 255 (2).

Wallace, P.F. 1992a *The Viking age buildings of Dublin,* 2 vols. Medieval Dublin Excavations 1962–81, Ser. A. Vol. 1. Dublin.

Wallace, P.F. 1992b The archaeological identity of the Hiberno-Norse town. *J.R.S.A.I.* **122**, 35–66.

Walsh, C. 1997 *Archaeological excavations at Patrick, Nicholas and Winetavern Sts, Dublin.* Dingle. Brandon Books/Dublin Corporation.

White, N.B. 1943 *Extents of Irish monastic possessions 1540–1541, from manuscripts in the Public Record Office, London.* Dublin. Irish Manuscripts Commission.

CHAPTER V

Dendrochronological analysis of oak wood samples

David Brown

INTRODUCTION

The Paleoecology Centre, Queen's University, Belfast, received 12 oak wood samples from the archaeological excavations at Winetavern St/Wood Quay, Dublin. This report will give a brief analysis of each sample, using the Belfast sapwood estimates of 32 ±9 years when estimating the felling date range. This figure is added to the last surviving heartwood ring where the sapwood is incomplete.

The samples have been allocated the following reference numbers:

QUB number	Context / sample number	QUB number	Context / sample number
Q8886	164.1	Q8892	800.5
Q8887	800.29	Q8893	246.1
Q8888	166.16	Q8894	246.8
Q8889	166.34	Q8895	246.17
Q8890	166.54	Q8896	1055.3
Q8891	800.4	Q8897	1055.1

RESULTS

Sample Q8886: Revetment timber 164.1.

This sample contained 62 annual growth rings when measured, including 22 sapwood rings that are complete. The centre of the tree is present. The tree-ring obtained from this sample was compared with a suite of Irish tree-ring chronologies. No significant or consistent correlation values were found. This sample is too short to provide a dendrochronological date.

Sample Q8887: Revetment timber 800.29 (from revetment F164).

This sample contained 62 annual growth rings when measured. The centre and bark are present on the sample. It has been identified as a hazel tree and cannot be dated by dendrochronology.

Sample Q8888: Revetment timber 166.16.

This sample contained 72 annual growth rings when measured, including 28 sapwood rings that are complete. The centre of the tree is present. The tree-ring series obtained was compared with a suite of Irish chronologies. No significant or consistent correlation values were found.

Sample Q8889: Revetment plank 166.34.

When measured this sample contained 230 annual growth rings, including 2 sapwood rings that are not complete. The rest of the sapwood proved impossible to measure. The centre of the tree is not present. The tree-ring series was compared with a suite of Irish tree-ring chronologies. Extremely significant and consistent correlation values were found. These show that the last measurable ring was for the year AD **1169 ±9 years.**

Sample Q8890: Revetment plank 166.54.

When measured this sample contained 125 annual growth rings, including 20 sapwood rings that are not complete. The centre of the tree is not present. The tree-ring series obtained was compared with a suite of Irish tree-ring chronologies. Extremely significant and consistent correlation values were found. These indicate that the last surviving ring was for the year AD 1187. The best estimated felling date will be AD **1199 ±9 years**.

Sample Q8891: Wooden plank 800.4 (F177).

This sample contained 253 annual growth rings when measured, including 16 sapwood rings that are not complete. The centre of the tree is not present. The tree-ring series obtained was compared with a suite of Irish tree-ring chronologies. Extremely significant and consistent correlation values show that the last surviving ring was for the year AD 1166. The best estimated felling date range for this tree will be AD **1182 ±9 years**.

Sample Q8892: Wooden plank 800.5 (F177).

This sample contained 226 annual growth rings when measured, including 40 sapwood rings that are complete. The tree-ring series obtained was compared with a suite of Irish tree-ring chronologies. Extremely significant and consistent correlation values were found. These indicate that the last surviving ring is for the year AD 1188. With the sapwood complete the felling year for this tree will be AD **1188**.

Sample Q8893: Revetment timber 246.1.

This sample contained 245 annual growth rings when measured, including 24 sapwood rings that are not complete. The centre of the tree is not present. The tree-ring series obtained from this sample was compared with a suite of Irish tree-ring chronologies. Extremely significant and consistent correlation values were found. These indicate that the last surviving ring was for the year AD 1194. The best estimated felling date range of the tree will be AD **1192 ±9 years but after** AD **1194.**

Sample Q8894: Revetment timber 246.8.

This sample contained 100 annual growth rings when measured. The sapwood is present but unmeasurable. The centre of the tree is present. The tree-ring series obtained was compared with a suite of Irish tree-ring chronologies. No significant or consistent correlation values were found. At the present time it is impossible to date this tree-ring pattern.

Sample Q8895: Revetment timber 246.17.

This sample contained 163 annual growth rings when measured, including 17 sapwood rings that are not complete. The centre of the tree is not present. The tree-ring series obtained from this sample was compared with a suite of Irish tree-ring chronologies. Very significant correlation values were found. These indicated that the last surviving ring was for the year AD 1188. The best estimated felling date range for the tree will be AD **1203 ±9 years**.

Sample Q8896: Revetment timber 1055.F.

This sample contained 94 annual growth rings when measured. The sapwood or the heartwood-sapwood boundary is present. The centre of the tree is not present. The tree-ring series was compared with a suite of Irish tree-ring chronologies. These comparisons produced no significant or consistent correlation values. At the present time it is impossible to date this tree ring pattern.

Sample Q8897: Revetment timber 1055.1.

This sample contained 122 annual growth rings when measured, including 23 sapwood rings that are not complete. The centre of the tree is present. The tree-ring series obtained from this sample was compared with a suite of Irish tree-ring chronologies. Significant and consistent correlation values were found. These indicate that the last surviving ring was for the year AD 1195. The best estimated felling date range for this tree will be AD **1204 ±9 years**.

POSSIBLE INTERPRETATIONS

Figure 42 shows the relative and absolute date of the samples. Two of the three samples from revetment F166 dated. Sample Q8890 gave an estimated felling date range of AD **1199 ±9 years.** Sample Q8889, however, has an estimated felling date of AD **1169 ±9 years**, a date range much earlier than other samples and which suggests re-use of this timber. None of the samples from revetment F164 dated, being too short to obtain dendrochronological dates. The samples from revetments F246 and F1055 are thought to be contemporary with each other and with revetment F166. The samples from context number F177, samples Q8891 and Q8892 indicate a felling date of AD **1188**; if these timbers are from later structure then re-use is indicated.

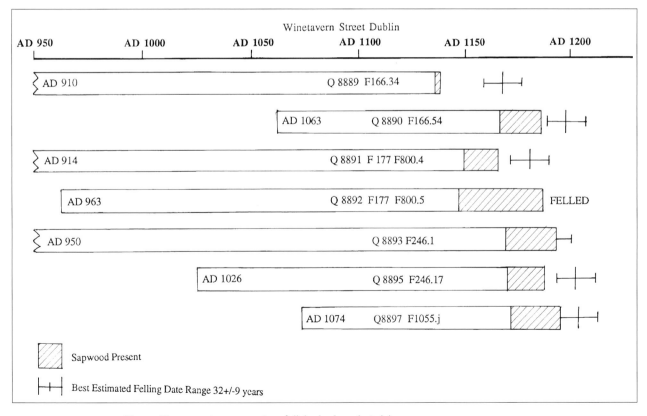

Fig. 42: Diagrammatic representation of all dendrochronological dates

CHAPTER VI

Analysis of sediment samples

Dr Peter Coxon

Context no.	Sample identification	Nature of sample and brief comment on origin
F128	WQ 5, 7, 8	Moderately sorted and poorly sorted sand and gravel deposited as a gravel bar, probably during a flood event. See 1 under Discussion below.
F137	WQ 1, 2, 3, 4	Laminated clays and silts deposited under quiet water deposition. Possibly intertidal laminations. Low organic content. See 2 under Discussion below.
F139	WQ 12, 13, 14	Organic clays and silts (WQ 14 is particularly organic). See 3 under Discussion below and Fig. 44.
F151	WQ 10, 11	Poorly sorted (WQ 10) and moderately sorted sand and gravel. WQ 10 may be disturbed or part of an unsorted flood deposit.
F174	WQ 9	Organic silt; see 2 under Discussion below.
F191	WQ 24	Stratified sand and gravel, possibly reworked as it is very poorly sorted (see Fig. 43). Its stratification could equally be produced by artificial throwing down of material.
F207	WQ 15, 22	Poorly sorted sand and gravel (see Fig. 43), either disturbed or a coarse flood deposit.
F221	WQ 21, 23	Organic silts (see Fig. 44) containing bone, charcoal, roots and some clasts. Probably reworked (see 3 under Discussion below) or flood redeposition of organic detritus.
F222	WQ 20	Silt with some organic content.
F237	WQ 25	Silt with some organic content.
F238	WQ 26	Silt with very high organic content (see Fig. 44 and 3 below).
F239	WQ 27	Silt with very high organic content (see Fig. 44 and 3 below).
F277	WQ 6	Poorly sorted sand with pebbles.

Table 1: Identification of samples analysed

INTRODUCTION

The excavations at Winetavern St/Wood Quay observed by the author in May 1993 consisted of a number of gravel bars banked against and interdigitating with silt-rich and clay-rich fine sediments, lying against and behind a wooden revetment. A number of simple analyses (detailed in Table 1) were carried out in order to assess the physical nature of the sediment sequence.

Pl. I: Area II from north near completion of excavation, showing baseplates of revetment F166 in foreground, with wall F150
(north wall of Structure A) to the south and revetment F164 in background

Pl. II: Revetment F164 (Phase 2) from north

Pl. III: Revetment F166 (Phase 3): Main baseplate and subsidiary baseplates, from east

Pl. IV: Cross-section through revetment F166 at upright 166.4, from west. The silt behind the revetment (F221, still visible at far right) has been eroded and replaced by sand and gravel, because of the lack of full boarding.

Pl. V: Detail of junction of west end of revetment F166 (on right) and north end of revetment F246 (at top)

Pl. VI: Revetment F1055 from west, partially excavated

Pl. VII: Section face showing deposits of organics, gravels and estuarine mud (F137) outside (north of) revetment F166

Pl. VIII: Phase 5: north wall of Structure A (F150), from north-east

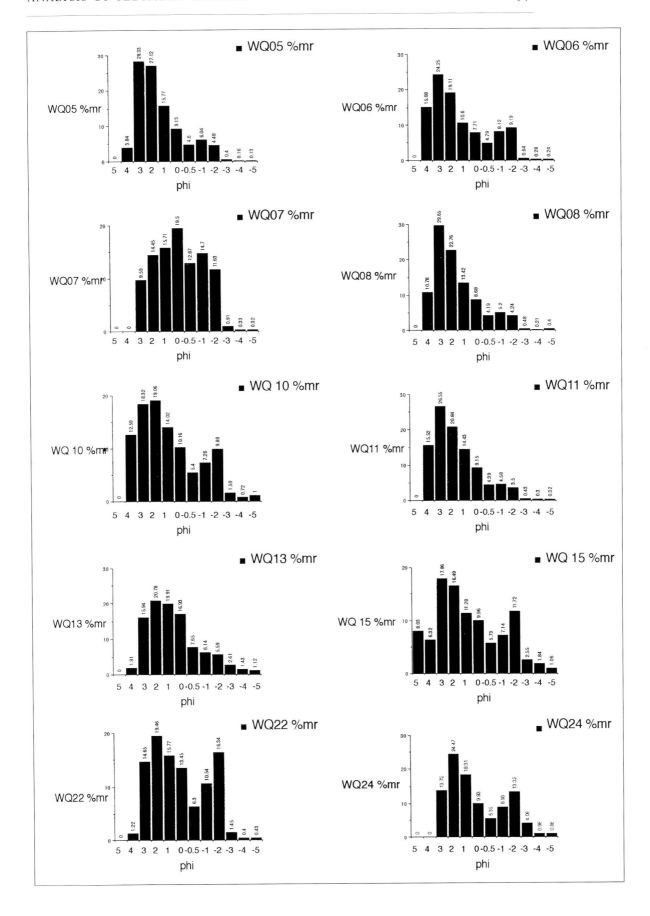

Fig. 43: Winetavern St/Wood Quay: particle size analyses

METHODS

Particle size analysis

Standard measurements (Gale and Hoare 1991) of the distribution of particle grain size were carried out on ten samples and the results are shown graphically on Figure 43. The graphs show the relative percentages of the different grain sizes by weight and the grain size fractions are as follows:

Phi size	Grain size (mm)	Category
5	0.031	coarse silt
4	0.063	very fine sand
3	0.125	fine sand
2	0.250	medium sand
1	0.5	coarse sand
0	1.0	very coarse sand
−0.5	1.5	very coarse sand
−1	2.0	granule
−2	4.0	pebble
−3	8.0	pebble
−41	6.0	pebble
−53	2.0	pebble

Samples with a spread of weight between the different size fractions (e.g. WQ 10, WQ 15 and WQ 22) are poorly sorted relative to the others. Samples with distinct peaks show sorting (for example, WQ 05 and WQ 06 are sorted, albeit weakly). Thus the graphs show the distribution of sediment size in the facies tested.

Loss on ignition

Sixteen samples were taken from the finer sediments deposited in the section and subjected to a standard loss on ignition test (Gale and Hoare 1991) to estimate the organic carbon content (see Fig. 44).

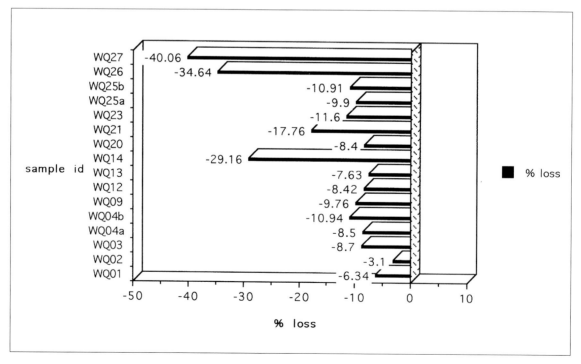

Fig. 44: Winetavern St/Wood Quay: loss on ignition data

Palaeocurrent analysis

The long axes of clasts within gravely sediments and the dip of foreset deposition were noted in the sand and gravel bars. This allows an estimation of the palaeocurrent operating during the deposition of the material.

Thin-sectioning

Two thin sections were prepared from grey clay horizons (F137) on the outside of the revetment. These were cut and then prepared by G.A.P.S. in London.

RESULTS

The results of the various techniques are outlined on Figures 43 and 44 and Table 2 and are discussed within the text below.

DISCUSSION

The depositional environments recognisable here can be subdivided and explained in terms of characteristics apparent in some of the sediments:

1. Sand and gravel bar sedimentation under fluviatile conditions.

2. Clay and silt sedimentation in quiet water.

3. Organic clay and silt which has possibly been reworked.

1. Sand and gravel bar sedimentation under fluviatile conditions.

The sections contain abundant evidence of channel bar sedimentation that must have occurred during flood events of the river. Examples of these bars (which appear in three dimensions as elongate lenses, fans or drapes of coarser sediment) could be seen as the gravels labelled F128 on the sections. Palaeocurrent analyses of these bars produce typical results with foreset dips and imbricate clasts showing a wide spread of flow directions. The predominant flow in the bars measured (including F128) was towards the east-south-east. These sand and gravel bars are moderately sorted showing that some water sorting has occurred but that they were probably deposited in flood conditions (with the river in spate) with a relatively short travelling distance of the material and an overall low degree of sorting.

Some of the sand and gravel was apparently organic (for example, F139) and this was subjected to a loss on ignition test giving a result of 7.63%. Although a relatively low concentration of organic material, this is high for such a gravel bar suggesting local incorporation of organics and a low travel distance for this particular unit of sand and gravel. A gravel bar behind the revetment (F207/ WQ 22) was poorly sorted (bimodal) as was an overlying stratified gravel unit (F191/ WQ 24). Such sediments are not unusual in natural gravel bars and probably represent material that has not travelled far during flood events. On the other hand there is a strong possibility that these sediments may have been post-depositionally disturbed.

2. Clay and silt sedimentation in quiet water.

Interdigitating with the gravel bars are clays and silts with variable organic content (see Pl. VII). These sediments have been analysed and are predominantly silt-sized with some clay. Sediment from F137 (grey clay) was tested both by loss on ignition (WQ 01, WQ 02, WQ 03 and WQ 04 [two samples tested WQ 04a and WQ 04b] : 6.34%, 3.1%, 8.7% and 8.5–10.94% respectively) and a sample (TS 1, just below WQ 02) was taken for thin sectioning. The thin sections show that the silts are poorly laminated with normally graded sequences fining up. The lamination is not immediately apparent to the naked eye. The lamination within these sediments suggests deposition in standing or slowly moving water. Such lamination would not occur in disturbed material. The uniform low organic content of these silts (note five samples tested from F139) is also notable and they are predominantly minerogenic. These faintly laminated silts were most likely laid down in slow moving water where enough time was available for the finer sediment to settle out. It is not possible to estimate the depth of water involved.

3. Organic clay and silt which has possibly been reworked.

Some of the samples taken for loss on ignition show distinctly higher values of organic carbon content. This may be naturally occurring organic detritus contained within the sediment or it may be secondary, allochthonous, organic material. Samples containing noticeably higher organic contents include WQ 14 (F139) with 29.16%, WQ 21 (F221) with 17.76%, WQ 26 (F238) with 34.64% and WQ 27 (F239) with 40.06%. These samples have relatively high organic contents and notably three are from behind the revetment. The silty clay of WQ 21 was associated with vivianite (a mineral product of bone), abundant root fragments, charcoal and pebble clasts.

CONCLUSIONS

The sediment sequences observed in the 1993 Winetavern St/Wood Quay sections are commonly associated with estuarine or fluviatile situations where flood events occur producing poorly sorted gravel bars within fine sediment accumulations. The fine sediment (silt and clay, often referred to as 'mud') has been laid down under quiet water deposition and is in part laminated, suggesting sluggish water conditions with some water depth. Certain facies contain high organic contents, bone, pottery and large clasts within a fine matrix and the properties of these sediments suggest that they have either been reworked or that they have had detritus thrown into them, as they occur proximal to human activity.

REFERENCES

Gale, S.J. and Hoare, P.G. 1991 *Quaternary sediments*. Belhaven Press.

PART II

The finds

This section is devoted to discussion of the artefactual material recovered during the excavation, under several different headings. In most cases, the various discussions are accompanied by Inventories of the material concerned, in which the following abbreviations and conventions are used:

B: Breadth	M: Moulded dimension
D: Diameter	S: Sided dimension
H: Height	T: Thickness
L: Length	W: Width

All measurements are in millimetres, unless otherwise stated.

All finds have been given a National Museum of Ireland registration number, which is in three parts, beginning with the site identifier (**93E24**), and thereafter the context number of the find, followed by its individual number. For the sake of brevity, however, the site identifier (93E24) is not included in references to objects in the following reports. Thus the full registration of the copper alloy stick pin, listed below as 1071.2, is actually 93E24.1071.2, where 1071 is the context number of the find (that is from layer F1071), and 2 its individual number. The finds have been lodged with the National Museum of Ireland.

CHAPTER VII

The medieval pottery

Cliona Papazian

Almost 7,000 sherds of medieval pottery were recovered from deposits associated with a series of reclamation phases and post-reclamation occupation which, on the evidence of the pottery, probably date from the late 12th century to the late 13th century. While locally made pottery dominates the assemblage (Table 1), English and Continental imports account for a significant proportion representing wares from possibly 19 different production sites.

ware	sherd count	%	weight	%
Dublin/Leinster	4,186	60%	69.386 kg	67%
English	1,221	17%	20.938 kg	20%
French	1,498	22%	12.491 kg	12%
Spanish/German	39	1%	0.429 kg	1%
Totals	**6,944**		**103.244 kg**	

Table 1: The Winetavern St/Wood Quay assemblage by sherd count and weight

METHODOLOGY

The assemblage was examined and sorted into groups, then counted and weighed. The pottery was recorded on a separate sheet for each context/feature, another for each phase/level and finally on a site summary spreadsheet. There are disadvantages to using sherd counts as a system of quantification (Vince 1977; Orton & Tyers 1990) and this was offset to a degree by weighing the groups. As can be seen from Table 1, French sherds, being thin walled, tend to fragment into smaller pieces giving disproportionately larger values for count than weight. For simplicity sherd counts are used when describing the frequency of each group but the reader should refer back to Table 1 when considering such values. It is accepted that the preferred method of quantification is estimated vessel numbers, but given the time allowed for examination and recording the author opted for the quickest, objective and most efficient method.

The imported groups are first discussed, followed by the local wares. Within each section (1: French; 2: English; 3: Spanish and German; 4: Dublin wares) the pottery groups are presented in approximate chronological order. The appellation for imports is common name; the local Dublin wares are described by fabric codes 001 – 004 with common names. The pottery groups are discussed individually; because detailed fabric descriptions are available for most of the groups, this information is not duplicated here and the reader is referred to the relevant texts. Where known, references are also given to published examples of vessel forms for each group.

The known dates for each group are outlined, based on dating evidence from urban sites in England and Ireland. Among the quoted parallels are a number of assemblages from other Dublin sites (Cornmarket, Ross Road/Christchurch Place, Back Lane and High St) for which reports have been prepared by the author but are as yet unpublished. The 'master dates' thus arrived at are discussed in the light of the stratigraphic and dendrochronological evidence from Winetavern St/Wood Quay. Pottery is described as residual only where it appears likely to the author that it occurs in stratigraphic levels later than the known terminal dates for the ware in question. Finally, the ceramic sequence is discussed, albeit in three unequal periods.

THE IMPORTED WARES

Approximately 40% of the medieval pottery was imported. Other sites excavated nearby, for which figures are available from previous work by the author, include Back Lane, Ross Road/ Christchurch Place, Cornmarket, Dublin Castle and High St. The respective figures are reproduced here for comparison (Table 2). In this author's experience the amounts of imports from the High St sites are anomalous, especially when compared with other contemporary assemblages such as the pottery from the pre-Norman and later fosses at Cornmarket and at Ross Road/ Christchurch Place.

site name	% English	% French	% misc. continental
Back Lane	11%	13%	
Ross Road/Christchurch Place	15%	14%	1%
Cornmarket	4%	5%	1%
Dublin Castle	3%	7%	
4–5 High St	35%	10%	
1–3 High St	48%	48%	
9–12 High St	11%	41%	

Table 2: Percentages of imported wares (based on sherd counts) from selected Dublin sites

The assemblage from Winetavern St/Wood Quay is directly comparable to that from P.F. Wallace's Wood Quay excavations, in which c.40% of sherds were also imported (C. McCutcheon, pers. comm.). The relatively high concentration of imports from this site is further evidence of localized concentrations of imports which are particular only to some contemporary sites. The factors which lead to such localized concentrations can only be imagined until the majority of Dublin sites are studied in tandem, but it seems likely that as yet unknown socio-cultural factors may be at work.

1. FRENCH WARES

Phase	1	2	3	4	5	6
Activity:	pre-reclamation & first reclamation		second and third reclamation		medieval occupation	post-medieval/ site clearance
Suggested date:	Late 12th		1st half 13th		2nd half 13th	post-medieval
GROUP	SHERDS					
French monochrome	11	45	247	86	32	65
Breton		2		1		1
French whiteware			15	1	3	4
French cooking		1	6			2
Rouen			13	9	1	12
Orleans			1	1	2	7
Saintonge green	1	7	121	226	274	290
Saintonge polychrome					4	1
all over green						6

Table 3: Medieval French imports by period, group and sherd count

1.1 NORTHERN AND NORTH-WESTERN FRENCH WARES

Northern French monochrome

Fabric and Forms: See Gahan and McCutcheon (1997, 307), McMahon (1991, 61) and Vince (1983i, 220–2); mostly jug forms, frequently decorated with cord impressions and short, diagonal incised lines. Some rim fragments have 'dummy spouts' (Fig. 45:203.1). Dummy spouted vessels were also made in the Saintonge and it has been suggested that such vessels were used as honey pots (R. Thompson, pers. comm.). Gahan and McCutcheon (1997, Fig. 11:14.11) illustrate an almost complete 'honey pot' in Saintonge green-glazed ware.

Dating and Frequency: These wares are known from Bristol where they predate Saintonge wares (Ponsford 1983, 222). In Dublin northern French monochrome wares are usually found with Saintonge green glazed wares, although in the earliest levels northern French monochromes usually occur with greater frequency. In London, northern French monochrome wares are contemporaneous with Rouen wares (Vince 1985, 48) and are found throughout the late 12th to mid-13th centuries. In Waterford a date range within the 13th century is suggested (Gahan and McCutcheon 1997, 307). At Winetavern St/Wood Quay northern French monochrome wares are first found in pre-reclamation and in initial reclamation deposits. They are most frequent in Phase 3 deposits associated with the second reclamation episode of c.1200 and by Phase 5 they probably occur as residual finds. An overall date range from the late 12th to mid-13th century is suggested by the stratigraphic evidence and the associated pottery.

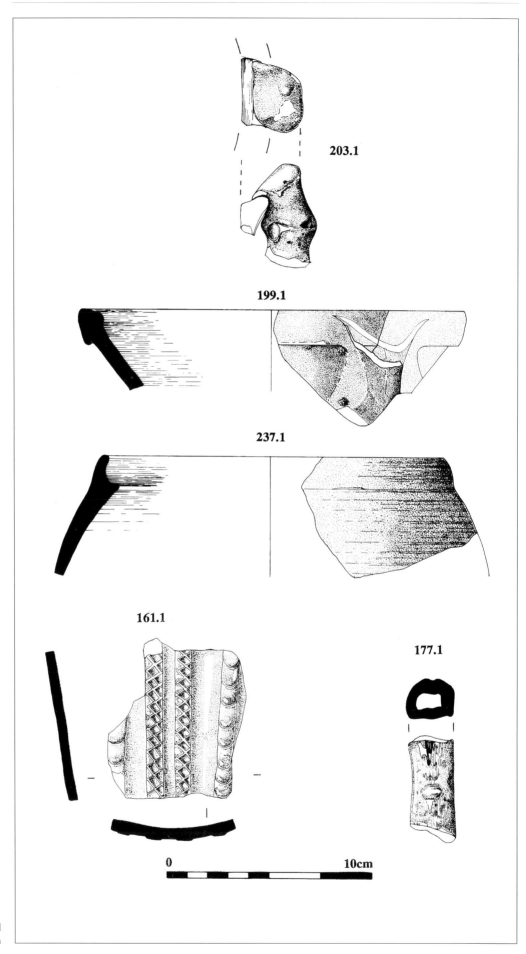

Fig. 45: Imported
pottery: French

Breton

Fabric and Forms: See Allan (1984, 37) and Papazian (1989, 44). None illustrated.

Dating and Frequency: Allan (1984, 37) suggests an early to mid-13th century date for these wares. At Ross Road/Christchurch Place they were first present in contexts dated to the late 12th century and an overall date range from the late 12th to mid-13th century seems likely. At Winetavern St/Wood Quay two sherds were recovered from contexts associated with the first reclamation episode, so a date from the late 12th century seems likely. In subsequent phases these wares are only evidenced by single sherds and it seems likely, from the date ranges given above, that by Phase 5 Breton wares occur only as residual finds.

Northern French whiteware

Fabric and Forms: Fabric is similar to, but coarser than northern French monochrome, and fires to a brilliant white colour. Forms and decorative motifs are very similar to both northern French monochrome and Rouen and therefore a production source in northern France seems likely. None illustrated.

Dating and Frequency: At Ross Road/Christchurch Place an overall date range from the mid/late 12th century to the early 13th century was suggested. Northern French whitewares are first found at Winetavern St/Wood Quay in Phase 3 contexts associated with the second reclamation episode of c.1200. They are only represented in subsequent phases by a few sherds which, given the suggested date ranges for Ross Road/ Christchurch Place, are probably residual.

Northern French cooking wares

Fabric and Forms: See Davidson (1972). Two cooking pots are illustrated, a collared rimmed cooking pot with tubular spout (Fig. 45 : 199.1) and a cooking pot with lid seating (Fig. 45 : 237.1). This form is also known from Waterford (Gahan and McCutcheon 1997, Fig. 11 : 9.10).

Dating and Frequency: Dated in Waterford from the 11th to 13th centuries (Gahan and McCutcheon 1997, 304), at Winetavern St/Wood Quay these wares are only found in Phase 2 and Phase 3 contexts, suggesting a maximum date range from the late 12th to early 13th century. This confirms the dating for northern French cooking wares from Ross Road/Christchurch Place.

Rouen

Fabric and forms: See Barton (1965) and Vince (1983, 1985). Only one type of Rouen jug is known from Winetavern St/Wood Quay, the classic dichrome jug decorated with scale pellets (Fig. 45 : 161.1).

Dating and Frequency: The evidence from Ross Road/Christchurch Place and from 1–3 High St indicates that Rouen imports first occur in Dublin in contexts dating to the late 12th century. At Winetavern St /Wood Quay Rouen imports are first found in Phase 3 contexts associated with the second reclamation episode of c.1200. The associated pottery supports a date at the beginning of the 13th century. Rouen imports are also found in succeeding phases. Allan (1983, 198) suggests a terminal date for Rouen wares in the middle or last quarter of the 13th century.

Orléans-type

Fabric and Forms: See Allan (1984, 21) and Gahan et al. (1997, 122–23). Typical forms include hollow handled jugs decorated with diagonally incised grooving (Fig. 45 : 177.1 and Fig. 46 : 160.1); see Allan (1984, 71, Fig. 32: no 888) for a complete jug illustration, and Gahan et al. (1997, Fig. 51 : 6) for a variation.

Dating and Frequency: At Ross Road/Christchurch Place Orléans-type wares are first present in early 13th-century contexts. At Winetavern St/Wood Quay they are first found in Phase 3 (second reclamation episode) contexts of the early 13th century. As all the fragments are from the same vessel, the sherds from subsequent phases are residual.

1.2 SOUTH-WESTERN FRENCH WARES

Saintonge green glazed ware

Fabric and Forms: See Barton (1963a), Platt and Coleman-Smith (1975) and Vince (1983i, 225–8). Forms from Winetavern St/Wood Quay include jugs, a 'honey pot' fragment (Fig. 46 : 17.1), a mortar (Fig. 46 : 146.1) and a dripping pan fragment (Fig. 46 : 15.1). A similar dripping pan was recovered from an early 13th century context at Ross Road/Christchurch Place. Dripping pan forms are known in London in a variety of fabrics from the late 12th/early 13th century onwards (Vince 1983ii, 465). Gahan and McCutcheon (1997, Fig. 11:14.11) illustrate an almost complete 'honey pot'.

Dating and Frequency: Barton (1963a, 201–04) and Allan (1983, 199) suggest a wide date range from the end of the 12th century to the end of the medieval period. At Ross Road/Christchurch Place, Saintonge green glazed wares are first present in contexts dating at the earliest to *c*.1175 (based on the presence of Ham Green 'B' wares). At Winetavern St/Wood Quay, they first occur in late 12th century contexts (Phases 1 and 2) but occur with greatest frequency in contexts dated from the mid-13th century onwards (Phases 4 and 5); the rise in the relative frequency of Saintonge wares is characterised by a corresponding decline in the amounts of Northern French monochromes found (Table 3).

Saintonge polychrome ware

Fabric and Forms: Fabric as for Saintonge green glazed, above; only jugs are known. None illustrated.

Dating and Frequency: The maximum date range is thought to be from *c*.1257–1330; Saintonge polychrome is first present at Winetavern St/Wood Quay in Phase 5 contexts (probably later 13th century); there are no residual finds.

Saintonge all over green glazed ware

Fabric and Forms: See Papazian (1989, 40) and Gahan and McCutcheon (1997, 316).

Dating and Frequency: Contemporaneous with polychrome wares, Saintonge all over green glazed ware occurs at Winetavern St/Wood Quay only in Phase 6 contexts as residual finds.

1.3 LATE MEDIEVAL FRENCH IMPORTS

Beauvais Green Glazed

Fabric and Forms: See Hurst et al. (1986, 106) and Meenan (1997, 345). None illustrated.

Dating and Frequency: Beauvais green glazed ware is dated to the 16th century (Hurst et al. 1986, 108); six sherds were recovered at Winetavern St/Wood Quay, all residual.

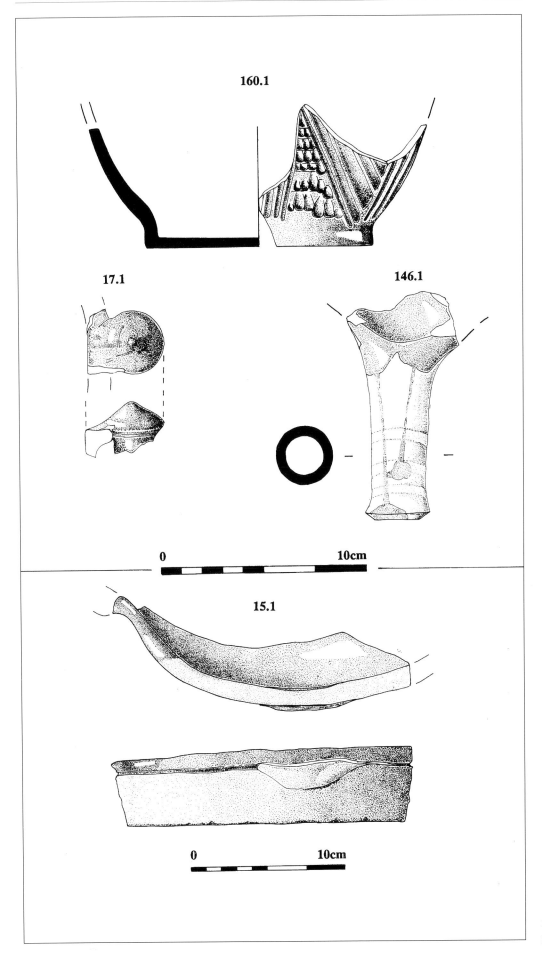

Fig. 46: Imported pottery: French

2. SPANISH AND GERMAN WARES

Phase	1	2	3	4	5	6
Activity:	*pre-reclamation & first reclamation*		*second and third reclamation*		*medieval occupation*	*post-medieval/ site clearance*
Suggested date:	Late 12th		1st half 13th		2nd half 13th	post-medieval
GROUP	SHERDS					
Merida/Iberian red						29
Iberian coarse						11
Paffrath			2			

Table 4: Medieval Spanish and German imports by period, group and sherd count

2.1 SPANISH IMPORTS

Merida-type wares / Iberian red micaceous

Fabric and Forms: See Hurst et al. (1986, 69–70) and Meenan (1997, 340). None illustrated

Dating and Frequency: At Ross Road/Christchurch Place these wares were first found in contexts dating to the early 13th century, although at Cornmarket they were found associated with Saintonge polychromes. None of the Merida ware found at Winetavern St/Wood Quay was recovered from contemporary medieval contexts and is therefore residual.

Iberian Coarsewares

Fabric and Forms: See Hurst et al. (1986, 66) and Meenan (1997, 340). 160.1 (Fig. 47) is a straight sided bowl with no published comparanda. Ms Rosanne Meenan confirmed the identification of 160.1 as an Iberian coarseware and commented further that the vessel form was unusual.

Dating and Frequency: Vince (1985, 81) suggests that pottery from the Iberian peninsula is first found in London in mid-13th century contexts. A total of 5 sherds were recovered at Winetavern St/Wood Quay, all of which were from post-medieval contexts and may therefore be residual.

2.2 GERMAN IMPORTS

Paffrath wares

Fabric and Forms: See Jennings (1981, 26). 171.1 (Fig. 47) is from the rim of a ladle.

Dating and Frequency: Jennings (1981) suggests a 12th to 13th century date range for these wares. At Exeter they dated from the late 12th to the early 13th century (Allan 1984, 45). Paffrath wares occurred in Waterford in 12th and 13th century contexts (Gahan and McCutcheon 1997, 320) and in Cork in early 13th century contexts (Gahan et al. 1997, 120–21). Two sherds occurred at Winetavern St/Wood Quay in Phase 3 contexts of early 13th century date.

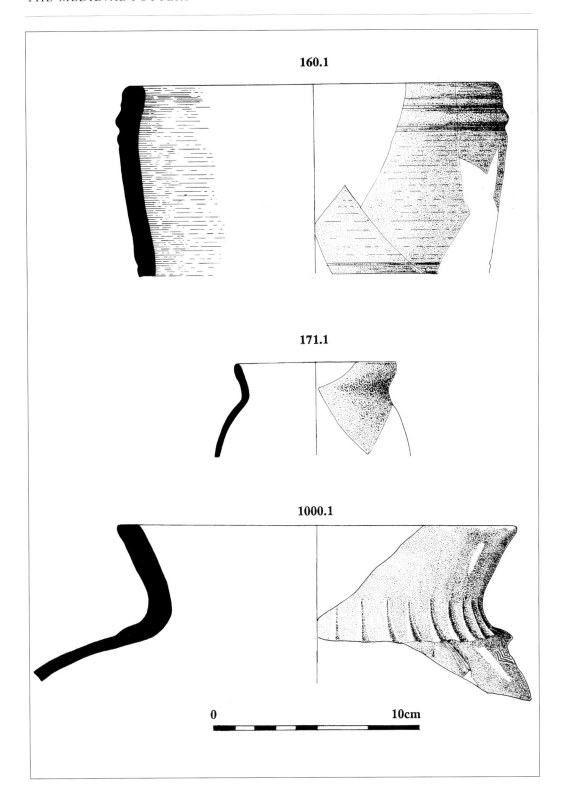

Fig. 47: Imported pottery: Spanish (160.1), German (171.1), English (1000.1)

3. ENGLISH WARES

In character with the overall profile of assemblages from medieval sites in Dublin, the bulk of the English imports at Winetavern St/Wood Quay can be provenanced to the Ham Green potteries in Bristol and to unknown production sites located in or near Bristol. Less common imports include north Devon wares and cooking wares from an unknown production source.

Phase	1	2	3	4	5	6
Activity:	*pre-reclamation & first reclamation*		*second and third reclamation*		*medieval occupation*	*post-medieval/ site clearance*
Suggested date:	Late 12th		1st half 13th		2nd half 13th	post-medieval
GROUP		SHERDS				
Ham Green 'B'	31	70	344	213	40	289
Ham Green cooking	3	7	62	75	7	12
Bristol/French		2	14			12
Minety			7	5	4	4
SE Wilts			1	2		3
SW English cooking			6			
N Devon			1			
Redcliffe					6	1

Table 5: Medieval English imports by period, group and sherd count

Ham Green 'B' wares

Fabric and Forms: See Barton (1963b; 1988) and Ponsford (1991). None illustrated.

Dating and Frequency: Ponsford (1991, 98) suggests that 'B' jugs can be dated *c.*1175–1250 with some forms datable to *c.*1275. In common with Ross Road/Christchurch Place, the greatest frequency of Ham Green wares at Winetavern St/Wood Quay occurs in contexts datable to within the first half of the 13th century (Table 5).

Ham Green cooking wares

Fabric and Forms: See Barton (1963b; 1988). None illustrated.

Dating and Frequency: These wares are contemporaneous with Ham Green 'B' wares; at Winetavern St/Wood Quay the greatest frequency is in contexts of Phases 3–4, which can be dated to the first half of the 13th century (Table 5).

Bristol / French(?) wares

Fabric and Forms: A possible unknown Bristol or French import, the fabric not recognised by the author. None illustrated

Dating and Frequency: A rare import, occurring at Winetavern St/Wood Quay mainly in contexts of Phases 2 and 3, which indicates an overall date range in the late 12th and early 13th centuries.

Minety wares

Fabric and Forms: See McMahon (1991, 60) and Vince (1983i, 137–45, 1988, 262–64). 1000.1 (Fig. 47) is a tripod pitcher rim decorated with fingernail nicking and wavy comb decoration.

Dating and Frequency: Minety tripod pitchers are found at Bristol Castle in contexts dated to *c.*1125, although they are known from earlier, late 11th century contexts at Ewen, Gloucestershire (Redknap 1990, 85). They occur in Waterford and Cork in contexts of the late 12th and 13th centuries (Gahan and McCutcheon 1997, 297; Gahan et al. 1997, 118). Vince (1988, 266–7) suggests that Minety wares from the Dublin excavations have a date range from the 12th to 13th centuries. At Ross Road/Christchurch Place Minety wares are first found in late 12th century contexts. They first occur at Winetavern St/Wood Quay slightly later, in early 13th century (Phases 3 and 4) contexts and are also found in Phase 5 contexts associated with Saintonge polychromes indicating an overall date range within the 13th century (Table 5).

South-east Wiltshire wares

Fabric and Forms: See Vince (1988, 264) and Gahan and McCutcheon (1997, 292–93). None illustrated.

Dating and Frequency: At Waterford the evidence indicated that these wares were being imported from the early 12th century and throughout that century, but infrequently in the 13th century. In Dublin, Wiltshire wares are found contemporaneously with Minety wares at Ross Road/ Christchurch Place, although always as a rare import. At Winetavern St/Wood Quay these wares occur for only a short period within the first half of the 13th century; by Phase 6 they are certainly residual.

South-west English cooking ware

Fabric and Forms: See McMahon (1991, 59–60). None illustrated.

Dating and Frequency: McMahon (1991, 59) suggests a late 12th-century date; the evidence from Ross Road/Christchurch Place confirms this, but the Winetavern St/Wood Quay sherds are slightly later, dating to the early 13th century.

North Devon gravel tempered ware / Dyfed gravel tempered ware

Fabric and Forms: English or possibly Welsh (Dyfed) gravel tempered wares; see Papazian (1989, 33). None illustrated.

Dating and Frequency: At Exeter these wares dated to the mid-13th century (Allan 1984, 6). At Winetavern St/Wood Quay they only occur in contexts datable to the early 13th century.

Redcliffe wares

Fabric and Forms: See Vince (1983i, 52, 1988, 260–61) and Gahan and McCutcheon (1997, 301). None illustrated.

Dating and Frequency: Vince (1983i, 52–3) suggests a starting date in the mid- to late 13th century. In Waterford, Redcliffe wares occur primarilydated to the later 13th century (Gahan and McCutcheon 1997, 303). At Winetavern St/Wood Quay they are contemporaneous with Saintonge polychromes in Phase 5 (later 13th century) contexts.

4. DUBLIN AND NATIVE WARES

Phase	1	2	3	4	5	6
Activity:	pre-reclamation & first reclamation		second and third reclamation		medieval occupation	post-medieval/ site clearance
Suggested date:	Late 12th		1st half 13th		2nd half 13th	post-medieval
GROUP	SHERDS					
Fabric 004	7	27	783	748	186	275
Fabric 004 cooking		3	253	310	27	155
Fabric 001		1	32	42	46	55
Fabric 002			6	18	704	362
Fabric 003			11	14	31	90

Table 6: Medieval Dublin wares by period, group and sherd count

Fabric 004: Dublin hand built glazed and cooking pot wares

Fabric and Forms: For macroscopic fabric description see Papazian (1989, 112); for petrological analysis see ibid., 140–2; for an account of the forms recovered at Dublin Castle see ibid., 116–18. Most of the 004 forms from Winetavern St/Wood Quay are glazed wares, with only 11% cooking wares, in contrast with Back Lane where 42% of the 004 assemblage are cooking wares. Indeed most of the Winetavern St/Wood Quay medieval pottery, regardless of type, are glazed table wares rather than cooking or other food preparatory vessels. None illustrated.

Dating and Frequency: At 4–5 High St fabric 004 wares are known from contexts dated to the late 12th century. The evidence from Ross Road/Christchurch Place indicates that fabric 004 wares are the earliest Dublin wares found on the site, as these were found in late 12th century contexts. Fabric 004 wares are also the earliest local wares found at Winetavern St/Wood Quay, occurring first in Phase 1 deposits and present in each subsequent phase. The evidence from Cornmarket indicates that these wares have a probable terminal date in the latter half of the 13th century, when fabric 002 wares are found in increasing numbers. This is confirmed by the evidence from this site; the increase in fabric 002 noted from Phase 5 can be dated to the second half of the 13th century by associated pottery.

Fabric 001: Dublin cooking ware

Fabric and Forms: For macroscopic fabric description see Papazian (1989, 125); for petrological analysis see ibid., 136–8; for a gazetteer of known vessel forms see ibid., 128–32. None illustrated.

Dating and Frequency: Fabric 001 wares are first present at Winetavern St/Wood Quay in Phase 2 contexts, dating to the late 12th century. Thereafter this ware is found in each subsequent phase in consistently small amounts. It is not yet certain whether this ware has a 16th century or earlier terminal date.

Fabric 002: Dublin Glazed Wares

Fabric and Forms: For macroscopic fabric description see Papazian (1989, 68); for petrological analysis see ibid., 138–9. None illustrated.

Dating and Frequency: Fabric 002 wares are first found at Winetavern St/Wood Quay in Phase 3 contexts, which can be dated to the early 13th century. There is a perceptible increase in the amounts of this ware from Phase 5, accompanied by a corresponding decline in the amounts of fabric 004 recovered. The large amount of this ware from Phase 6 is probably explicable as upcast caused by the disturbance and partial clearance of the medieval ground surface by later post-medieval building activity. Evidence from other Dublin sites studied by the author suggests that fabric 002 wares have a terminal date in the 16th century.

Fabric 003: Dublin temper-free wares

Fabric and Forms: For macroscopic description see Papazian 1989, 96–7; for petrological analysis see ibid., 142; a description of forms is given in ibid., 116–18. None illustrated.

Dating and Frequency: Fabric 003 wares are contemporary with fabric 002 wares at Winetavern St/Wood Quay, although they do not account for a significant proportion of the medieval pottery assemblage. This may be explained by the fact that the main floruit of these wares (from the 14th to 16th centuries) is later than the surviving archaeological stratigraphy on this site.

THE CERAMIC SEQUENCE

The dating evidence for the assemblage from Winetavern St/Wood Quay is based on the stratigraphic evidence and is buttressed by comparison with the ceramic sequences from other Dublin sites. The sequence discussed below represents a relative, not absolute sequence and may be subject to refinement when more closely datable assemblages are excavated.

The late 12th century

The dendrochronological dating for Phase 3 (second reclamation episode) suggests a terminus ante quem of c.1195–1201 AD for Phases 1 and 2 and the associated stratigraphy. Therefore it is possible to suggest a starting date for this assemblage in the later 12th century. The pottery from the pre-reclamation (Phase 1) and first reclamation (Phase 2) deposits is similar to the pottery types found in contemporary deposits at other Dublin sites. The amount of pottery from the earliest archaeological layers is small relative to that from Phase 3 and 4 contexts. English, northern French and south-western French imports constitute the bulk (83%) of the pottery and local wares (17%) do not form a significant part of the assemblage. Contemporary assemblages from Ross Road/ Christchurch Place and from Cornmarket have a different composition with local wares accounting for between 50% to 75% of the pottery. While the evidence suggests considerable variation between different sites, however, the overall pattern of imports is fairly consistent, with Ham Green glazed wares accounting for the majority of English imports. Pottery from known and unknown production centres in northern France are more common than south-western imports from the Saintonge. This pattern prevails until the mid-13th century when Saintonge imports predominate.

The early to mid-13th century

Dendrochronology provides a *terminus post quem* of c.1195–1201 AD for the deposits associated with the second reclamation episode. The excavator suggests that these deposits accumulated fairly rapidly and therefore the pottery recovered was probably deposited in the early years of the 13th century. Saintonge polychromes are present in Phase 5 deposits and the pottery in Phase 4 (third reclamation episode) deposits should predate these wares. Thus an overall date range from the early to mid-13th century seems likely for the pottery from the second and third reclamation episodes. This conclusion is supported by historical evidence for the completion of reclamation on the site, with the construction of a stone quayside wall, by c.1260 AD (see Chapter II above).

The most significant changes in the character of the assemblage of this period is the increase in the volume of pottery deposited (by a factor of 18) and the increase in the frequency of local wares; now accounting for 60% of the contemporaneous assemblage. The relative frequency of imports remains largely unchanged in the pottery from deposits associated with the second reclamation episode (Phase 3) but by the third reclamation episode (Phase 4) Saintonge imports occur with greater frequency. This increase is marked by a corresponding decline in the amounts of northern French monochromes. Rare imports include Orléans-type, Paffrath and North Devon gravel tempered wares.

The middle to the end of the 13th century

The dating of the post-reclamation activity is based on the presence of Saintonge polychromes and also on the increase in the frequency of Dublin fabric 002 wares – a phenomenon which seems to occur on other Dublin sites studied by the author in contexts dating from the mid-13th century. The overall volume of local wares increases slightly although imports still account for 35% of the contemporary assemblage. For the first time French imports are more frequent than English imports and from the mid-13th century Redcliffe imports are found. It seems probable that northern French monochromes and whitewares are residual by the second half of the 13th century. The general absence of Dublin fabric 003 wares suggests that the Winetavern St/Wood Quay assemblage predates the *floruit* of this ware, which is dated from the 14th century onwards.

Post-medieval and residual pottery

A large quantity of the medieval pottery was recovered as residual upcast material in later, post-medieval deposits and as clearance from removal of the overburden. Consequently the stratigraphy at Winetavern St/Wood Quay, being a truncated sequence, does not represent the true sequence of medieval activity and use of the site. At most the material covers a span of little over a century.

CONCLUSIONS

The medieval pottery assemblage from Winetavern St/Wood Quay dates from the late 12th century to the end of the 13th century. Most of the medieval pottery was recovered from deposits associated with the second and third reclamation episodes (Phases 3 and 4) although much of it occurred as residual finds in post-medieval and later contexts. In common with most Dublin assemblages, local wares are, from the early 13th century onwards, the most important source of medieval pottery. Dublin fabric 004 glazed and cooking wares have a suggested date range from the mid-12th century and first appear at Winetavern St/Wood Quay during the late 12th century. Fabric 004 wares continue to dominate the medieval assemblage until the middle of the 13th century when fabric 002 wares dramatically increase (Table 6). Fabric 001 cooking wares first appear in contexts associated with the first reclamation episode and occur in small amounts in each subsequent phase. Cooking wares of all types are not frequent and the assemblage mostly consists of glazed jugs and other tablewares.

The earliest wares found are predominantly English imports from Bristol. Northern French imports occur earlier than Saintonge imports, which although present from the late 12th century do not occur with great frequency until the second half of the 13th century. English wares continue to be imported throughout the first half of the 13th century but thereafter the amounts imported decline, the only definite later 13th century English imports coming from the Redcliffe potteries in Bristol. Spanish and German wares are rare pottery types and do not seem to have been an important source of imported pottery in the medieval period.

REFERENCES

Allan, J.P. 1983 The importation of pottery to southern England *c*.1200–1500. In Davey and Hodges 1983, 193–208.

Allan, J.P. 1984 *Medieval and post-medieval finds from Exeter 1971–80*. Exeter Archaeological Reports **3**.

Barton, K.J. 1963a The medieval pottery of the Saintonge. *Arch. J.* **120**, 201–14.

Barton, K.J. 1963b A medieval pottery kiln at Ham Green, Bristol. *Trans. Bristol & Gloucs. Arch. Soc.* **82**, 95–126.

Barton, K.J. 1965 Medieval pottery at Rouen. *Arch. J.* **122**, 73–85.

Davidson, B.K. 1972 Castle Neroche: an abandoned Norman fortress in south Somerset. *Proceedings of the Somerset Archaeological Society* **116**, 16–58.

Gahan, A. and McCutcheon, C. 1997 Medieval pottery. In M.F. Hurley, O.M.B. Scully and S.W.J. McCutcheon (eds), *Late Viking age and medieval Waterford: Excavations 1986–1992*, 285–336. Waterford. Waterford Corporation.

Gahan, A., McCutcheon, C. and Twohig, D.C. 1997 Medieval pottery. In R.M. Cleary, M.F. Hurley and E. Shee Twohig (eds), *Skiddy's castle and Christ Church, Cork: Excavations 1974–77 by D.C. Twohig*, 108–129. Cork. Cork Corporation.

Hurst, J.G., Neal, D.S. and Van Beuningen, H.J.E. 1986 *Pottery produced and traded in north-west Europe 1350–1650*. Rotterdam Papers **6**.

Jennings, S 1981 *Eighteen centuries of pottery from Norwich*. East Anglian Archaeology **13**.

McMahon, M. 1991 Archaeological excavations at Bridge St Lower, Dublin. *P.R.I.A.* **91C**, 41–71.

Meenan, R. 1997 Post-medieval pottery. In M.F. Hurley, O.M.B. Scully and S.W.J. McCutcheon (eds), *Late Viking age and medieval Waterford: Excavations 1986–1992*, 338–55. Waterford. Waterford Corporation.

Orton, C. and Tyers, P. 1990 Slicing the pie – a framework for comparing ceramic assemblages. *Medieval Ceramics* **14**, 55–6.

Papazian, C. 1989 *The medieval pottery from the Dublin Castle excavations*. M.A. thesis submitted to University College Cork, unpublished.

Platt, C., and Coleman-Smith, R. 1975 *Excavations in medieval Southampton 1953–69*, 2 vols. Leicester. University Press.

Ponsford, M. 1983 North European pottery imported into Bristol 1200–1500. In Davey and Hodges 1983, 219–24.

Ponsford, M. 1991 Dendrochronological dates from Dundras Wharf, Bristol and the dating of Ham Green and other medieval pottery. In E. Lewis (ed.) *Customs and ceramics: essays presented to Kenneth Barton*, 81–103. Wickham. A.P.E.

Redknap, M. 1990 The pottery from Ewen, Gloucestershire. In R. Reece (ed.), *Excavation, survey and records around Cirencester*, 64–86. Cotswold Studies vol. 2. Cirencester.

Vince, A.G. 1977 Some aspects of pottery quantification. *Medieval ceramics* **1**, 63–74.

Vince, A.G. 1983 *The medieval pottery industry of the Severn valley*, 3 vols. Ph.D. thesis submitted to the University of Southampton, unpublished.

Vince, A.G. 1985 The Saxon and medieval pottery of London: a review. *Med. Arch.* **29**, 25–93.

Vince, A.G. 1988 Early medieval English pottery in Viking Dublin. In MacNiocaill and Wallace 1988, 254–70.

CHAPTER VIII

Medieval boat and ship timbers

Aidan O'Sullivan

The ship and boat timbers described here were found associated with four different waterfront structures, re-used as cladding, uprights or as general infill. Nine individual timbers and two groups of multiple planking were identified as of nautical origin. There were two stems, two groups of planking, four knees, one possible breasthook, one possible cross-beam, one ship oar and two further timbers of possible nautical function. These timbers confirm the importance of excavation for revealing the maritime origins of medieval Dublin.

METHODOLOGY

The recording of boat and ship timbers has increasingly become a field of great complexity (McGrail 1987). The recent comprehensive publication of previous nautical timbers from the medieval Dublin excavations (McGrail 1993) has been extensively drawn from in this study. Reference has also been made to various publications of the Skuldelev ships (Crumlin-Pedersen 1986a; Olsen and Crumlin-Pedersen 1967, 1990) and the publication of the ship timbers from the Bergen excavations (Christensen 1985). Furthermore, the author made a useful visit to the Vikingeskibshallen, Roskilde, Denmark in April 1995, where the Skuldelev ships were carefully examined for comparative purposes.

Detailed measured descriptions according to McGrail's guidelines are necessary to ascertain the function of each timber. As part of a deliberate policy of detailed wood recording during the excavations, the boat and ship timbers were maintained in good condition throughout the excavation, assigned special numbers on Wood Record Sheets and tightly wrapped in plastic sheeting, before storage in warehouse conditions. They were then recorded by means of 1:10 drawings on permatrace with written free-text descriptions in notebooks. These measurements and drawings were carried out prior to conservation and can therefore be considered as accurate. Wood species identifications were carried out either by naked eye or through the use of a microscope. All the nautical timbers are now in the process of being conserved by the National Museum of Ireland.

The Inventory descriptions of the Winetavern St/Wood Quay boat and ships timbers are ordered in a sequence of stems, planking, knees, breasthook, cross-beam and oar, following the standardised format adopted by McGrail (1993). The textual discussion is based on this Inventory and provides comparative material from previous Dublin excavations. There are real problems in identifying the function of disassembled ships timbers; a forked timber may be a knee, floor timber or breasthook. Even then it can be difficult to ascertain the angle in which it was used, thus differentiating between hanging, standing and lodged knees. Derived attributes are provided to establish the timber's function. These Inventory entries are therefore provided here with the understanding that other scholars may well recognise alternative functions. Two additional timbers of possible nautical function are also included although these could have served as timber elements in a dryland structure.

HULL STRUCTURAL ELEMENTS

Stems

Stems in the Nordic shipbuilding tradition were the foremost and aftermost timbers which were scarfed at their end to the keel and to which the strakes were attached. There are two stems (214.1, 1500.3; Figs 48–49) in the Winetavern St/Wood Quay assemblage. These are quite similar in size and form, wedge-shaped in section with flat, continuous inboard faces and groups of nails along the inboard edge. There was no rabetting, the evidence suggesting the common use of overlapping strakes onto the stem. This combination of attributes would seem to suggest that they are stems of McGrail's (1987, 123–25) Type F, a type not previously been found in the Dublin excavations and known only from a 12th century 'cog' at Kollerup. Type F stems are not generally used in the Nordic tradition of boat building, suggesting that these timbers are a useful contribution to the Dublin material. Confusingly, however, McGrail (1993, 105) seems to identify a similar stem timber (DST53) as a Type A stem, despite the fact that it had no rabbetting. The (M/S) ratios (2.86 and 3.00) of the Winetavern St/Wood Quay stems suggest an origin in small ships or large boats. Their enclosed angles (16° and 25°) and radii of curvature (1.7m and 1.9m) are also quite similar, leaving open the possibility that these stem timbers derive from the same vessel.

Planking

There were two main groups of ship or boat planking. Nine planks reused in revetment F164 (Figs 50–58) were each identified as being from a small ship, although it is not possible to be certain that all are from the same ship. Another group of articulated boat planks was found together with the original keel, re-used as planking in the main revetment F166 (Fig. 59). The dimensions and shape of the keel suggests that this timber group derives from towards the end of a small *faering* boat, similar to the Gokstad 2 and 3 vessels. A similar sized keel is the Dublin timber T383. The original F166 boat was therefore probably not greater than 7–9m in overall length. Such small boats would have been used for small-scale transport and fishing in the vicinity of medieval Dublin.

Knees

Knees were crooked timbers used as brackets between two timbers at right angles. There were four knees in the Winetavern St/Wood Quay assemblage of boat and ships timbers. This includes two standing knees (1500.8, 800.33; Figs 60, 61), one possibly lodging knee (1500.9; Fig. 62) and one further knee (800.32; Fig. 63). The two standing knees (1500.8, 800.33) were joggled to fit against at least three clinker planks. A single knee (800.32) was notched on its underside to fit against a stringer. The knees were fastened to the strakes by means of carved treenails. The Winetavern St/Wood Quay knees have (M.S) products of 80, 98, 120 and 240 and derive both from small ships and ships. One knee (800.33) had a rounded cross-section on its upper arm which was perforated by a circular hole and had possible rope marks around its surface. It is possible that this projected slightly above the sides of the vessel.

Possible breasthook and cross-beam

Breasthooks were fitted horizontally inboard of a forward or after stem and attached to the side-planking. There is one possible breasthook (1040.7; Fig. 64) in the Winetavern St/Wood Quay assemblage but it was in very poor and damaged condition, which made ascertaining its function difficult. It was cut from a naturally forked timber, with dowel holes and a step drilled into the sides and an irregular perforation through the width surface (possibly for rigging). Breasthooks of 13th/14th century date were found at Bryggen and have been considered to be a late Viking introduction. There is the alternative possibility that this timber is a bulkhead.

Cross-beams were timbers extending across the width of the vessel. A possible cross-beam (164.3; Fig. 65) was also found at Winetavern St/Wood Quay. This was an incomplete length of timber, cut to a T-shaped cross-section, with a series of nails and nail holes for planking. An apparently similar cross-beam is illustrated from Skuldelev 2 (Olsen and Crumlin-Pedersen 1990, 111).

PROPULSION

Ship oar

There is one oar from the Winetavern St/Wood Quay assemblage (1500.11; Fig. 66). This is an important addition to the Dublin nautical timbers, as only one possible oar has previously been discovered in the Dublin excavations. This is a late 12th-century broken blade (T377) of uncertain design and doubtful identification from Fishamble St. The Winetavern St/Wood Quay timber is quite unlike this piece, being much more clearly an oar, and is in fact more similar in plan and cross-section to the oars from Kvalsund 1 and Kvalsund 2 and in (L/B) ratio to both of the Gokstad 1 oars (McGrail 1993, 68, Fig. 45). Interestingly, these Scandinavian examples date from an earlier period, the 8th and 9th centuries AD. The Winetavern St/Wood Quay oar is a further example of the long continuity of Norse ship-building traditions. The oar is of incomplete length but its size and narrow blade suggest that it was used for propelling a large sea-going ship in open water.

BOATS AND SHIPS FROM 12TH CENTURY
WINETAVERN ST/WOOD QUAY

Although the Winetavern St/Wood Quay sample is relatively restricted in size, there are a remarkably wide range of boat and ship timber types represented. The timbers have been assessed in terms of their M/S ratios, M.S products, shapes, dimensions and manufacture and compared with the extensive Tables compiled by McGrail (1993, Tables 1, 2, 5, 6, 16 and 21). The timbers can be seen to derive from a small boat, large boats/small ships and from both small and larger ships. The oar is a further useful indicator of large sea-going ships docking at Dublin. The results are presented in Table 1.

Timber	Type	(M.S.)	Vessel
214.1	Stem/intermediate	280	Ship
1500.3	Stem	243	Ship
164	Planking	–	Large boat/small ship
166	Planking & keel	96	Small boat
1500.8	Knee	98	Large boat/small ship
800.33	Knee	120	Large boat/small ship
1500.9	Knee	240	Ship
800.32	Knee	80	Large boat/small ship
164.3	Cross-beam	238	Small ship
1500.11	Oar	(Lb/Bb) 7.8	Sea-going ship

Table 1: Boats and ships represented by the Winetavern St/Wood Quay timbers

THE DUBLIN SHIPWRIGHTS

Trees and woodland

The recording of the boat and ship timbers was carried out with a view to reconstructing the parent trees and local woodland sources (Goodburn 1991, 1994). Species were identified and an estimated tree-ring count made on each timber. The direction of the grain, the relative knottiness of the wood and the use of crooked timbers were also carefully recorded. Almost all of the timbers were of oak (*Quercus sp.*), although the oar was fashioned from straight-grained, fast-grown ash (*Fraxinus excelsior*). Willow and ash were used as treenails. Oak wedges were occasionally used to tighten the treenails. It seems likely that local oaks were used for the stems, planks and knees. A range of archaeological and dendrochronological evidence suggests that there was a native Dublin shipbuilding industry, perhaps with a boat-yard situated along the Liffey valley. The Skuldelev 2 boat, for example, has been shown to have been made from Dublin grown oaks (Bonde and Crumlin-Pedersen 1990).

By the late 12th century AD, the Dublin woodlands had been utilised intensively for centuries, particularly for hazel, ash and alder underwood rods and poles (O'Sullivan 1994a). Oak was the clearly preferred species for larger houses, waterfront structures and for ships timbers. The trees used in the Winetavern St/Wood Quay boat and ship timbers appear to have been wide in girth, fairly knotty with heavy side branches (Fig. 40). The planks were taken from wide, straight-grained, knot-free oak trunks. The stems were taken from slow-grown, slightly curved limbs, the knees from forked branch-trunk junctions. A single breasthook was also taken from a trunk-branch fork. Both the sapwood and pith was often visible on the knees, so that they appear to have been fashioned either from topwood branches or from the lower trunks of immature trees. The former case is more likely. A range of woodland sources is possible for the Winetavern St/Wood Quay timbers, including hedgerow or large woodland trees for the planks, pasture-grown or open woodland oaks for the stems, knees and bulkhead.

Woodworking techniques and tools

The manner of conversion of the trunks to timber was either by cleaving with wedges or hewing with axes. The stems have wedge-shaped sections that correspond to the radial growth characteristics of oak. The planks may have been sawn but clear evidence for this was not present. A single timber (800.31) seems to have been sawn across its end. Sapwood was left on some timbers, such as the knees, but definitely removed from the stems. The treenails were fashioned from cleft pieces of timber (possibly seasoned) rather than roundwood branches, which would probably reduce shrinkage. The joinery found on the boat and ships timbers included augured treenail holes, joggled outboard surfaces on knees for fitting against clinkered planks and scarfs on the ends of the stem, cross-beam and some planking. The preserved tool marks indicates the use of broad, T-shaped axes for the hewing of some surfaces (Christensen 1986, Crumlin-Pedersen 1986b, O'Sullivan 1994b). An iron axe blade (122.2) was found during the present excavation.

Conclusion

The excavation has produced important new boat and ships timbers to add to those previously found in the Dublin excavations. There is evidence for at least one small boat, possibly for fishing or use as a ferry across the river. There are also a number of timbers which suggest at least one and probably two vessels of the large boat / small ship type. There are stems and a knee from at least one ship, while an narrow oar definitely suggests another sea-going ship. The boats and ships seem mostly to be from the Nordic tradition of shipbuilding, although some stems may be from the cog style of ship building. These boats and ships were the engines which generated the growth and expansion of the port of medieval Dublin.

INVENTORY

214.1 Stem/intermediate timber. Fig. 48.

Stem (or intermediate timber judging by the possible presence of scarfing at either end) radially
fashioned from a slow-grown oak trunk; wedge-shaped in cross-section and curved in length. The
inboard and outboard edges are damaged and one face bears number of irregularly spaced
indentations, possibly also the result of damage. This stem has a stepped, continuous inboard face.
There is a vertical keel scarf at the lower end, but no evidence for rabbetting. A continuous dark
stain along the inboard edge may indicate the overlap with planking, which was itself possibly
bevelled. The closest similarity is with McGrail's DST53, although the scantling of 214.1 is larger.
There is a row of nails 0.02m from the inboard trailing edge, spaced at 0.10–0.15m intervals along
the length of the stem on either face. A cluster of 11–13 nail fastenings and nail holes (possibly in
three rows) are also clustered around the lower end on opposing sides. There are traces of caulking
and two plugs on one side face at lower end. The upper end also has traces of a damaged scarf. The
(M/S) ratio is 2.8; the enclosed angle is *c.*160 and the radius of curvature is approximately 1.70m.
The stem is probably from a large boat or small ship.   Species: Oak (*Quercus* spp.)   L: 1.63m
S: 0.10m   M: 0.28m   (M/S): 2.8   (M.S) 280   Phase 3.

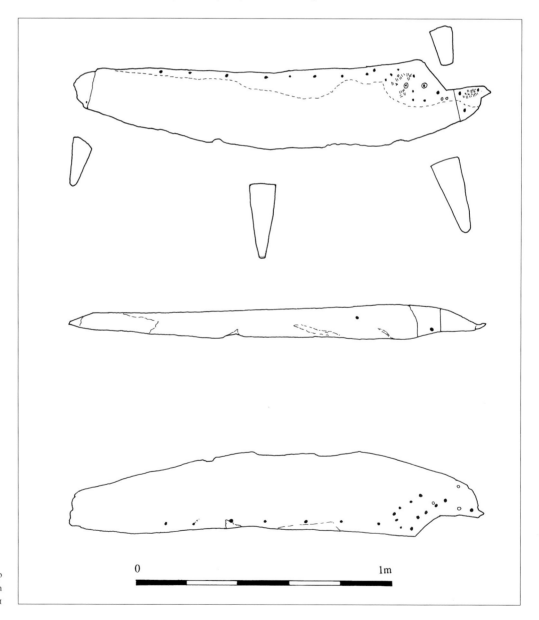

Fig. 48: Ship
timbers: Stem
214.1

0   1m

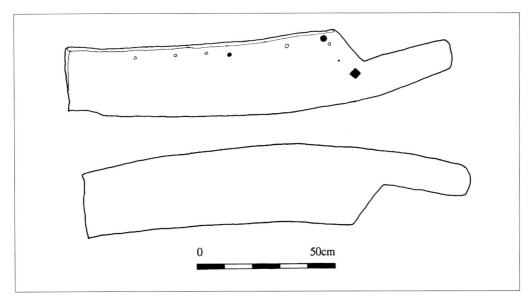

1500.3 Stem Fig. 49.

Stem radially fashioned from a slow-grown oak trunk; wedge-shaped in cross-section and slightly curved in length. The inboard and outboard edges are in good condition. This stem has a flat, continuous inboard face. There is a vertical keel scarf at the lower end, but no evidence for rabbetting. A continuous dark stain was found along the inboard edge may indicate the overlap with bevelled planking. The stem is quite similar to 214.1 and should be of similar type. There is a row of four to six nails and nail holes 0.02m from the inboard trailing edge, spaced at 0.10–0.20m intervals along the length of the stem on either face. The nail holes measure 4.0–5.5cm in depth. The nail shanks measured up to 0.8cm wide, the circular nail heads 2.0cm wide. A large diamond-shaped nail head or rove was situated beside the scarf joint at the lower end, clenched on the opposite side. The upper end is cut straight across. The (M/S) ratio is 3.00; the enclosed angle is 250 and the radius of curvature is approximately 1.9m. The stem derives from a small boat or ship.   Species: Oak (*Quercus* spp). L: 1.4m   S: 0.09m   M: 0.27m   (M/S): 3.00   (M.S): 243   Phase 3.

F164: Ship's planking group 1

A group of disarticulated ship's planking re-used in the late 12th-century revetment F164 (Pl. III); it was recorded during excavation by means of an elevation drawing and further details of nautical interest were recorded after excavation. This detailed study confirmed that the planking was not originally an articulated unit, and the planks are therefore presented here as individual timbers.

Plank 1 (Fig. 50)

Radially fashioned oak plank; length 1.62m, complete breadth 0.28m, maximum thickness 30mm. The straight edge is chamfered and the other edge is also slightly chamfered, with a triangular notch cut into the edge. Along the straight edge, there are six tree-nail holes for fastening to a stringer, spaced at 0.13m–0.55m intervals. The treenail holes measure 0.20m–0.23m in diameter. In addition there are nine nail holes in this straight edge, in which there are three corroded iron nails. On the opposite irregular edge there are two nail holes. The scantlings of the plank and the size of treenail holes suggest the plank derives from a large boat or small ship.

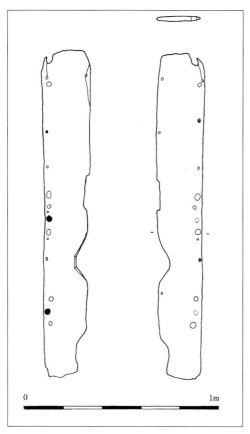

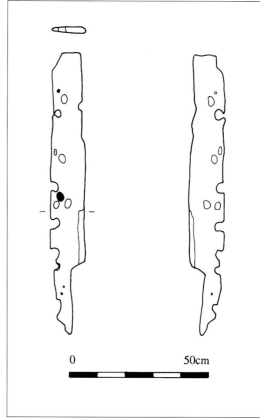

Fig. 50 (left): Ship
timbers: F164, Plank 1

Fig. 51: Ship timbers:
     F164, Plank 2

Plank 2 (Fig. 51)

Radially fashioned oak plank; incomplete length 0.99m, incomplete breadth 0.13m, maximum
thickness at upper edge 22mm. The lower edge has seven incomplete treenail holes, 0.19m–0.22m
in diameter, at c.0.08m–0.12m intervals. There are three other treenail holes inserted 0.40m from
the narrow edge, at 0.18m–0.20m intervals. There are nails at either end, one group of two nails
at the broken end and a single nail beside a treenail hole at the other end. There is also a corroded nail in the middle, which may be from a repair patch.

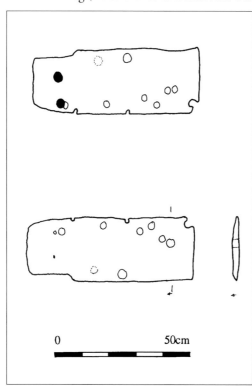

Plank 3 (Fig. 52)

Radially fashioned oak plank; length 0.61m, breadth 0.22m, thickness 24mm. There are five treenail holes (one vestigial) along one edge (18–20mm in diameter, at 0.15m–0.19m intervals), possibly fastenings for a stringer. Two closely spaced treenail holes near the plank midline may have been for fastening against a framing timber. There are vestigial nail holes at the feather edge. There are two nails with corroded heads (35mm in diameter) situated at right angles across the plank. The opposite edge has a corroded nail shank and a treenail hole. This short rectangular plank is probably a repair patch.

Fig. 52: Ship timbers:
     F164, Plank 3

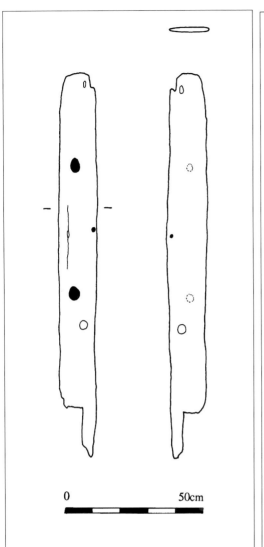

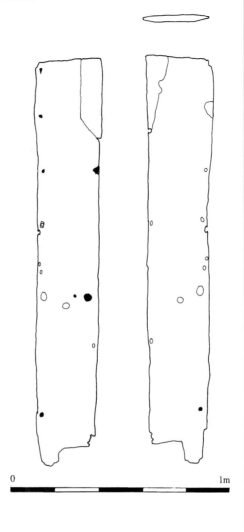

Fig. 53 (left): Ship timbers: F164, Plank 4

Fig. 54: Ship timbers: F164, Plank 5

Plank 4 (Fig. 53)

Radial oak plank; incomplete length 1.36m, breadth 0.17m, thickness at upper edge 22mm. There is a single complete treenail hole (30mm diameter) near the upper edge and a possible vestigial treenail hole at one end. There is single nail shank on the upper edge and two points of metal staining on either side. There are two large, corroded dome-shaped nail heads along the plank midline.

Plank 5 (Fig. 54)

Radial oak plank; incomplete length 1.79m, breadth 0.26m–0.38m, maximum thickness 40mm. There are two treenails, 15–20mm diameter, one by the upper edge and a second with a nail on the plank midline. There are five nails and four nail holes (two coalesced), 10mm in diameter, at 0.22–0.25m intervals along the upper edge. There are two large nail heads, 35mm diameter and 0.55m apart and a single nail hole at the lower edge.

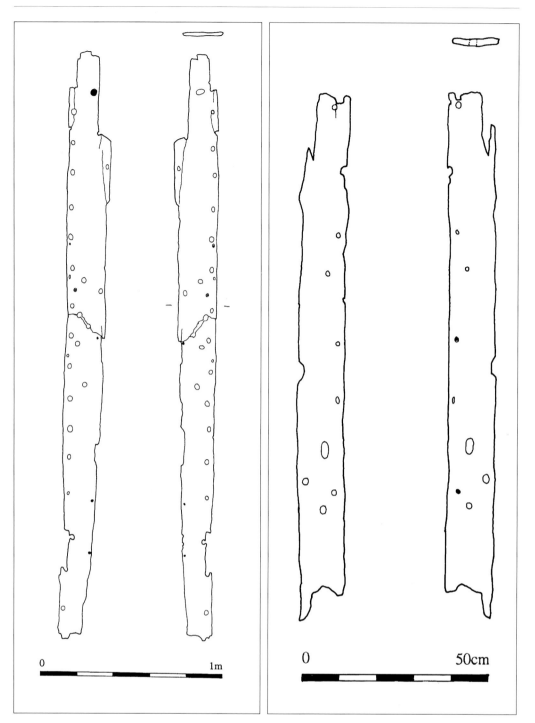

Fig. 55 (left): Ship
timbers: F164, Plank 6

Fig. 56: Ship timbers:
F164, Plank 7

Plank 6 (Fig. 55)

Radial oak plank; length 3.23m, breadth tapers from 0.23m to 0.13m, maximum thickness 17mm.
There are nineteen treenail holes along the upper edge, with a single treenail in situ. The treenails
measure 20–35mm in diameter and are spaced at regular intervals of between 0.09m and 0.19m,
with a mean spacing of 0.16m. There are four treenail holes in the middle of the plank, along the
midline at 0.16m intervals. There are three nail shanks along the lower edge and a dome-shaped
nail head with a rectangular rove on the inboard side through the plank near the opposite end.
The additional treenail holes may be for fastening to frames.

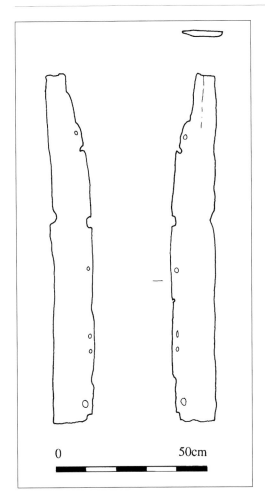

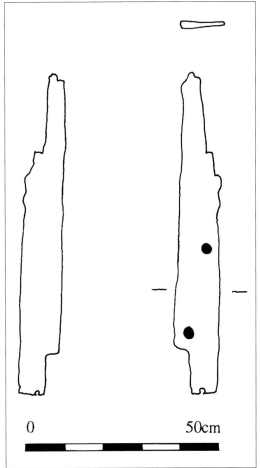

Fig. 57 (left): Ship timbers: F164, Plank 8

Fig. 58: Ship timbers: F164, Plank 9

Plank 7 (Fig. 56)

Radial oak plank; incomplete length 1.38m, breadth 0.12m, maximum thickness 25mm. There are six nail holes, one vestigial at the edge and two of which have nail shanks in place, along the narrow edge. The nail holes are spaced at 0.16m intervals. There are three treenail holes, two along the plank midline.

Plank 8 (Fig. 57)

Radial oak plank; incomplete length 1.12m, breadth 0.13m–0.07m, maximum thickness 0.20m. There are two possible opposing vestigial treenail holes on the upper and lower edges and a third treenail at the other end; the treenail holes measure 21mm in diameter. There are six nail holes along the lower feather edge, which measure 15mm diameter at *c*.0.10m intervals. The tapering curve suggests that the plank derives from the end of a large boat or small ship.

Plank 9 (Fig. 58)

Radial oak plank fragment; incomplete length 0.81m, breadth 0.12m, maximum thickness 0.18m. There are two dome-shaped, corroded nail heads either side of the plank midline.

166.17–39 Boat planking group 2

This was an articulated group of multiple boat planks and a single keel. The timbers were reused as planking in the main revetment F166 (Ill. 13). It was recorded in situ by means of both a

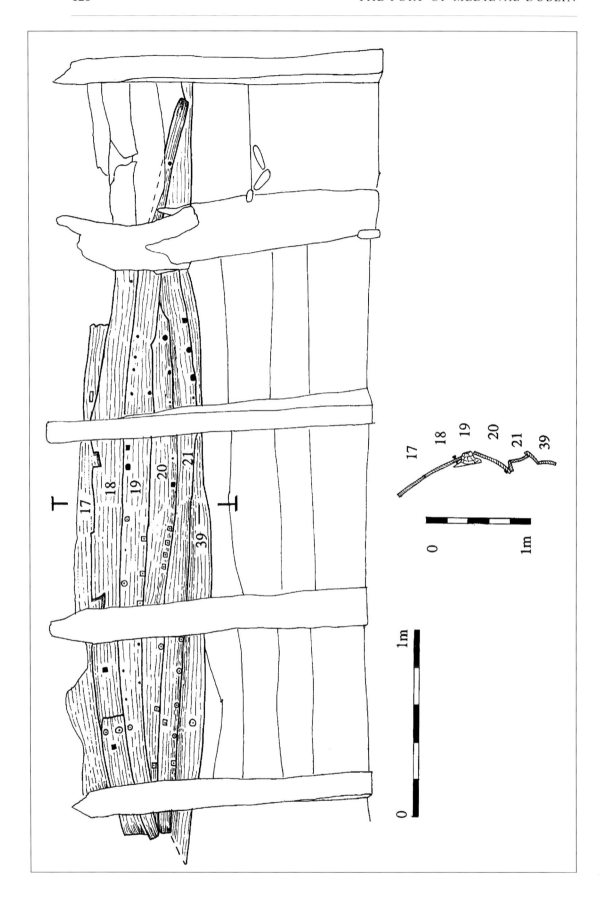

Fig. 59: Detail of elevation of revetment F166, showing ship timbers *in situ*

detailed 1:20 elevation drawing and cross-section (Fig. 59). Unfortunately, because of its location at the top of the revetment, the planking was in a very poor state of preservation and it has not been possible to make a closer record subsequent to excavation.

The oak keel (166.19) measures at least 1.5m in length, 12cm in breadth (S) and 8cm in thickness (M), with an (M/S) ratio of 0.67. The small (M.S) product (96) suggests it derives from a boat. The keel has an average deadrise of *c*.30°, placing it between the middle and end of the boat. This is confirmed by the apparent convergence of the planking at the eastern end of the revetment. It was not possible to examine the scarfs. The keel appears to be non-rabbeted and the garboard strakes were attached by means of internally roved nails. These nails were spaced at regular intervals of 10cm. It has a Y-shaped section and dimensions which make it quite comparable with those of the Gokstad 2 and 3 *faering* boats. A similar sized keel is the Dublin timber DST383. The original boat was therefore probably not greater than 6–9m in overall length.

There appears to have been at least two, possibly four, surviving runs of planking on either side of the keel. These planks typically measure at least 1.8m in length and *c*.25cm in width. There are both rectangular roves and round nail heads visible on the internal surfaces. The nails are typically spaced at regular 18cm intervals. Plank 17 had two treenail holes for fastening it to a frame timber.

1500.8 Standing knee (Fig. 60)

Fashioned from a natural slow-grown oak trunk-branch junction, with pith present in the centre of both arms and sapwood retained. There are tool marks from a broad, flat axe visible on outboard face of the vertical arm. The (M/S) ratio of the vertical arm is 0.5 and it is joggled to fit three clinker strakes, *c*.30mm thick and 0.22m broad. It is fastened to these strakes by six treenails, the lowest two of which are still in position. The two lowest treenails were inserted close together, the remainder at intervals of 0.8m. No fastenings were visible on the horizontal arm. The plank convergence was *c*.18°, situating the knee towards the end of the ship; the included angle was 114°, making the flare angle of the side 24° at this point. The joggling and enclosed angle suggest that it was a standing knee. The scantlings suggest it derives from a large boat or small ship. Species: Oak (*Quercus* spp.) LV: 0.58m LH: 1.05m M: 0.07m S: 0.14m (M.S): 98 (M/S): 0.5 Phase 3.

800.33 Standing knee (Fig. 61)

Fashioned from a natural slow-grown oak trunk-branch junction, with pith present in the centre of both arms and sapwood retained on the inboard face; the wood was quite knotty. The (M/S) ratio of the vertical arm is 1.0 and it is joggled to fit three clinker strakes, *c*.50mm thick and 0.20m broad. It is fastened to these strakes by two treenails 25mm in diameter. The top of the vertical arm is rounded in cross-section, perforated through its thickness by a circular hole 20mm in diameter and with possible rope marks around the top. This may have extended above the side of the ship with rigging running through and around the arm. There were three treenails through the horizontal arm and a notch on the underside of the horizontal arm possibly to fit against a timber. The plank convergence was *c*.35°, placing the knee towards the end of the ship; the included angle was 120°, making the flare angle of the side 30° at this point. The joggling and enclosed angle suggest that it was a standing knee and the scantlings suggest it derives from a large boat or small ship. Species: Oak (*Quercus* spp). LV: 0.80m LH: 1.02m M: 0.08m S: 0.15m (M.S): 120 (M/S): 0.54 Phase 3.

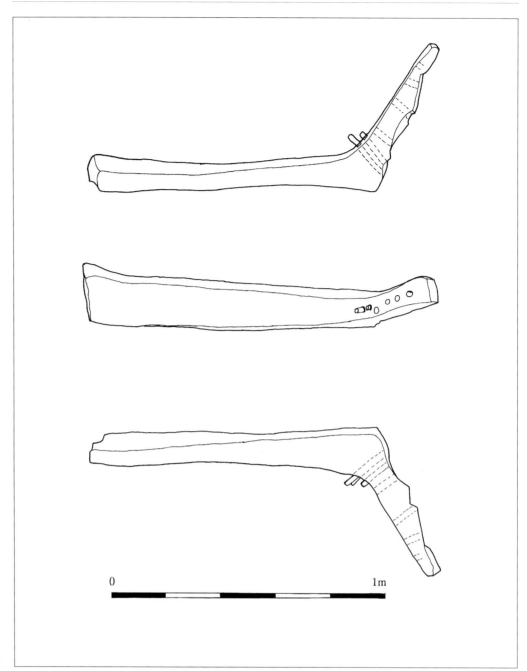

1500.9 Knee (Fig. 62)

Fashioned from a natural slow-grown oak trunk-branch junction, with pith present in the centre of both arms and sapwood retained on the inboard face; the wood was quite straight grained. The horizontal arm is incomplete. The (M/S) ratio of the vertical arm is 0.67. It has a single groove cut in the outboard face of the vertical arm, possibly for placing against a stringer. It was fastened to the strakes by two widely spaced treenails, 25mm in diameter. The horizontal and vertical arms are both rectangular in cross-section. No fastenings were visible on the horizontal arm. The length profile of the horizontal arm is quite bowed. The plank convergence was $c.5°$, placing the knee in the midships. The included angle was $c.100°$. The relatively small enclosed angle and lack of joggling suggest that it was either a standing knee, a lodging knee or a timber between floor timber and keelson. The scantlings suggest it derives from a ship.   Species: Oak (*Quercus* spp).
LV: 0.65m   LH: 0.95m+   M: 0.10m   S: 0.24m   (M.S): 240   (M/S): 0.42   Phase 3.

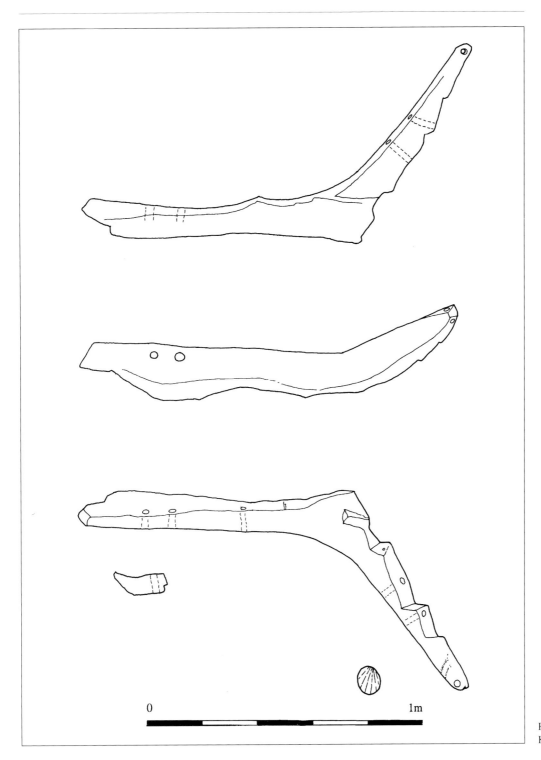

0   1m

Fig. 61: Ship timbers:
Knee 800.33

800.32 Knee (Fig. 63)

This is a small knee, fashioned from a natural oak trunk-branch junction. The (M/S) ratio of the vertical arm is 0.32. It was fastened to the strakes by three treenails 25mm in diameter, one of which is present within the augur hole. The top of the vertical arm narrows to a rounded end. There were three augured holes through the horizontal arm. A single hole near the end had an intact dowel. There was a notch on the underside of the horizontal arm, near the junction with the outboard face. The plank convergence was *c.*20° placing the knee towards the end of the vessel; the included angle was 120°, making the flare angle of the side 30° at this point. The scantlings suggest it derives from a large boat or small ship.   Species: Oak (*Quercus* spp).   LV: 0.30m LH: 0.40m   M: 0.05m   S: 0.16m   (M.S): 80   (M/S): 0.32   Phase 3.

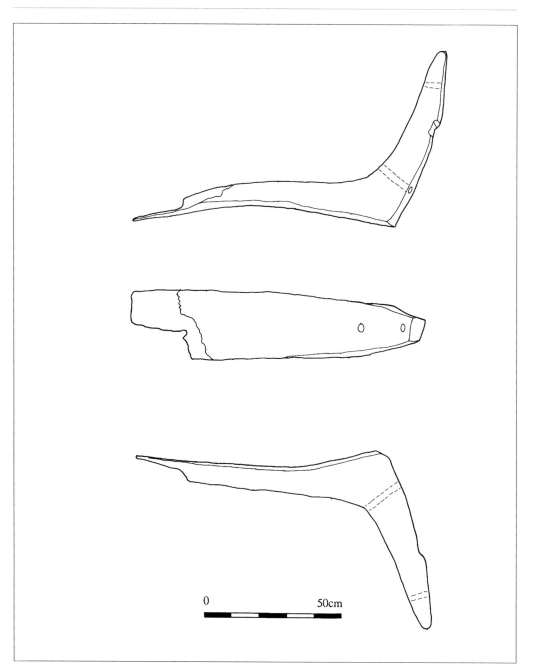

Fig. 62: Ship timbers:
Knee 1500.9

0   50cm

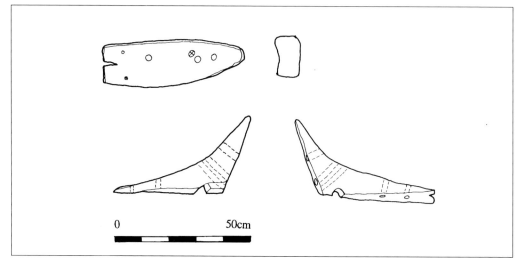

0   50cm

Fig. 63: Ship timbers:
Knee 800.32

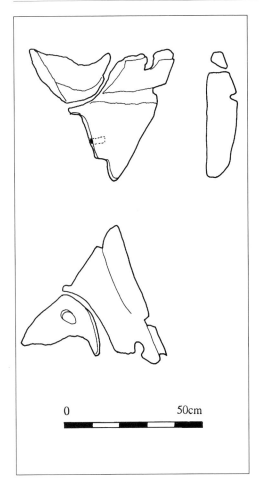

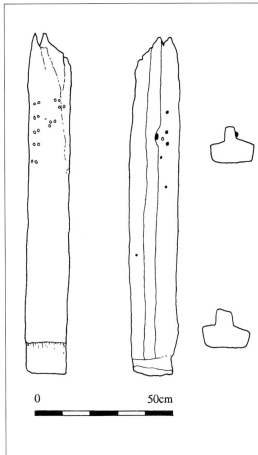

Fig. 64 (left): Ship
timbers: Breasthook
1040.7

Fig. 65: Ship timbers:
Cross-beam 164.3

1040.7 Possible breasthook (Fig. 64)

Fashioned from a natural fork of knotty oak timber. The timber is quite damaged, broken into
two pieces and the surfaces are much rotted. Two blind dowel holes were drilled into either side
to a depth of 4.5cm and there are traces of a step cut into the opposite side. It has an internal angle
of 65°. Species: Oak (*Quercus* spp). L: 0.47m B (S): 0.52m T (M): 0.10m Phase 3.

164.3 Possible cross-beam (Fig. 65)

Incomplete length of straight oak timber, T-shaped in section, which is similar to cross-beams
illustrated from Skuldelev 2, although these had integral knees. Edge-butted scarf at one end, 12cm
in length; the other end is broken. A cross beam in Skuldelev 5 appears to have been attached at
right angles to a stringer by a scarf. There are groups of twin-spaced nails driven through the
surface on either side of projecting ridge (ten on one side, seven on the other), possibly to hold
floor planks. If this is a cross-beam timber, then the scantlings suggest a small ship. L: 1.2m
M: 0.14m S: 0.17m (M.S): 238 (M/S): 0.83 Phase 2.

1500.11 Oar (Fig. 66)

Finely-made ship's oar, in three pieces with incomplete shaft; the shaft widens gradually to a sub-
rectangular blade with rounded end. The blade has worn surfaces, although the feather edges are
intact. The shaft is elliptical in cross-section and the blade is bi-convex in section. Probably used
for rowing at sea, it was carved from moderately grown ash trunk with straight grain. It is not like
the other known Dublin example, DST377 and is most similar in shape to earlier oars from

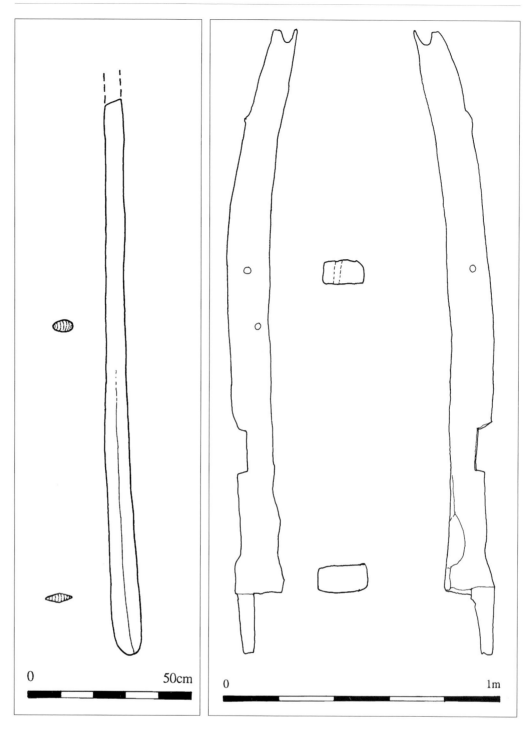

0   50cm

0   1m

Kvalsund 1, Kvalsund 2 and in (L/B) ratio to the Gokstad 1 oars.   Species: Ash (*Fraxinus excelsior*).
L: 162cm   L (blade): 70cm   B: 9cm   T (blade): 2.5cm   L/B (blade): 7.8   Phase 3.

800.31 Possible nautical timber (Fig. 67)

Curving beam, tangentially cut from a trunk, of rectangular cross-section. A single lap-joint 16cm
in length and 4cm in depth is cut on the convex side. The thickest end has a projecting tang due
to cross-cutting. There are two augured holes, 2cm in diameter, at the middle of the timber. One
is drilled entirely through the timber, the other is blind. Its function is unclear.   Species: Oak
(*Quercus* spp.).   L: 221cm   B: 15cm   T: 10cm   Phase 2.

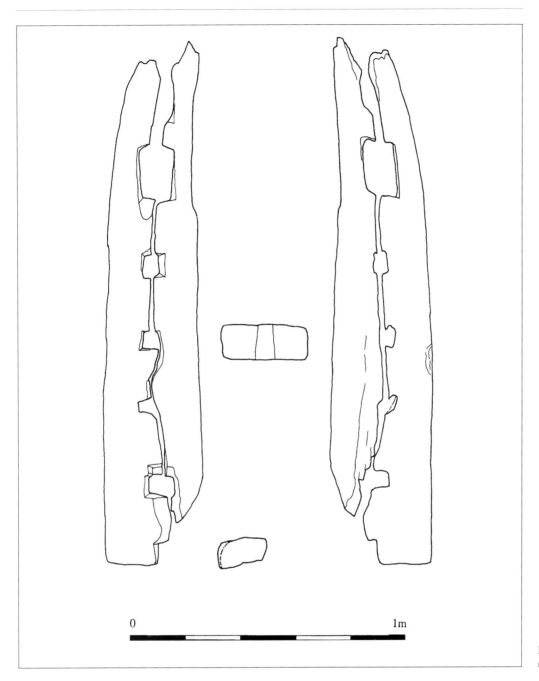

0   1m

164.4 Possible nautical timber (Fig. 68)

Large radial oak beam, the sides curving slightly in one direction towards the narrower end, of
rectangular cross-section. There are four square mortises (*c.*12cm x 13cm) at 20cm intervals and a
fifth, rectangular mortise (20cm x 14cm) spaced along its length. The timber was re-used as a vertical
in revetment F164; its original function is unclear.   Species: Oak (*Quercus* spp).   L: 185cm   B: 31cm
Th.: 13cm   Phase 2.

REFERENCES

Bonde, N. and Crumlin-Pedersen, O. 1990 The dating of wreck 2 from Skuldelev, Denmark. *NewsWARP*
      7, 3–6. Exeter. Wetland Archaeology Research Project.

Christensen, A.-E. 1985 Boat finds from Bryggen. *Bryggen Papers* **1**, 47–280. Oslo University Press.

Christensen, A.-E. 1986 Tools used in shipbuilding in ancient and more modern times. In Crumlin-Pedersen and Vinner 1986, 150–9.

Crumlin-Pedersen, O. 1986a Aspects of Viking age shipbuilding. *Journal of Danish Archaeology* **5**, 209–228.

Crumlin-Pedersen, O. 1986b Aspects of wood technology in medieval shipbuilding. In Crumlin-Pedersen and Vinner 1986, 138–49.

Crumlin-Pedersen, O. and Vinner, M. (eds) 1986 *Sailing into the past.* Roskilde. The Viking Ship Museum.

Goodburn, D. 1991 Waterlogged wood and timber as archives of ancient landscapes. In J. Coles and D. Goodburn (eds.), *Wet site excavation and survey,* 51–3. Exeter. Wetland Archaeology Research Project.

Goodburn, D. 1994 Trees underground: new insights into trees and woodmanship in south-east England *c.*AD 800–1300. *Bot. Jnl. Scotland* **46**, 658–62.

McGrail, S. 1987 *Ancient boats in N.W. Europe.* London. Longman.

McGrail, S. 1993 *Medieval boat and ship timbers from Dublin.* Medieval Dublin Excavations 1962–81, Ser. B, vol. 3. Dublin. Royal Irish Academy.

Olsen, O. and Crumlin-Pedersen, O. 1967 Skuldelev ships II. *Acta Archaeologica* **38**, 73–174.

Olsen, O. and Crumlin-Pedersen, O. 1990 *Five viking ships from Roskilde fjord,* 2nd edition. Roskilde. Vikingeskibshallen.

O'Sullivan, A. 1994a Trees, woodland and woodmanship in early medieval Ireland. *Bot. Jnl. Scotland* **46** (**4**), 674–81.

O'Sullivan, A. 1994b The craft of the carpenter in medieval Ireland; some hints from book illuminations. *Irish Association of Professional Archaeologists Newsletter* **19**, 18–22.

CHAPTER IX

Building materials

A small but significant assemblage of building materials provides evidence of the earliest periods of occupation and construction on the site, in the wake of the reclamation phase. Most of this material consists of ceramic roofing tiles but a small number of stone architectural fragments and roofing slates were also recovered. All of this material points to the construction of buildings of some substance and importance on the site during the later Middle Ages, after completion of the reclamation programme.

ARCHITECTURAL FRAGMENTS (FIG. 69)

The present small sample is an addition to several architectural fragments which have been found on the Wood Quay site. While the nearby Christchurch cathedral is obviously a possible source, the presence of substantial secular structures on the site, such as the 13th-century Guildhall, should not be overlooked. The relatively simple mouldings recovered in the present excavation could well have come from such buildings. In all cases the stone has been identified by Mr Ivor P. Harkin, of the National Museum of Ireland, as oolitic limestone. This clearly indicates that the fragments are of imported building stone, almost certainly from southern England, and the most likely source is the well-known quarry at Dundry, near Bristol. However, it has not been possible to locate the stone to a precise source, and it should not automatically be assumed that it is from Dundry. Indeed, some differences in the geology of the pieces may indicate more than a single source.

15.5 Medium-sized moulding, possibly from a vault rib; almost rectangular block, flat dressed (although not vertical) on three sides; fourth side displays two rounded grooves with roll/fillet (now missing) in between. The stone has been identified as an oolite, which contains bivalve fossil fragments, possibly of *Inoceramus dubius*; this suggests that the stone is from the Lower Inferior Oolite of the Middle Jurassic. H: 83 W: 170 D: 107 Phase 5.

93.4 Fragment of a small moulding; two engaged demi-rolls, one with fillet. The stone has been identified as an oolite, with a small percentage of mafic minerals and translucent mica. H: 59 W: 72 D: 50 Phase 5.

96.2,3 Two fragments of roll moulding 5.4cm in diameter. Phase 5.

2000.12 Large fragment of moulding; one dressed right-angled return on one side. The stone has been identified as an oolite, with many visible translucent mica flakes and possibly glauconite; it also contains some larger rounded rock fragments. Unstratified.

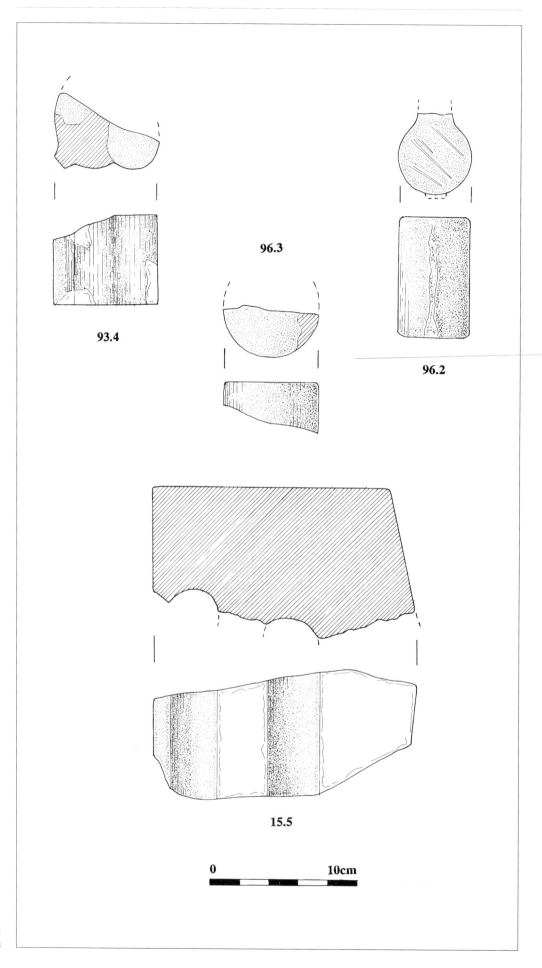

96.3

93.4

96.2

15.5

0   10cm

Fig. 69: Architectural
fragments

ROOFING TILES AND SLATES

Joanna Wren

The Winetavern St excavation produced an assemblage of eighty-nine sherds of roof tile, including examples of curved tiles, medieval ridge tiles and pegtiles and pantiles. The different tile types are discussed with reference to assemblages from other excavated sites in Dublin, notably Dublin Castle, Patrick St, Parliament St and Temple Lane/Crow St, for which reports have been prepared by the author but are as yet unpublished. All of the sherds were weighed as the most accurate way of establishing quantities of each type within different time periods. All percentages mentioned therefore are of the total weight of a particular tile or fabric types.

Curved roof tiles

There are five sherds of curved roof tile (300g) made in completely oxidised pink earthenware fabrics. 17% are from contexts in the earliest phase of reclamation dating to the late 12th century. The other 83% come from the later phases of reclamation in the first half of the 13th century. Curved roof tiles occur regularly on sites in Dublin in contexts dating from the 11th century onward. This type of tile continued in use throughout the Middle Ages.

Ridge tiles and pegtiles

There are eighty-one sherds of tile made in three local fabrics which have been identified previously by the author and thin-sectioned.

DT1 is a hard, very coarse fabric. It oxidises to brick red, with the degree of oxidisation varying considerably from sherd to sherd. It contains poorly sorted composite grains of quartz, feldspar and mica, some flint and sandstone and possible calcareous material and ore fragments. There are twenty-nine sherds (3675g) of tile in this fabric. Eight of them have been identified as coming from crested ridge tiles and sixteen are from pegtiles. 64% are from the later phases of reclamation (Phases 3 and 4), dating to the first half of the 13th century and 36% come from late or post-medieval contexts (Phases 5 and 6). Tiles made in this fabric have been found previously at other Dublin sites in contexts dating from the 13th to early 14th century and substantial waste from a kiln producing pegtiles and ridge tiles in DT1 fabric was uncovered at Cornmarket in Dublin (A. Hayden pers comm).

DT2 is a hard coarse fabric, partly oxidised to brick red with a grey core. It contains well sorted inclusions of quartz, feldspar, white mica, pyroxene calcareous material (calcite or limestone) flint and grass. Grass is common in medieval tile fabrics, as potters added plant extracts to clay to improve its malleability and cohesiveness (Sheppard 1976, 52). The tile sherds are partly covered by an olive green lead glaze. Fifty sherds are made in DT2 fabric, all of them being from crested ridge tiles. 3% were found amongst the earliest occupation material on the site, dating to the second half of the 13th century, 87% come from late to post-medieval contexts and 10% are unstratified. Tiles in this fabric are found regularly on sites in Dublin and normally date to the 13th and 14th centuries.

Two sherds (142.2c, 2d) have the remains of high knife cut cockscomb cresting. Tiles with this type of cresting were produced in both Ireland and Britain throughout the 13th and much of the 14th century (Dunning 1975, 103). Two other sherds (142.2a, 2b) were decorated with applied strips across their exterior faces. These are an imitation of a style popular in Bristol from the late 13th-century onwards (Rahtz 1960, 246). The Bristol tiles combined cockscomb cresting with thumbed strips applied criss-cross to their exterior faces; the strips are said to be in imitation of cross stringing in thatching. Four examples were found in the previous National Museum of Ireland excavations on the 13th century waterfront at Wood Quay (Wren 1987). All four sherds from the present assemblage come from a late or post-medieval occupation layer (F142), but tiles can stay on a roof for well over a century (Harvey 1972, 35) and these tiles were probably made in the 13th/14th century.

DT3 is a hard and rough fabric, partly oxidised to brick red with patches of grey. It contains very well sorted inclusions of quartz, mica, feldspar, sandstone, flint and grass. Two sherds of this fabric were present, both partly covered by a mottled green and yellow lead glaze. Crested ridge tiles made in this fabric are common on Dublin sites and date to the late 14th and 15th centuries. Both of the present sherds come from a late or post-medieval occupation layer (F144).

Post-medieval roof tiles

There is one sherd of pegtile (148.4), made in a sandy post-medieval red earthenware. It comes from a layer of ash in a late or post-medieval level of occupation material. Pegtiles continue in use to the present day.

Two sherds of pantile were found amongst intrusive material in the later two phases of reclamation material (F134, F137) dating to the first half of the 13th century. Pantiles were introduced to Ireland in the late 17th century and continued in use to the beginning of the 20th century. They have a distinctive S-shaped profile and were mortared to the roof with their long edges overlapping.

Roof finial

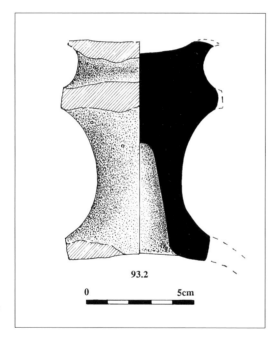

Fig. 70: Ceramic roof finial 93.2

The excavation produced one sherd of roof finial (93.2; Fig. 70), in this case from the top of a globular 'bottle-neck' finial made in DT2 fabric. Finials of this type had a wheel thrown globular body, surmounted here by a tubular neck, which has broken from the body. The top of the neck is closed and it cannot have functioned as a roof ventilator, but must have been purely decorative. Decorative finials were commonly placed at either end of the roof attached to the ridge tiles. Bottle neck finials were common in London in from the 13th to the 15th century (Pearce, Vince and Jenner 1985, 48) and the present sherd is from a later 13th century context.

Roof slate

Two pieces of sandstone (31.2, 141.3) were found amongst late or post-medieval occupation debris. One piece (31.2) had the remains of a nail hole 9mm wide and both probably came from roofing slates. Stone has been used as a roofing material from the 13th to the 20th century (Wren 1987).

REFERENCES

Dunning, G.C. 1975 A ridge-tile crest from Lyveden, with notes on ridge-tiles with knife-cut crests in England and Wales. *Journal of the Northampton Museum and Art Gallery* **12**, 97–103.

Harvey, J 1972 *Conservation of Buildings*. London. J. Baker.

Pearce, J.E., Vince A.G. and Jenner, M.A. 1985 *A dated type series of London medieval pottery*. London. London and Middlesex Archaeological Society Special Paper No. 6.

Rahtz, P. 1960 Excavation by the town wall, Baldwin St, Bristol. *Trans. Bristol & Gloucs. Arch. Soc.* **79**, 221–50.

Sheppard, A.O. 1976 *Ceramics for the archaeologist*. Washington.

Wren, J. 1987 *Crested ridge-tiles from medieval town sites in Leinster, 1200–1500*. Unpublished M.A. thesis submitted to the Department of Archaeology, University College, Dublin.

FLOOR TILES

No complete floor tiles were found in the excavation but several fragments were recovered. The majority of fragments are either plain, or so worn as to be undiagnostic, but fragments of two two-colour tiles and two line-impressed tiles were found. The designs on these tiles, as far as they can be made out, all appear to be previously noted by Eames and Fanning (1988, design nos T84, T103, L14, L52/55) and all four designs are previously recorded from other locations in Dublin. Indeed, with the exception of T84 (known from St Mary's Abbey, Dublin), all of the designs are recorded at nearby Christ Church cathedral and it may well be that the cathedral is the ultimate source of the fragments recovered in the present excavation. However, as with the architectural fragments (see above), the possibility must be borne in mind that the tile fragments could derive from high-status secular buildings in the Winetavern St/Wood Quay area. The two-colour fragments are both from contexts associated with the later 13th-century building, Structure B (see Chapter III above) but as there is no evidence for a tile pavement associated with this building, they are probably redeposited, much as the architectural fragments 93.4 and 96.2,3 (see above) and stone mortar fragments 93.3 (see Chapter XI, below) were reused in the area of paving F93. All tile fragments appear to be of manufactured from local fabrics, with calcite and mica inclusions evident.

INVENTORY

Two-colour tiles

15:2 Corner of tile of Eames' and Fanning's design no. T103. L: 73 W: 64 T: 29 Phase 5.

99:2 Worn fragment with one straight edge, possibly of Eames' and Fanning's design no. T84, although the circle in the corner seems to be open, rather than solid; glaze almost entirely worn away. L: 80 W: 48 T: 32 Phase 5.

Line-impressed tiles

144:5 Corner fragment of Eames' and Fanning's design no. L14; glaze almost entirely worn away; traces of mortar/plaster on base. L: 81 W: 70 T: 22 Phase 6.

2000:4 Worn fragment with one straight edge, probably of Eames' and Fanning's design no. L52 or L55; glaze on upper surface almost entirely worn away L: 75 W: 48 T: 23 Unstratified.

Plain or undiagnostic tiles

15:3 Plain, glazed fragment with part of one straight edge. L: 73 W: 71 T: 27 Phase 5.

35:2 Plain fragment with plaster(?) on upper surface; no original edges. L: 65 W: 54 T: 46 Phase 5.

45:2 Waster(?) fragment with flat, sand-marked base and uneven, thumbed upper surface; one straight edge.   L: 96   W: 85   T: 30   Phase 6.

49:2 Smaller fragment of same tile as 45.2 with one intact corner.   L: 79   W: 50   T: 37 Phase 6. (45.2 and 49.2 join to form a tile fragment at least 134mm long, 85mm wide and 37mm thick.)

141:4 Plain, glazed corner fragment; traces of mortar/plaster on base.   L: 58   W: 50   T: 24 Phase 6.

151:6 Plain fragment with one straight edge, all traces of glaze worn away; base missing.   L: 90 W: 63   T: 31+   Phase 3.

160:2 Plain fragment with one straight edge, almost all traces of glaze worn away; traces of mortar/plaster on base.   L: 71   W: 50   T: 23   Phase 6.

170:2 Plain fragment with one straight edge; no evidence of glaze.   L: 66   W: 66   T: 33 Phase 3.

2000:1 Plain corner fragment with dark green glaze on upper surface; sand-marked base.   L: 94 W: 81   T: 30   Unstratified.

2000:2 Plain fragment with one straigth edge; dark green glaze on upper surface.   L: 85   W: 84 T: 37   Unstratified.

2000:3 Plain corner fragment; no evidence of glaze.   L: 90   W: 82   T: 30   Unstratified.

REFERENCES

Eames, E.S., and Fanning, T. 1988 *Irish medieval tiles*. Dublin. Royal Irish Academy Monographs in Archaeology 2.

CHAPTER X

The leather finds

Daire O'Rourke

Ninety-nine pieces of worked leather were recovered in the excavation, the majority of which related to footwear. This material came entirely from the reclamation deposits associated with the wooden waterfronts and can be dated from the late 12th to mid-13th centuries, although the bulk (over 70%) of the material is from Phase 3 (early 13th century) deposits. The leather in general consisted of discarded pieces, with most in poor condition. Some showed signs of repair and all are typical of this period in Dublin.

FOOTWEAR

The footwear is all made in the turnshoe technique, where the upper and sole were stitched together while wet and inside out. The shoe was then turned the right way around, with the grain side of the upper and sole outwards. A thin strip of leather, the rand, was usually stitched between the upper and the sole. This strengthened the lasting seam and helped in keeping the shoe watertight.

Uppers

Of the vamp and upper pieces, eight are undiagnostic, but among the remaining pieces nine different varieties of footwear can be identified. The most common variety, of which there are eight pieces, is the upper type which is thonged at the side. 151.18 (Fig. 71) is a good example of this type. In this case, the shoe or ankle boot is wrapped around the foot, then an insert stitched between the left hand wing and quarter. As well as stitching, the shoe would be laced at the side through thong holes placed at the edge of the wing and quarter. Other pieces belonging to this category of footwear are 139.15, 151.12, 151.13, 186.2, 237.2, 238.4 and 238.12 (Fig. 71). 237.2 is distinctive as a vertical line of decorative stitching, formed by a line of stitch holes on the flesh side of the leather, runs down the left hand wing/quarter area.

139.15 is also slightly different as it follows the wrap-around technique. The vamp – the only piece of the upper extant – is distinct from the heel and quarters. It has a vertical line of seven small thong holes on the right hand side of the wing. This vamp, along with 151.12 and 186.2, shows evidence for lining along the thong hole area, by way of a line of stitch holes on the flesh side of the vamp. All these uppers are made of calf skin.

126:3 (Fig. 71) is the only example in the present assemblage of another variety of upper. While in the minority in this assemblage, however, it is a very common style of footwear found throughout 13th-century levels in Dublin and Waterford. This style of upper is distinct in a number of ways. A continuous line of slits with some thonging *in situ* runs just below the top edge of the upper. The leather at the right hand side of the instep extends to an exaggerated point up

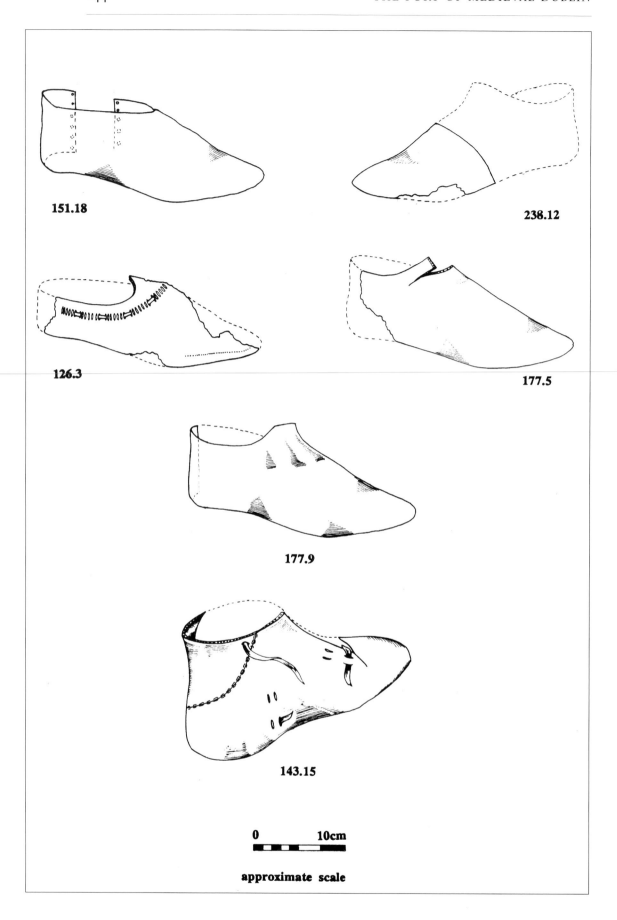

Fig. 71: Leather footwear: uppers

the foot, and there is evidence for a thin toe cap encircling the toes. Only the right hand side of this upper is extant, and it too is of calf skin.

The third variety of upper represented, of which there are six examples, is a simple wrap-around style, seamed at the side. 138.2 is typical of this type; it is a 'slip-on' child's shoe for the right foot. The quarters are cut lower than the heel and a whipped seam runs along the top edge. This type of seam is quite common in most shoes and seems to have fulfilled a dual purpose. By stitching the top edge of the upper, it helped in preventing the splitting of the leather into its grain and flesh layers; this would happen if ineffective tanning methods had been used. However, it also served to accomodate a top band. This was a strip of leather, often decorated with slits and other devices, that was stitched along the top edge to increase the height of the heel and quarters of the shoe. Other examples of this style of upper are 129.2 of sheep/goat skin, 138.4 and 223.3, both of deer skin, 177.5 (Fig. 71) and 177.9 (Fig. 71), both of calf skin and 238.5 of goat skin.

The wrap-around pattern is also found in ankle boots, of which there are four examples in the present assemblage. 137.5, 195.5, 199.2 and 1066.2 are all similar in style. There is no evidence for fastening in 137.5, 195.5 or 199.2 and the only difference to the footwear mentioned above is in the height of the quarter. The ankle boots are simply wrapped around the foot and seamed at the side. 195.5 and 199.2 are clearly children's footwear, the former being made of calf skin and the latter of deer skin. 1066.2 was fastened via three crude slits along the instep.

Another more complex style of ankle boot, of which there are three examples in the present assemblage, is of interest as the uppers are all composite and there is some evidence for fastenings. 143.15 (Fig. 71) and 239.5 (Fig. 72) are similar; the former is an ankle boot, which is in the wrap-around tradition, but an extra piece of leather has been stitched at the top to facilitate the wrap-around pattern. This was fastened by a thong, threaded through two rows of vertical slits. It is in very bad condition and had been worn until the heel was totally ripped. 239.5 (Fig. 72) is more correctly termed a boot as it would have reached to the lower calf. As with 143.15, an extra piece of leather – a triangular insert – would have been stitched between the bottom left hand quarter and wing. Here three vertical lines of slits on the right hand quarter were used for fastening. There is also a number of crude thong holes on the left hand side of the upper. The third example, 195.7, is a child's boot upper of calf skin. It is for the right foot and is made in the wrap-around style. The upper is in two pieces, the top of the left hand quarter being made of a seperated piece of leather.

The four remaining upper pieces all have detached vamps. 139.17 consists of vamp and sole; the vamp has a V-shaped instep and the quarters and heel would have been stitched here. 238.11 is similar, except that the instep is cut to form two points at each side of the foot. This type of shoe is also quite common from 13th-century Dublin contexts. 172.2 (Fig. 72) is an unusual vamp; there are three slits on the right hand side of the wing with some thonging *in situ* and crude slits along the left hand side of the wing. The vamp is complete but shows secondary stitching at the toe. 151.10 is the heel and quarters of a boot; the left hand quarter extends to a proto-latchet which has two slits for fastening.

Inserts

As noted above, most footwear was made in the wrap-around technique and frequently, in order to complete the pattern, extra smaller pieces of leather – inserts – were stitched to the upper. Three such inserts, all detached, occur in the present assemblage. 151.14 is rectangular in shape and stitched all round; it is made from calf skin. 195.4 is a long triangular piece, made from sheep/goat skin. It is stitched on three sides, the other side being cut. These inserts could belong to any type of upper. 1049.3 (Fig. 72) has thong holes at the edge for a side-fastened upper; the leather was unidentified.

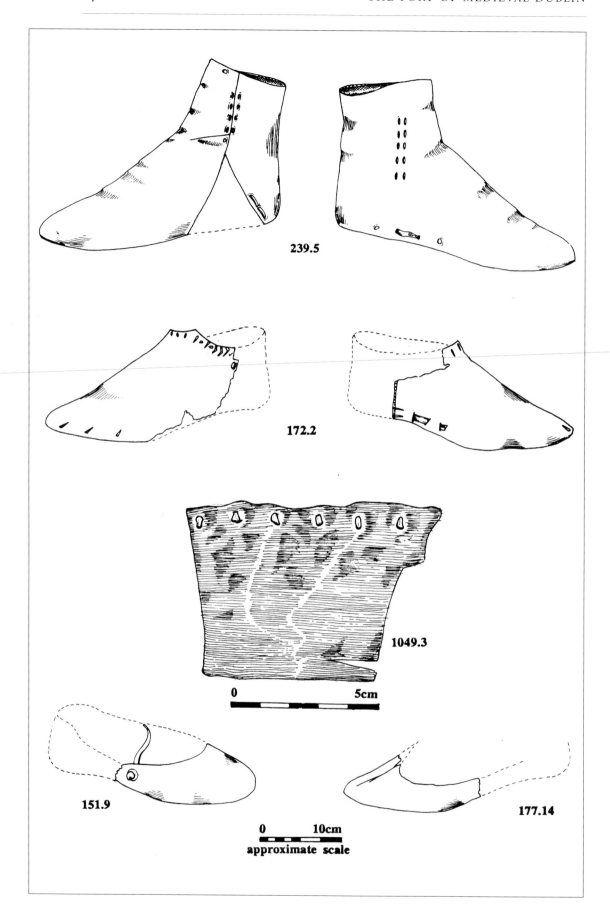

Fig. 72: Leather footwear: uppers

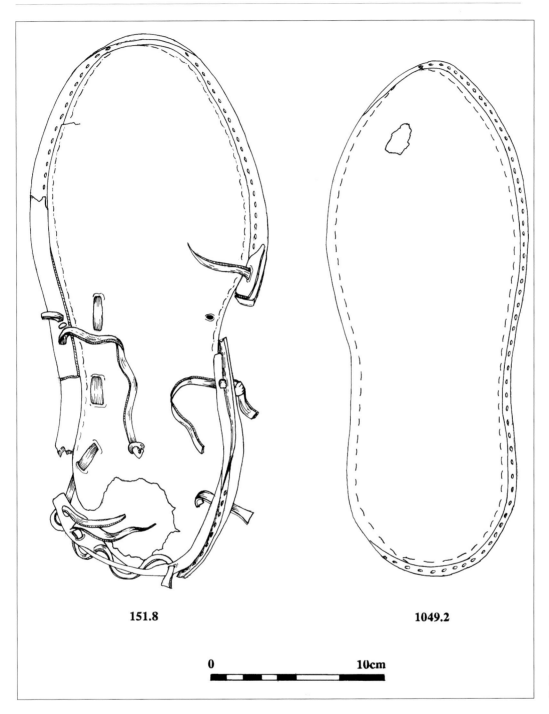

151.8   1049.2

0   10cm

Fig. 73: Leather
footwear: soles

Soles

Forty soles and sole fragments were excavated, fifteen of which were in a very fragmentary
condition. The soles have both round and pointed toes and are for both right and left feet. Many
soles show signs of wear, such as 1049.2 (Fig. 73), where a hole has been worn in the tread of the
sole. 151.8 (Fig. 73) is a very good example of wear and repair. It is for the right foot and has been
repaired along the left hand side of the waist with a crude leather thong. Two pieces of rand are
still in evidence, stitched around the seat. The waist and seat show evidence for patching. Soles,
like uppers, were sometimes composed of various different pieces of leather. Three such sole pieces
or half soles were excavated, 151.24, 171.6 and 238.6; all are from the tread of the sole.

OTHER WORKED LEATHER

Binding strips

Five binding strip fragments were excavated. They would have been stitched, probably to the edges of clothing or other textiles, to stop the material fraying. 125.3, 177.4 and 1060.2 (Fig. 74) are all long strips of leather which are folded along their length and stitched; 125.3 is made of sheep/goat skin and the others of calf skin. 186.3 and 186.4 are of a different style. The former is quite broad (20mm), with three lines of stitch holes along its length; the latter is narrower and has been cut along one side. The leather is too abraded to permit identification.

Belts and straps

Five belts or straps were excavated. 137.6 and 238.8 are similar; both are stitched around the edge; the former is made of cow hide and the latter of deer skin. 238.8 also has a number of perforations along its length. 149.3 (Fig. 74) shows evidence for where the buckle was stitched. 182.2 is slightly unusual, as it consists of two pieces of leather stitched together along their length; one end is cut to a point, where there is one perforation. 171.4 (Fig. 74) is quite decorative; a line of decorative stitching runs along each edge, and seven domed copper alloy mounts are inserted along the length, with perforations for two more at either end, and three perforations for a buckle. This piece resembles spur straps from medieval London illustrated in Clark (1995, Fig. 111, 112; see esp. nos 383, 384), although the mounts are apparently not arranged in two distinct groups as would be expected on a spur strap. As the piece is clearly incomplete it may well be part of a spur strap, but this cannot be regarded as certain.

Sheaths

Six sheaths were recovered, all made of calf skin. Various medieval English ordinances relating to leather workers refer to the exclusive use of calf skin in sheaths and scabbards. Four of the sheaths, 138.3 (Fig. 75), 138.5 (Fig. 76), 149.4 (Fig. 76) and 177.3 (Fig. 75), were seamed along the back, either along the centre or slightly off-centre. 1060.3 (Fig. 76) was originally seamed along the side with crude thong holes. Some of the sheaths are decorated. The decoration is organised into panels, and in general is composed of lines of hatching, vertical lines and lozenges. 138.3, 138.5, 149.4 and 1060.3 are wider at the top to accomodate the handle, and narrow lower down for the blade. This is quite common in 13th-century sheaths. In a number of instances, represented here by 149.4 and 1060.3, crude thong holes are cut into the side of the sheath of suspend it from a belt or strap. Evidence from other sites points to the cutting of the thong holes after decoration had been executed. The perforations are always crude and point to the owners of the sheaths or scabbards undertaking this work themselves.

Undiagnostic

There are seven undiagnostic leather pieces, one of which is of some interest. 234.3 (Fig. 74) is a roughly cut, round piece of leather with a small perforation towards the edge; it is 64mm in diameter and is made of calf skin. A number of similar pieces have been found on excavated sites in Dublin and it is possible that they were tags attached to bundles of leather for identification purposes, that is a possible selling device. 177.8 (Fig. 74) is a large piece of deer skin with stitch holes around the edge.

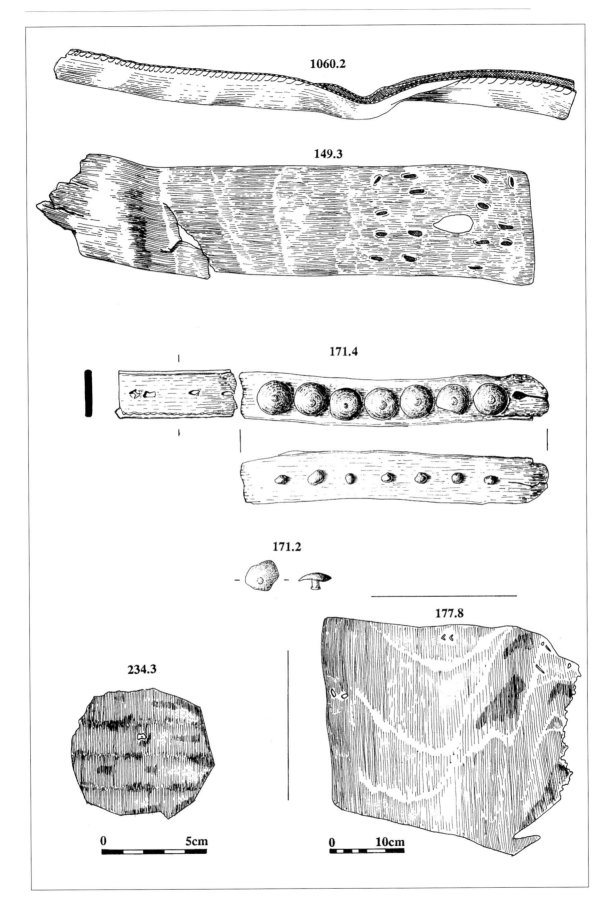

Fig. 74: Leather: strip (1060.2), belts/straps (149.3, 171.4) and undiagnostic (234.3, 177.8)

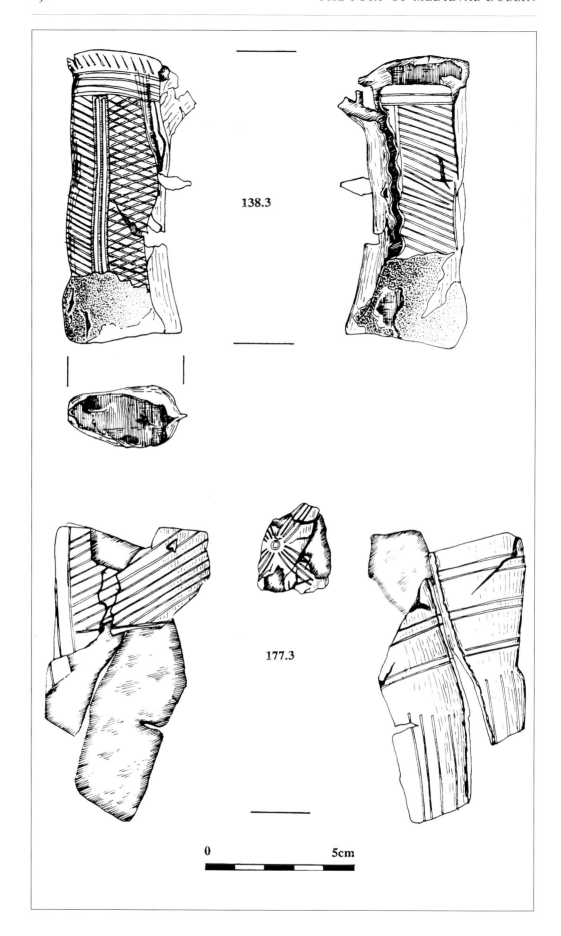

138.3

177.3

0   5cm

Fig. 75: Leather sheaths

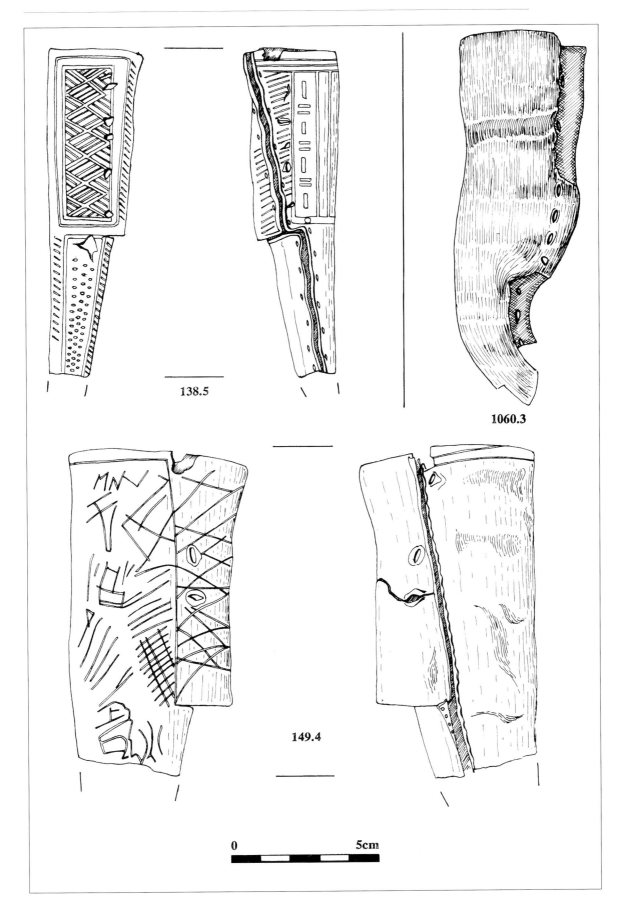

Fig. 76: Leather sheaths

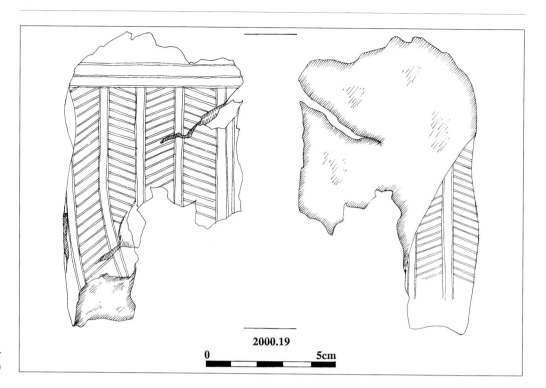

Fig. 77: Leather
sheath (2000.19)

COBBLING AND RE-USE OF LEATHER

Thirteen objects show evidence for cobbling and/or re-use of leather; this does not include the
three half soles mentioned above, which are also a good indication that every piece of leather was
used. A number of items show evidence for patching, for example 151.8, where the tread and waist
area of the sole was heavily patched. 149.3 is a possible patch for a sole. It is crudely cut in the
shape of a tread but there is no evidence for stitch holes; it may have been placed inside a shoe.
139.13, 151.9 (Fig. 72), 172.2 (Fig. 72), 239.2 and 239.5 (Fig. 72) all show evidence of crude repairs
to soles and/or uppers. Other pieces show evidence for being cut up and the leather re-used, for
example 151.22, 151.23, 177.14 (Fig. 72) and 238.9. 199.3 is a large piece of calf skin left over from
leather working; it measures 292mm by 137mm and is probably from the underbelly of the animal,
where the hide would not be of the best quality.

HIDES USED IN LEATHER MANUFACTURE

For the diagnostic objects, the breakdown of hides used was as follows (see Fig. 78).

Cow:	40.0 %	Sheep/goat	6.6 %
Calf:	31.8 %	Goat	1.1 %
Cow/calf	1.1 %	Unidentifiable	5.5 %
Deer	7.7 %		

Thus 72.9 % of the leather was bovine in character. This is not unusual, as a large proportion
of the objects concerned were shoe soles. By their nature soles have to be thick to protect the foot,
and cow hide is thick and durable. Deer skin was used in a variety of forms, including for shoe
uppers, a strap and in two unidentified objects. The sheep and goat skins were used only in
footwear. Overall, the variety of leathers used is typical of the period.

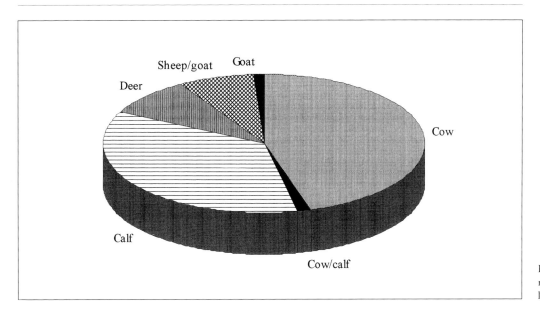

Fig. 78: Hide species
represented in
leather artefacts

CONCLUSIONS

The leather finds from the excavation are all typical of the late 12th/13th centuries. Most of the material relates to footwear, which is typical of the leather finds from medieval urban contexts in Ireland. A wide variety of different styles of footwear are in evidence, indicating that a good cross-section of fashions was in use in 13th-century Dublin. The use of sheep, goat and deer skins, along with the popularity of bovine hides, is also indicative of this period.

REFERENCES

Clark, J. (ed.) 1995 *The medieval horse and its equipment c.1150–1450.* Museum of London, Medieval finds from excavations in London: 5. H.M.S.O.

INVENTORY

Uppers

126.3 Upper and sole fragment, with left hand side torn away. Right hand side extends to quarter, where leather is torn. A line of slits with some thonging in situ lies just below top edge; a whipped seam runs along top edge. A line of stitch holes runs just around toe, where toe strengthener would have been stitched.   Calf skin.   L: 249   H (quarter): 47.   Phase 4.   Fig. 71.

129.2 Upper and sole, torn. Upper of wrap-around pattern, torn along left side; right quarter extends to beyond heel; triangular reinforcer in situ; toe torn away.   Sheep/goat skin.   L: 215   H (quarter): 71.   Phase 4.

137.5 Ankle boot of wrap-around pattern for left foot. Upper still stitched to sole. Right hand quarter ends in butt seam; triangular heel stiffener *in situ*. Abraded.   L: 258   H (quarter): 108.   Phase 3.

138.2 Child's shoe, wrap-around pattern, for right foot. Lasting seam torn away; heel rises at back, seamed on left hand side; whipped seam along top edge. Calf skin.   L: 190   H (quarter): 38   H (heel): 63.   Phase 3.

138.4 Child's shoe upper, very fragmentary, consisting of parts of vamp, heel and quarters. Both ends of quarters end in butt seams where wings would have been stitched; traces of decorative seam run along centre of vamp.   Deer skin. L (upper): 149   L (sole): 182   H (heel): 59.   Phase 3.

139.13 Vamp. Lasting seam partly cut and partly torn away; evidence for repair by secondary stitching along right hand side of lasting seam; right hand wing ends in butt seam, left hand side torn; butt seam runs along instep.   L: 180.   Phase 3.

139.15 Vamp, complete but with some cuts. Square-shaped instep, right hand side ends in butt seam with line of seven small perforations, evidence for a lining on flesh side of upper; whip seam runs along instep and butt seam at left hand side of wing.   Calf skin.   L: 201   H (wing): 74. Phase 3.

139.16 Vamp and sole. Round instep with traces of a butt seam; both wings torn; pointed toe. Calf skin.   L: 232   H (wing): 69.   Phase 3.

139.17 Upper and sole. Vamp complete but very torn and fragile; V-shaped instep; left hand wing ends in butt seam, right hand wing torn; sole complete.   Calf skin. L (upper): 254 L (sole): 250 H (wing): 70.   Phase 3.

143.15 Ankle boot of wrap-around pattern, completed by extra triangular piece at top. Poor condition; vamp torn away from rest of upper but extant; heel worn down and badly ripped; two pairs of vertical slits on both quarters.   Calf skin.   L: 217   H (quarter): 156.   Phase 4.   Fig. 71.

151.9 Child's vamp, with thong repair; cut for re-use of leather.   Calf skin.   W: 86.   Phase 3. Fig. 72.

151.10 Heel of ankle boot. Right hand side torn; left hand side extends up into proto-latchet with two thong holes; an insert would have been stitched into left hand quarter.   Calf skin.   L: 207 H: 185.   Phase 3.

151.12 Vamp, cut and torn; pointed toe, cut at vamp for re-use of leather; 3–4 thong holes at left hand wing for fastening.   L: 160.   Phase 3.

151.13 Quarter fragment, possibly related to 151.12; three holes for fastening, torn; whip seam along top edge.   Calf skin.   L: 145   H (quarter): 83.   Phase 3.

151.15 Vamp for left foot, undiagnostic; torn along right hand side.   Calf skin.   L: 123.   Phase 3.

151.18 Ankle boot upper. Right hand quarter stretches to just beyond ankle, with six perforations along edge; left hand wing also has thong holes, where insert would have been stitched; left hand side of vamp torn.   Deer skin.   L: 310   H (quarter): 107.   Phase 3.   Fig. 71.

172.2 Vamp, unusual as secondary stitching present at left hand side of toe; three slits at right hand side of wing, crude slits at left hand side of wing.   Sheep/goat skin.   L: 167   W: 115. Phase 3.   Fig. 72.

177.5 Upper. Right hand side extends to quarter, where leather is torn; left hand side torn away. Calf skin.   L: 280.   Phase 3.   Fig. 71.

177.9 Vamp. Left hand side torn; right hand quarter extends to heel and ends in butt seam.   Calf skin.   L: 275   H (quarter): 92.   Phase 3.   Fig. 71.

177.14 Child's vamp, the centre of which has been cut away for re-use of leather; a line is scored on left hand side.   Cow/calf skin.   W: 89.   Phase 3.   Fig. 72.

186.2 Ankle boot quarter with four thong holes at one side; traces of lining on flesh side; whip seam along top edge.   Calf skin.   L: 197   H (quarter): 101.   Phase 3.

190.2 Vamp, undiagnostic; torn at instep; butt seam at right hand wing; lasting seam along bottom edge.   Calf skin.   L: 154   W: 115.   Phase 3.

195.5 Child's upper of wrap-around pattern, left foot; left wing extends to quarter where leather is torn; right wing ends in closed seam; triangular heel stiffener in situ; sole extant.   Calf skin. L: 208   H (quarter): 73.   Phase 4.

195.7 Child's boot of wrap-around pattern for right foot, made of two pieces; long triangular heel stiffener *in situ*.   Calf skin.   L: 193   H (quarter): 155.   Phase 4.

199.2 Vamp of child's ankle boot; instep torn; right wing ends in butt seam which continues along top edge of right wing; left wing torn; fragment of top band extant.   Deer skin.   L: 221. H (wing): 157.   Phase 3.

223.3 Vamp/upper. Left wing extends to quarter where it is torn; right wing extends to quarter where it ends in butt seam; slit runs up vamp from instep to toe.   Deer skin.   L: 180.   Phase 3.

237.2 Upper. Right wing ends with two thong holes, continues to quarter where it is torn, and is stitched with a whip seam; line of stitch holes run on inside of quarter which are visible on grain side and thus decorative in nature.   Calf skin.   L: 273.   H (quarter): 73.   Phase 3.

238.4 Upper of wrap-around pattern. Left quarter has slit with three thong holes on either side, used for fastening; right side of upper is torn away; sole extant.   Sheep/goat skin.   L: 240 H (quarter): 63.   Phase 2.

238.5 Child's upper. Left wing with instep and top of right wing have been cut away.   Goat skin. L: 143   H (quarter): 73.   Phase 2.

238.10 Upper and sole. Left side of upper torn away, as is part of right side; trace of slit in instep; no evidence for fastening.   Calf skin.   L: 221   Phase 2.

238.11 Vamp. Torn around toe; cut at instep to two points to fit snugly around foot.   Calf skin. L: 143.vPhase 2.

238.12 Vamp and quarter of boot. Slit in instep which has been stitched; vamp badly torn; quarter has eight thong holes at left side, stitched along sides; lasting seam torn away; evidence for repair along lasting seam.   Calf skin.   L: 305   H (quarter) 118.   Phase 2.   Fig. 71.

239.4 Possible upper fragment, stitched around all sides.   Calf skin.   L: 135.   W: 80.   Phase 3.

239.5 Boot upper of wrap-around pattern for right foot, almost complete. Extra triangular piece, stitched to bottom left side of wing, would have completed this pattern;two thong holes along left side edge of upper; toe pointed; good evidence for repair.   Calf skin.   L: 276   H (quarter): 193. Phase 3.   Fig. 72.

1066.2 Boot of wrap-around pattern, extending from right hand wing to left hand quarter; top half of seam stitched with butt seam, lower half is cut, with five crude thong holes; crudely cut rectangular insert completes pattern; butt seam runs along top edge of left wing (otherwise torn) and along edge where vamp was stitched to quarter; piece of thong in situ at wing; boot fastened via three crude slits along height of instep; two further crude slits run along top edge.   Cow/calf skin.   L: 250   H (quarter): 135.   Phase 3.

Inserts

151.14 Insert for shoe, rectangular, stitched all round.   Calf skin.   L: 124   W: 47.   Phase 3.

171.7 Top band. Long strip folded in two along its length and stitched with whip seam.   Calf skin.   L: 333   W: 3.   Phase 3.

195.4 Long triangular insert; butt seam along top and bottom edges; whip seam along one side; cut along other side.   Sheep/goat skin.   L: 185   W: 80 (max.), 20 (min).   Phase 4.

1049.3 Insert for side fastened upper; whipped seam along two sides, butt seam along other two sides; six thong holes for fastening; evidence for lining on flesh side of upper to strengthen thong holes. Source unidentified.   L: 66   W: 51.   Phase 2.   Fig. 72.

Soles

137.7 Two sole fragments.   Phase 3.

137.9 Sole fragment.   Phase 3.

137.10 Sole fragment.   Phase 3.

139.6 Two sole fragments.   Phase 3.

139.7 Sole, torn at waist; toe torn at lasting seam; waist very narrow.   L: 153.   Phase 3.

139.8 Sole fragment.   Phase 3.

139.9 Sole, right foot. Left side of tread torn; pointed toe.   L: 226.   Phase 3.

139.10 Two very fragmentary pieces of sole.   Phase 3.

139.11 Seat of sole, cut across top edge and at right side.   L: 71.   Phase 3.

139.12 Possible patch for sole cut in shape of tread; no stitch holes; cut crudely around edge. L: 141.   Phase 3.

139.14 Two sole fragments.   Phase 3.

149.2 Sole for left foot. Pointed toe; lasting seam torn at seat AD cut away in parts from right side of tread.   L: 222.   Phase 4.

151.8 Sole for right foot with lasting seam and rand. Sole repaired on left side at waist with crude leather thong; evidence for stitching across waist where sole was heavily repaired. Lasting seam stitched with leather thong, would have been stitched around seat; seat torn in centre; two pieces of rand stitched around seat.   L: 275   W (tread): 102   W (rand) 11.   Phase 3.   Fig. 73.

151.11 Seat of sole, crudely cut all around for re-use.   L: 88.   Phase 3.

151.16 Sole for left foot; seat torn in centre.   L: 228.   Phase 3.

151.17 Sole for right foot; rounded toe.   L: 251.   Phase 3.

151.19 Sole for right foot, delaminated.   L: 60.   Phase 3.

151.20 Sole for right foot; very narrow waist.   Phase 3.

151.21 Sole fragment.   Phase 3.

151.22 Sole for left foot; right side cut away.   L: 250.   Phase 3.

151.23 Sole, cut away for re-use; very pointed toe.   L: 127.   Phase 3.

151.24 Half sole for right foot, torn at waist.   L: 155.   Phase 3.

171.5 Sole for right foot; left side of seat torn.   L: 220.   Phase 3.

171.6 Half sole, stitched across waist and tread.   L: 143.   Phase 3.

177.6 Sole; tread torn; hole worn in seat.   L: 160.   Phase 3.

177.7 Sole; tread torn away.   L: 174.   Phase 3.

177.10 Sole for right foot; rounded toe, hole in left side of tread.   L: 251.   Phase 3.

177.11 Sole, in poor condition; tread worn away.   L: 243.   Phase 3.

177.12 Sole. Delaminated; tread worn away; seat cut around for re-use of leather.   L: 180.   Phase 3.

177.13 Child's sole; pointed toe; seat torn at corner.   L: 170.   Phase 3.

223.2 Sole fragment. Right side of tread and end of seat torn.   L: 211.   Phase 3.

238.6 Half sole. Pointed toe and tread; stitched across just below tread.   L: 136.   Phase 2.

238.7 Child's sole; seat worn away in centre.   L: 137.   Phase 2.

239.2 Sole for right foot. Delaminated; seat badly torn with some evidence for repair.   L: 214. Phase 3.

1046.2 Child's sole and two pieces of rand; straight, slightly pointed toe. Cow hide.   L: 146. Phase 2.

1049.2 Sole, straight; hole on left side of tread; tear in tread and seat. Cow hide.   L: 272.   Phase 2. Fig. 73.

Binding strips

125.3 Piece of binding folded along its length; two lines of long slits along the length; torn at each end.   Sheep/goat skin.   L: 113   W: 12.   Phase 4.

177.4 Binding strip; folded over and stitched along its length with whip seam.   Calf skin.   L 185. Phase 3.

186.3 Binding strip, folded over along its length, with three lines of stitch holes; abraded.   L: 257 W: 20.   Phase 3.

186.4 Binding strip, folded over along its length, with one line of stitch holes; crudely cut along one side.   L: 364   W: 13.   Phase 3.

1060.2 Binding strip, folded over along its length and stitched with whipped seam; torn at either end.   Cow/calf skin.   L: 250   W: 14.   Phase 2.   Fig. 74.

Belts/straps

137.6 Belt with stitch holes along three sides, torn at one end.   Cow hide.   L: 167.   Phase 3.

149.3 Strap, cut around sides and torn at one end; stitch marks for holding buckle at other end. Cow hide.   L: 233   W: 51.   Phase 4.   Fig. 74.

171.4 Strap with seven copper alloy studs *in situ*, with perforations for two more at each end, also three perforations for a buckle; buckle end has been cut; a line of decorative stitching runs along each edge.   Cow hide.   L: 194   W: 20   T: 3.   Phase 3.   Fig. 74.

182.2 Belt. Two pieces stitched together, cut to a point at one end and crudely cut at other; one perforation near pointed end.   Cow hide.   L: 149   W: 27.   Phase 3.

238.8 Strap, torn at both ends; line of stitch holes along each side and a number of perforations along length.   Deer skin.   L: 258   W: 42.   Phase 2.

Sheaths

138.3 Top half of knife sheath, with fragment of blade *in situ*; seamed at back along centre, along top edge 6mm of leather is folded from grain side onto flesh side. Decorated front and back; front decoration consists of band of hatching in top 6mm, below which two rectangular panels are separated by two vertical lines and bordered at the top by four horizontal lines; left hand panel is hatched and right hand panel is cross-hatched. Back decoration consists of traces of horizontal lines at top; elsewhere hatched lines radiate from the seam.   Calf skin.   L: 85.   Phase 3.   Fig. 75.

138.5 Sheath, cut to accomodate handle and narrowing for blade; seamed at back, seam slants from top left corner to 10mm from edge and continues in centre with blade portion. Decorated front and back; front decoration consists of rectangular panel surrounded by continuous line, filled with vertical lines of conjoined hatched lozenges, background also hatched; in lower half of sheath decoration is confined in a long rectangular panel outlined by a double line, filled with vertical lines of pocking; edges decorated with slanting lines. On back, top half decorated with slanting lines bordering the seam, to right of which is a panel decorated with four short vertical lines seperated by pairs of horizontal lines; lower seam highlighted by radiating lines. Seven crude perforations run vertically along top half, with a tear at extreme left hand side.   Calf skin.   L: 96 W: 28.   Phase 3.   Fig. 76.

149.4 Top piece of sheath, cut to accomodate handle and narrowing for blade. Seamed at back to left of centre; two crude thong holes along right hand side. Decoration very crude and confined to front; lines are scored 4mm from top edge around sheath, below which are two panels; right hand panel decorated with crossed zig-zags, left hand panel filled with haphazard incised lines, extends to area of blade.   Calf skin.   L: 102   W: 50.   Phase 4.   Fig. 76.

177.3 Fragmentary sheath; seamed at back along centre. Decoration consists of hatched lines bounded at one side by double line; back has three pairs of spaced, parallel horizontal lines across seam; lower part has seven vertical lines.   Calf skin.   L: 74.   Phase 3.   Fig. 75.

1060.3 Crude sheath, seamed at side with crude thong holes; handle area slightly wider than blade area.   Calf skin.   L: 118   W: 14.   Phase 2.   Fig. 76.

2000.19 Sheath fragment; decorated in vertical panels filled with slanting lines in alternating directions.   Calf skin.   L: 98.   Unstratified.   Fig. 77.

Undiagnostic

137.8 Strip, tapering to one end, stitched with butt seam along two sides; cut across top. Sheep/goat skin.   L: 255.   Phase 3.

177.8 Large piece with stitch holes around edge.   Deer skin.   L: 310   W: 262.   Phase 3.   Fig. 74.

195.6 Three pieces stitched together, possibly some form of covering?   Source unidentified. L: 183   W: 154.   Phase 3.

199.3 Long piece leftover from working; very rough, from underbelly of animal.   Cow/calf skin. L: 292   W: 137.   Phase 3.

234.3 Roughly cut round piece with small perforation towards one side.   Calf skin.   D: 64. Phase 3.   Fig. 74.

238.9 Piece leftover from working.   Calf skin.   L: 165   W: 124.   Phase 2.

239.3 Large piece left over from working.   Deer skin.   L: 346   W: 342.   Phase 3.

CHAPTER XI

The small finds: stone, metal, wood, bone and antler

STONE ARTEFACTS

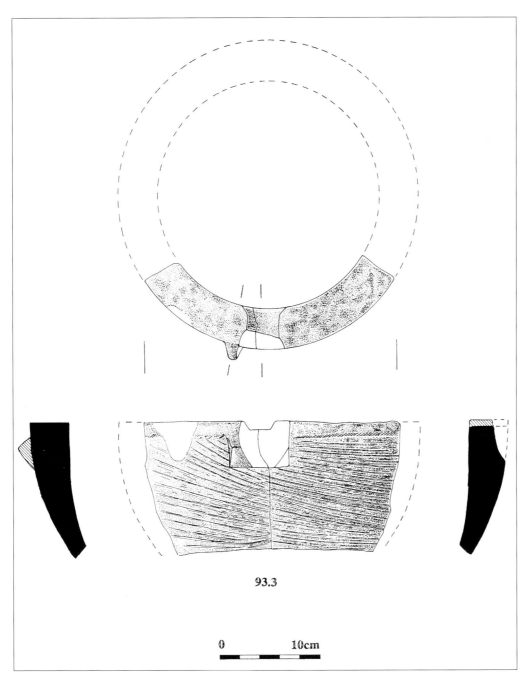

93.3

0   10cm

Fig. 79: Stone mortar (93.3)

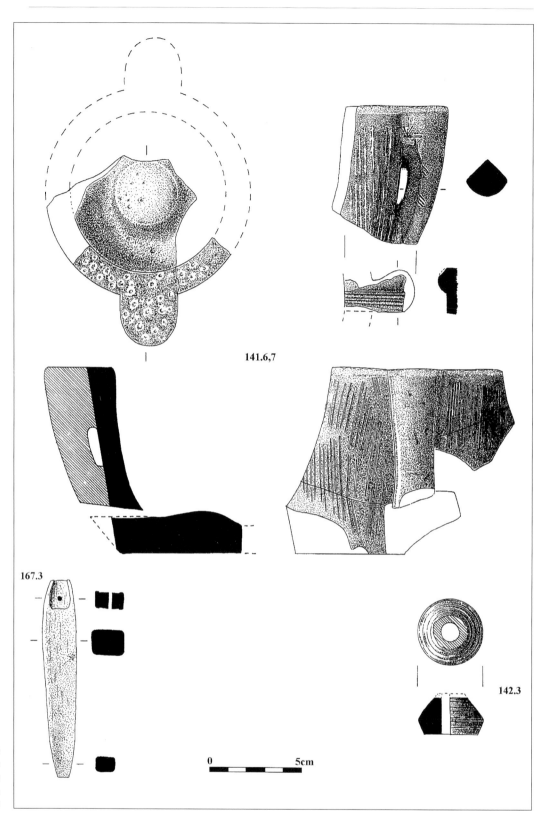

141.6,7

167.3

142.3

0   5cm

MORTARS (FIGS 79–80)

Six fragments were recovered which, however, represent only two mortars as four fragments are from a single vessel and the other two from a second. The latter mortar (93.3; Fig. 79) is from a 13th century context; of the former (Fig. 80), one fragment (2000.13) is unstratified and the others (141.6,7) are from a late or post-medieval context but are probably residual. In the most comprehensive recent discussion, Biddle and Smith (1990, 891) argue that mortars were a 13th-century introduction, at least in Winchester, which largely replaced querns for hand milling in the later Middle Ages. Examination of wear patterns on the Winchester mortars suggested two forms of use, either pounding or grinding (ibid., 891). A grinding pattern is characterised by wear on the lower part of the side and adjacent part of the base and on this basis it can be suggested that the mortars represented by the present fragments were both used for grinding. Geological identifications by Ivor P. Harkin, of the National Museum of Ireland, suggests that while one mortar (93.3) is made of probably local Carboniferous limestone, the other (141.6,7) is of fine-grained oolite, presumably imported from England.

93.3 Fragment (in two pieces) of mortar, originally *c*.30cm in external diameter (at rim) and 12.5cm in surviving height. Surviving fragment includes flat rim, 41mm thick, and a damaged lug with runnel; base absent. Horizontal tooling visible on outer face with a plain band 16mm deep at the rim; inner face displays sporadic pocking but is worn increasingly smoother towards base. The stone has been identified as a bioclastic limestone, possibly Carboniferous and probably local in origin.   Phase 5.

141.6a, b   Fragment of side (in two pieces) with flat rim; 35mm thick.   Phase 6.

141.7   Fragment of base, flat externally but with strongly convex wear pattern internally; up to 46mm thick at base.   Phase 6.

2000.13   Fragment of side with flat rim, 36mm thick and almost complete pierced and chamfered handle; approx. 3.4cm thick; transverse scoring on broken underside of handle.   Unstratified.

141.6a, 6b, 7 and 2000.13 all come from the same vessel, a mortar which was originally almost straight-sided, flat based, *c*.23cm in external diameter (at rim) and *c*.20cm in height, 35mm thick at the rim, with a base 46mm thick; vertical tooling is visible on the outer face throughout, apart from a plain, bevelled band 10mm thick immediately below the rim. The stone has been identified as a fine-grained calcareous oolite.

Flints

A number of pieces of apparently worked flint were recovered from contexts representing most phases of activity on the site (phases 2, 3, 4 and 6). They are presumably residual in these contexts, but whether their occurrence is entirely accidental cannot be established without a wider study of the occurrence of such material in medieval contexts.

7.3 Small piece of retouched flint, yellow/brown; part of cortex surviving.   L: 33   W: 18   T: 8. Phase 6.

139.4 Small piece of retouched flint, dark grey; bulb of percussion and part of cortex visible. L: 29   W: 23   T: 10.   Phase 3.

175.3 Medium-sized struck flint pebble, black; part of cortex survives.   L: 64   W: 39   T: 23 Phase 4.

1019.2 Small, broken piece of retouched flint, grey.   L: 27   W: 14   T: 7.   Phase 6.

1059.2 Multi-platformed core of black chert.   L: 59   W: 41   T: 39.   Phase 2.

Miscellaneous

136.2 Possible line- or net-sinker. Roughly oblong block of calcareous, fossiliferous oolite with opposing V-shaped indentations midway along long sides. The stone is probably a reused fragment of an architectural moulding, preserving one apparent right-angled corner.   L: 114   W: 75   T: 52   Phase 4.

142.3 Spindle whorl; truncated biconical shape with vertical central perforation 10mm in diameter. Body of whorl decorated with incised concentric lines.   D (external): 36   H: 19.   Phase 6.   Fig. 80.

151.7 Probable hone stone of fine-grained sedimentary rock, possibly a silicified siltstone; dressed sub-rectangular with rounded edges, but fractured at each end.   L: 78   W: 16   T: 14.   Phase 3.

167.3 Hone stone of fine-grained sandstone; oblong, of rectangular cross-section and tapering toward each end, both in outline and in profile. At the top is a sub-rectangular recessed panel, 13mm long and up to 10mm wide, on each face, presumably to receive a metal mount; a small simple perforation, 2mm in diameter, occurs centrally, 8mm from the top.   L: 96   W: 16   T: 12. Phase 5.   Fig. 80.

REFERENCES

Biddle, M. and Smith, D. 1990 Mortars. In M. Biddle, *Object and economy in medieval Winchester*, vol. ii, 890–908. Winchester Studies 7ii: Artefacts from medieval Winchester. Oxford, Clarendon Press.

WOODEN ARTEFACTS

Aidan O'Sullivan and Mary Deevy

The assemblage of wooden artefacts from the excavation was small, consisting mainly of broken bowls and several objects of uncertain function. In all, eight wooden artefacts were received for analysis. Detailed measurements and descriptions were made and recorded and comparative material was compiled from a brief literature search. The artefacts were thin-sectioned by razor blade, with the sections mounted on glass slide and viewed through 140x magnification. The species were identified through comparison with a published key (Schweingruber 1990). The only species definitely identified were ash (*Fraxinus excelsior*) and willow (*Salix* sp).

BOWLS (FIGS. 81, 82)

Fragments of five lathe-turned wooden bowls were recovered from the reclamation deposits (late 12th to mid-13th centuries). All are medium-sized, shallow vessels with sides narrowing from either a rounded or flat base to the rim. Decoration is minimal, confined to two parallel grooves incised on one example, which also had an inscribed maker's identification on the base. All the bowls are turned from ash wood, reflecting the suitability of this species for carving vessels and the likely common occurrence of this tree on local soils.

Lathe-turned wooden vessels are a ubiquitous find from excavations in medieval Dublin. The most common form in the 13th century was a simple, medium-sized vessel with a rounded or flat base and narrow rim. Decoration is also usually minimal on these types, often confined to a few concentric grooves incised on the outer body. Tradesman's marks are occasionally etched into the base. The Winetavern St/Wood Quay bowls are similar in size, form and lack of decoration to other assemblages of 13th-century bowls from such diverse settlements as Adare Castle, Co. Limerick (Sweetman 1979), Cork (Hurley 1982), Winchester (Keene 1990) and further afield at Novgorod (Kolchin 1989ii, Fig. 41).

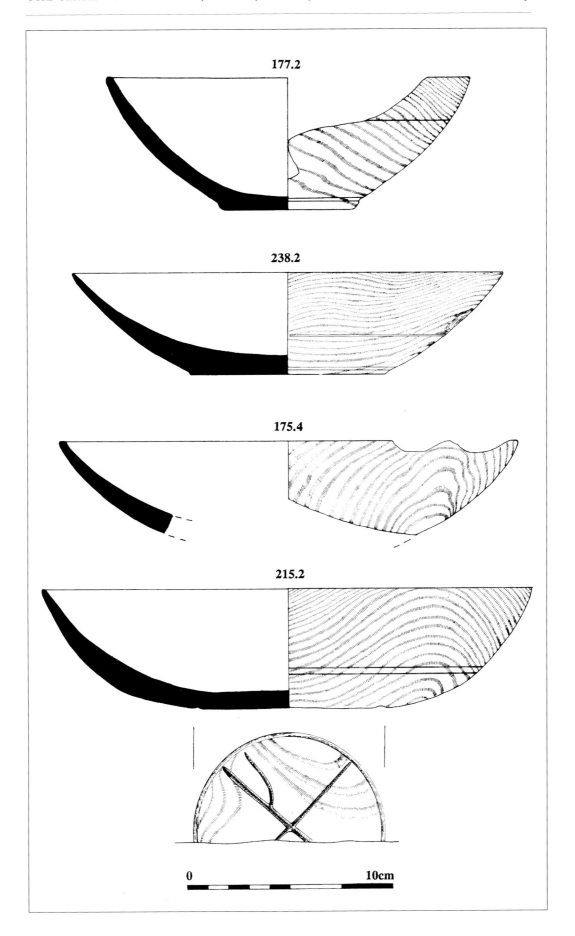

Fig. 81: Wooden bowls

The production of wooden bowls

The bowls would have been turned on a reciprocating pole-lathe, similar to those known from folklife studies (for example Ó Ríordáin 1940). Preliminary rough-outs for such bowls have been found at Tawnagh, Co. Mayo (NMI 1971, 234, Fig. 23) and elsewhere in Dublin (D. Murtagh, pers. comm.). The woodturner would have been one of the specialist craftsmen operating in Anglo-Norman Dublin. Excavations at High St in the 1970s uncovered a large amount of turning waste, leading to the interpretation that a lathe-turning workshop was situated in that vicinity (Ó Ríordáin 1971, 77), although it should be noted that the nature of a pole-lathe means that it can be carried about and assembled when needed (Barber 1984).

Species selection and craft traditions

The morphological similarities of these bowls would suggest some degree of specialist mass-production and, therefore, a constant supply of suitable timber. On present archaeological evidence, it appears that ash was definitely the preferred species for turned ware in Dublin, although alder, oak and yew were also occasionally used. There is also some historical evidence to support this conclusion, namely a reference in the *Account Roll of Holy Trinity Priory, Dublin*, to the purchase of 'cups of ashwood' (*ciphis de fraxino*) for ½d. (Mills 1891). Indeed craftsmen tend to be conservative in their choice of raw materials, repeatedly using the same wood for a specific task. This seems often to have been due to the recognition and preference of the properties of each species, which could include colour, taste, density, resistance to rot and ease of working (O'Sullivan 1990).

However, it is also possible that the preference for ash was due to the fact that it was readily obtainable in the vicinity of Dublin, given this species' preference for lime-rich, well-drained soils. The grain and tree-rings on the bowl surfaces seem to indicate that the wood came from very fast-grown timber, ash trees which were of no great age but measured up to 25cm in diameter. It is possible that the bowls were made from stout poles and small trunks growing in hedgerows or areas of mature coppiced woodland.

OTHER ARTEFACTS

Three further artefacts from the site (Fig. 82) consist of a willow toggle, a perforated fragment and a unique 'propellor-shaped' object. These add to the large number of artefacts of uncertain function known from medieval urban excavations. It seems likely that the toggle was used in fastening clothing. The most interesting artefact, the 'propellor-shaped' object 209.2 of early 13th-century date, may have had a function in holding cord or rope on a boat, or alternatively could be compared to the wooden swivels from Novgorod noted by Kolchin (1989, 129–30; Pl. 128), which he noted as having a range of possible uses. However, one of the terminal perforations on 209.2 is blocked with the apparent remains of a wooden rod or shaft, which seems to preclude the passing of cords through the perforations. A function within a loom, analogous to the 'dogs' identified by Kolchin (1989, 119; Pl. 119–120) at Novgorod, has been suggested for 209.2 by Maurice Hurley (pers. comm.). Significantly, Kolchin refers to rods passing through the apertures of such 'dogs', and thus the interpretation of 209.2 as a 'dog' seems most likely at present.

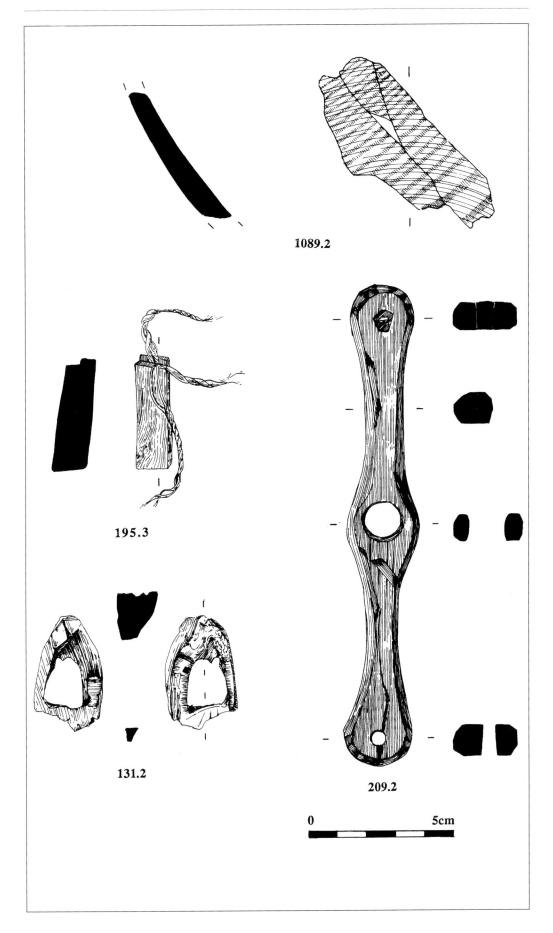

Fig. 82: Wooden artefacts: bowl (1089.2), perforated object (195.3), toggle? (131.2), propellor-shaped object (209.2)

INVENTORY

Bowls (Fig. 81)

175.4 Two small rim fragments of a lathe-turned bowl.   Species: Ash (*Fraxinus excelsior*).   D: 225
H: *c.*70   T: 8.   Phase 4.

177.2 Single fragment of a lathe-turned bowl. The flat base (7cm in diameter) thickens toward the
middle and narrows to the rim.   Species: Ash (*Fraxinus excelsior*).   D: *c.*180   H: 55   T: 7.
Phase 3.

215.2 Single fragment of a lathe-turned, medium sized bowl. The bowl had slightly convex sides
narrowing to the rim. The underside of the base (9cm in diameter) was slightly concave. Two
parallel incised grooves provide decoration on the external surface. Turner's marks on the base
consist of two intersecting lines with attached arc at the end of one. Whitish material adheres on
the inner surface.   Species: Ash (*Fraxinus excelsior*).   D: 240   H: 60   T: 10.   Phase 3.

238.2 Three fragments of a lathe-turned, medium sized bowl. The bowl had slightly convex sides
narrowing to the rim. The underside of the base (9cm in diameter) was slightly concave.   Species:
Ash (*Fraxinus excelsior*).   D: 210   H: 55   T: 10.   Phase 2.

1089.2 Single, small body fragment of a lathe-turned bowl.   Species: Ash (*Fraxinus excelsior*).
L: 75   W: 34   T: 9.   Phase 3.   Fig. 82.

Perforated object

131.2 Small fragment of charred wood; function unknown. Triangular in shape, it is pierced by an
irregular hole.   Species indeterminate.   L: 40   W: 25   T: 15.   Phase 4   Fig. 82.

Toggle?

195.2Small, finely worked rectangular piece of wood, narrowing to one end which has textile
material attached; associated with matted textile.   Species: Willow (*Salix sp.*).   L: 38   W: 14
T: 12.   Phase 4   Fig. 82.

Possible loom dog

209.2 Finely worked wooden object, straight with rounded expansions at terminals and in centre;
round perforations through either end and a larger one through central expansion; one terminal
perforation is blocked with remains of a wooden shaft. Function uncertain, but possibly a loom
dog.   Species indeterminate.   L: 160   W: 25   T: 8.   Phase 3   Fig. 82.

REFERENCES

Barber, J. 1984 Medieval wooden bowls. In D. Breeze (ed.), *Studies in Scottish antiquity presented to Stewart
     Cruden*, 125–47. Edinburgh. Donald.
Hurley, M. 1982 Wooden artefacts from the excavation of the medieval city of Cork. In Mc Grail 1982,
     301–12.
Keene, D. 1990 Wooden vessels. In M. Biddle, *Object and economy in medieval Winchester*, vol. ii, 890–908.
     Winchester Studies 7ii: Artefacts from medieval Winchester. Oxford, Clarendon Press.
Kolchin, B.A. 1989 *Wooden artefacts from medieval Novgorod*, 2 vols. Oxford. B.A.R. Int. Series 495.
McGrail, S. (ed) 1982 *Woodworking techniques before AD 1500*. Oxford. B.A.R. Int. Series 129.
Mills, J. 1891 *Account Rolls of the Priory of the Holy Trinity, Dublin 1337–1346*. Dublin. Royal Society of
     Antiquaries of Ireland. Reprinted Dublin, Four Courts, Press, 1996.

Morris, C.A. 1982 Aspects of Anglo-Saxon and Anglo-Scandinavian lathe turning. In Mc Grail 1982, 245–261.

NMI 1971 National Museum of Ireland: Archaeological acquisitions in the year 1968. *J.R.S.A.I.* **101**, 184–244.

Ó Ríordáin, A. B. 1971 Excavations at High St and Winetavern St, Dublin. *Medieval Archaeology* **15**, 73–85.

Ó Ríordáin, S.P. 1940 Pole-lathe from Borrisokane, Co. Tipperary. *J.C.H.A.S.* **45**, 28–32.

O'Sullivan, A. 1990 Wood in archaeology. *Archaeology Ireland* **4:2**, 69–73.

Schweingruber, F.H. 1990 *Microscopic wood anatomy*, 3rd edition. Birmensdorf. Swiss Federal Institute for Forest, Snow and Landscape Research.

Sweetman, P.D. 1980 Archaeological excavations at Adare castle, Co. Limerick. *J.C.H.A.S.* **85**, 1–6.

METAL ARTEFACTS

IRON

Iron objects survived in extremely poor condition with heavy corrosion, a feature not noted in the National Museum of Ireland excavations in the 1970s and which thus may be related to more recent conditions on the site. A large number of objects were unidentifiable lumps of corrosion and only those objects which could be identified with any degree of confidence are listed below. Of these, the vast majority are nails of various forms, most of which presumably derive from buildings or other structures which formerly existed on the site. A hinge pivot (99.4) probably derives from a door mounted within Structure B in the later 13th century (Phase 5). A particularly interesting discovery is what is almost certainly a broken axe blade (122.2) from the latest reclamation deposits on the site (Phase 4). It may well represent the type of woodworking tool with which the revetments were constructed and, indeed, may well have been broken and discarded on the site during the construction of the latest revetments.

Phase 3

1022.2 Probable nail, very corroded.   L: 50.

Phase 4

71.3 Probable nail shank.   L: 51.

102.4 Bar, very corroded; form obscured.   L: 112.

102.5 Oblong object of rectangular section, 23mm by 13mm; very corroded, form obscured. L: 96.

102.6 Curved object, very corroded, possible horseshoe fragment.   L: 98.

102.7 Oblong object of rectangular section, 18mm by 9mm; corroded, form obscured.   L: 106.

102.10–14 5 nails, 2 expanded-headed, 1 round-headed, 2 probable shanks.

103.3 Large nail/rivet, probably round-headed.   L: 110.

103.4–5 Two large nails, probably round-headed.

118.2 Clench nail/rivet, square-headed.   L: 57.

119.2 Probable nail, large shapeless head, broken.   L: 88.

122.2 Probable axe blade, heavily corroded but apparently with straight upper and lower sides and shallow, convex cutting edge; socket is missing, with straight break across blade at socket end. Blade 99mm long, 92mm wide at cutting edge, narrowing to 57mm at break at socket end, and 10mm in maximum thickness.

136.3 Probable nail, expanded-headed, but obscured by corrosion.   L: 57.

143.5–7 2 nails, round-headed.

143:8 Large amorphous piece of ferrous slag or dross; convex curve on one side suggests a possible fragment of furnace bottom (?).   L: 131   W: 90   T: 73.

143.9 Bar, rounded section, recurved at each end.   L: 87.

146.3–4 2 large nails, round-headed. Phase 4/5.

Phase 5

1.4 Large bolt/rivet, encrusted but apparently dome-headed.   L: 66.

1.5–16 12 nails, 5 round-headed, 1 square-headed, the remainder incomplete shanks.

15.7–20 14 nails, 6 round-headed, 2 expanded-headed, 6 probable shanks.

17.2, 9 Nail, shape of head obscured, and probable nail shank.

41.3 Nail, round-headed, shank incomplete.   L: 29.

68.3 Nail, expanded head, bent, incomplete.   L: 57.

89.2, 4–5 3 nails, round-headed, no. 2 with very large round head.

93.5–6 Nail, round-headed, bent, complete and probable nail shank.

96.8–28 21 nails, 6 round-headed, 3 apparently expanded heads, the remainder incomplete shanks.

96.29 Bar, straight, probably square-sectioned.   L: 177.

97.2 Large, round-headed nail/rivet, bent.   L: 52.

99.4 Hinge pivot.   L: 104.

99.5–22 18 nails, 7 round-headed, 4 expanded-headed, 7 probable shanks.

130.2 Large nail, probably round-headed.   L: 67.

135.3 Bar, apparently oval section, expanded at one end, probably due to corrosion.   L: 73. Phase 5/6.

154.2–8 5 nails, apparently round-headed, and 2 possible shanks, very corroded.

167.2 Large nail, round-headed.   L: 94.

Phase 6

6.3–5 3 nails, 2 round-headed, 1 incomplete shank.   L: 38.

12.2 Bar, probable nail shank.   L: 38.

28.2 Nail, probably round-headed, complete.   L: 61.

38.3 Heavily concreted looped object.   L: 85.

38.4 Large nail, possibly square-headed.   L: 82.

38.5 Iron bar, rounded at ends and in section; possible ingot?   L: 94.

45.3 Probable nail, expanded head, incomplete.   L: 66.

49.3–4 Nail, round-headed, bent and probable nail shank.

60.2 Probable nail or rivet; expanded at each end.   L: 66.

67.2 Small, short bar, now expanded at each end.   L: 32.

141.10 Bar, apparently rectangular section, *c.*24mm wide by 9mm thick, but obscured by corrosion; expanded at one end, probably due to corrosion   L: 151.

141.11 Bar, section obscured, apparently tapering toward one end.   L: 96.

141.12–15 4 large nails, probably round-headed.

141.16 Large nail/rivet, round-headed with lozenge-shaped rove at other end; possible ship's nail. L: 83.

142.5–8 4 nails, 3 round-headed, 1 incomplete shank.

142.9–15 8 nails, 7 round-headed, 1 probable shank.

142.10 Knife blade, back slightly curved, edge ragged, tang missing.   L: 135.

142.11 Bar, rounded section, tapering toward one end.   L: 80.

145.2 Large nail, round-headed.   L: 84.

148.5–7 3 nails, 2 round-headed, 1 probable shank.

1016.2 Curved, flat strip, 20mm wide by 2mm thick; probable knife blade.   L: 126.

1020.2 Nail, oval-headed.   L: 79.

1029.3 Probable nail fragment, very corroded.   L: 41.

COPPER ALLOY (FIG. 83)

Of the recognisable copper alloy artefacts, the most common type was buckles, with six examples represented. All but two of these were in 13th century contexts and the exceptions (140.2, from a phase 6 context and 2000.20, unstratified) are probably residual. The only other personal object was a stick pin (1071.2) from a late 12th century context. Two barrel padlocks from phase 6 contexts were probably residual and may have derived from the later 13th-century buildings on the site.

Phase 1

1071.2 Stick pin. Club-headed, stem swells slightly towards middle and tapers to point; decorated below head with series of short oblique lines on 3 sides.   L: 75   Fig. 83.

Phase 3

137.3 Buckle (?). Corroded object with two separate elements, one an open, trapezoidal frame with thick outside edge, the other a square frame with solid plates on each face, probably a buckle plate and apparently attached by a loop to the other frame.   L (frame): 32   W (frame): 22   L (plate): 25   W (plate): 22.

139.5 Plate, flat and roughly oval with 8 small perforations (*c.*2mm diameter) around outer edge; possible repair patch for a metal vessel?   L: 57   W: 41   T: 0.5   Fig. 83.

Phase 4

105.2 Ring/link (?). Roughly half of a circular ring of D-shaped section, with an expanded bifurcate terminal on one end; both ends broken and incomplete.   D (original): 14   W: 3   T: 2 Fig. 83.

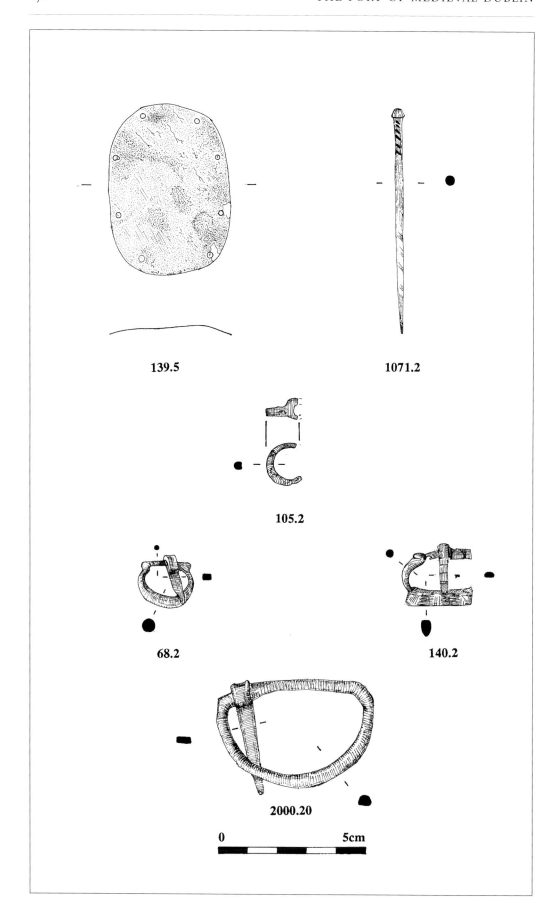

Fig. 83: Copper alloy artefacts: plate (139.5), stick pin (1071.2), ring/link (105.2), buckles (68.2, 140.2, 2000.20)

Phase 5

1.3 Sub-rectangular cake, corroded.   L: 51   W: 42 T:19.

15.6: Featureless fragment of sheet metal.   L: 62   W: 37   T: 2.

68.2: Buckle; oval frame with offset narrowed bar; simple, flat pin   L: 19   W: 15   T: 4   Fig. 83.

96.4: Buckle tongue; small square-sectioned bar, hooked at one end and pointed at other.   L: 19 T: 2.

96.5: Small rounded ball (?).   D: 14.

96.6: Buckle; probably rectangular double frame with plate, quite corroded. Staining of corrosion at one side suggests that pin was of iron.   L (frame): 20   L (overall): 35   W: 13   T: 5.

96.7: Fragments of narrow sheet, with two possible rivets.   L: 39   W: 11   T: 2.

99.3: Mount (?), corroded. Square head with scalloped or notched edges and dome-headed rivet set off-centre; narrower, projecting loop at base containing traces of small, round-sectioned bar. L: 29   W: 21   T: 8.

Phase 6

7.2 Bar, extremely corroded, section obscured.   L: 36.

26.2: Rivet or nail, corroded; large round head with short rectangular-sectioned shank, bent at end.   L: 27   D: 19.

140.2: Buckle, incomplete and in poor condition. Oval frame with narrowed, offset bar; traces of separate sheeting around bar may indicate former existence of plates. Outside edge of frame is straight, thickened and has traces of incised transverse lines. Pin flat and tapering.   L: 24   W: 20 T: 4   Fig. 83.

141.8: Barrel padlock, very corroded. Case has several longitudinal rods along its sides; end plate displays two rectangular holes for bolt; other end plate obscured by corrosion. Traces of fin on case; separate fragment of tapering tube survives.   L: 76   D: 38.

142.4: Barrel padlock, very corroded. Two probable rectangular holes for bolt visible in one end plate; traces of fin on case.   L: 65   D: 26.

1029.2: Piece of sheet with circular perforation, 10mm in diameter.   L: 91   W: 37.   T: 1.

Unstratified

2000.20: Buckle, rather crude D-shaped frame, of rounded cross-section at bar, becoming wider at outer edge; simple, flat pin, looped around bar.   L: 53   W: 37   T: 4   Fig. 83.

OTHER NON-FERROUS METALS

Silver

1056.2 Silver coin, in extremely poor condition, but identified by Mr Michael Kenny (National Museum of Ireland) as a Hiberno-Norse bracteate of the 'Kildare Round Tower' type (see Seaby 1984, Pl. XVI: 399); a mid-12th century issue date is likely, although the context is early 13th century (phase 3).   Not illustrated.

Pewter (?)

192.2 Pewter (?) disc, roughly round, rather battered, apparently quite plain; possibly a token?
D: 23   T: 1.   Phase 3.

Lead

141.9 Amorphous piece of lead sheet.   L: 56.   W: 53.   T: 15.   Phase 6.
146.2 Amorphous piece of lead sheet.   L: 50.   W: 32.   T: 11.   Phase 4.
160.3 Amorphous piece of lead sheet.   L: 68.   W: 39.   T: 15.   Phase 6.

REFERENCES

Seaby, W. 1984 *Sylloge of coins of the British Isles 32: Ulster Museum, Belfast, Part II: Hiberno-Norse coins.*
London. British Academy/Trustees of the Ulster Museum/Oxford University Press.

ARTEFACTS OF BONE AND ANTLER (FIG. 84)

Antler combs and bone 'toggles' are fairly typical finds from Irish medieval sites and both are represented, albeit slightly, in the present assemblage. Two composite combs of antler were recovered. One (213.2) is a double-sided comb with one row of relatively fine teeth and the other row of coarser teeth, features described by Dunlevy (1988, 369–70) as characteristic of her Class H. The contextual date, at the end of the 12th century or beginning of the 13th century is in line with the meagre dating evidence for this class noted by Dunlevy. The second comb (126.3) is incomplete but is single-edged, with a slightly curved back and bears decoration of incised parallel lines on the sideplates; these features tend to suggest that it belongs to Dunlevy's (1988, 366–67) Class F3 combs, although the contextual date in the first half of the 13th century is slightly later than the 10th–12th century date suggested by Dunlevy for the type. However, there is evidence that several artefacts recovered from the reclamation deposits are residual in their context, which should come as no surprise.

The 'toggle' (126.2) is a phalange with a central oval perforation; these are common finds in 12th and 13th century deposits, and while they are still commonly referred to as toggles many scholars suggest that they were in fact a form of musical instrument known as 'buzz-bones' or 'buzz-discs' (see Hurley 1997, 674–5 for discussion). An undoubted musical instrument is the fipple-flute (1004.2), made from a long bone of a large bird, such as a goose or swan. This is a less common object, although a number of examples are known from Dublin (Buckley 1988) and Waterford (Hurley 1997, 665), while it is a relatively common find from English medieval sites (see Megaw 1990). A second, similar bone (143.13) may have been intended for use as a flute but no actual signs of working are evident.

The most common bone artefacts from the present site, as from many others (for example Waterford; Hurley 1997, 685) are a series of short, cut sections of long bones, with the centres hollowed out to form short bone cylinders. A number of offcuts from the ends of the bones were also found; these too had been hollowed out, in some cases with two parallel perforations. Hurley (1997, 685) notes the occurrence of groups of offcuts at Waterford and Dublin and in this respect it may be significant that sixteen offcuts were found in a single context (F143) on the present site, although they were not definitely associated as a group. At Christchurch Place, Dublin, a set of seven of these cylinders were found strung on a leather thong (Donaghy 1992, 29 & fig.). An offcut from Waterford was also found with a piece of rope running through the central perforation and Hurley (1997a, 685) notes that many others display wear patterns consistent with such internal

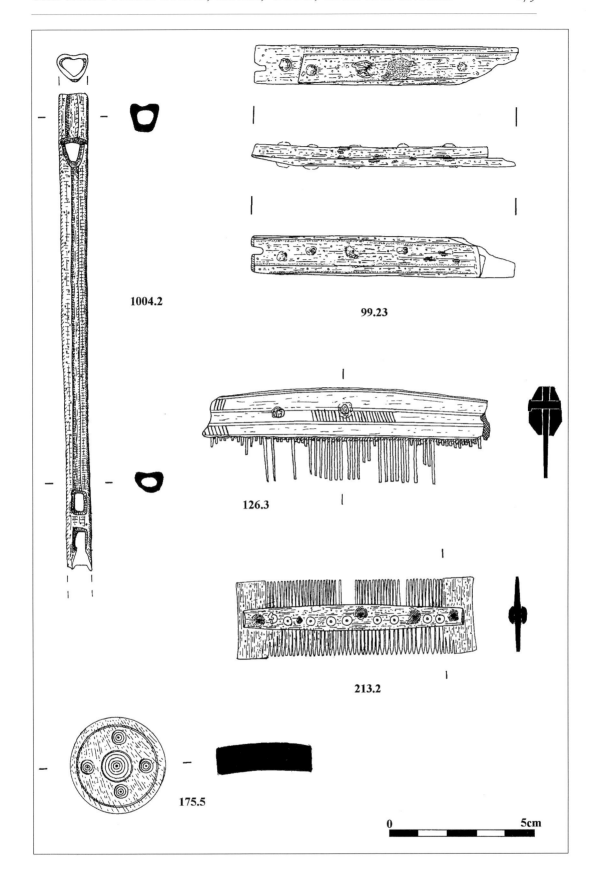

Fig. 84: Bone artefacts: fipple-flute (1004.2), rivetted plates (99.23), gaming piece (175.5), combs (126.3, 213.2)

stringing. The function of these objects is not certainly known; the range of suggestions has been summarised by Hurley (1997a, 685; 1997b, 263–65), who appears to find most of them unconvincing. He does not, however, rule out the possibility that they may have functioned as charms, hair curlers, spacers used in making netting, devices for rolling or twisting string, or as loom weights. These objects were found most frequently in Phase 3 deposits (early 13th century) and somewhat less frequently in the later 13th century Phases 4 and 5. Two examples from Phase 6 are probably residual while a single offcut from a Phase 2 deposit may be intrusive.

Apart from the combs, the only artefacts of antler recovered were a discoid gaming piece (175.5), a type which seems to be an Anglo-Norman introduction, with typical dot-and-circle decoration on one face, and two small, notched pegs (1056.4, 2000.17) of uncertain function; a range of uses have been suggested, including clamps, linchpins, pegs for stretching hides, cheekpieces for horse bridles, tools for making basketry or matting and netting needles (see Hurley 1997, 681–82).

Phase 2

238.3 Offcut from end of bone.   L: 49   W: 39.

Phase 3

169.2 Bone cylinder.   L: 33   W: 32.

171.3 Bone cylinder.   L: 31   W: 31.

177.15 Two bone cylinders.   L: 30 and 27.

209.3 Bone cylinder.   L: 30   W: 28.

213.2 Antler comb, double-sided, almost intact; probably five teethplates, each secured to sideplates by an iron rivet (two of which are missing); wide end-teeth and slightly concave ends; plain apart from a row of dot-and-circle motifs along centre of each side-plate.   L: 79   W: 25   T: 7.   Fig. 84.

1004.2 Fipple-flute, broken at one end, formed of a long, thin bone, probably of a large bird; knife (?) marks visible on all sides. At one end is the blow hole, while at the other are two sub-rectangular finger holes, each *c*.7mm by 5mm, and 6mm apart. Flute broken below second finger hole, so that it is impossible to say whether there were other holes. Fipple missing.   L: 159   W: 10   T: 9.   Fig. 84.

1039.2 Bone cylinder.   L: 26   W: 31.

1056.3 Offcut from end of bone.   L: 28   W: 42.

1056.4 Antler peg (?). Short tapering sliver with straight notch cut across one side.   L: 35   W: 10   T: 8.

Phase 4

126.2 Toggle. Phalange with central oval perforation, 8mm by 5mm.   L: 52.

126.3 Antler comb, single-sided with bevelled sideplates, incomplete at both ends; currently four teethplates, secured to sideplates by two iron rivets; many teeth missing; the facets on each sideplate are outlined by incised horizontal lines, with a zone 28mm wide of vertical hatching in the centre of each sideplate.   L: 97   W: 31   T: 11.   Fig. 84.

143.12 Sixteen bone cylinders of varying sizes, between 23mm and 38mm in length. No pieces definitely join and more than one bone seems to be represented.

146.5 Two offcuts from the ends of long bones.   L: 32 and 41.

175.5 Gaming piece. Flat disc decorated on one face with dot-and-circle motifs; at centre is dot surrounded by five circles with, outside this, four smaller motifs of dots surrounded by three circles. A single incised line runs just inside edge of disc. D: 32   T: 8. Fig. 84.

195.3 Offcut from end of bone.   L: 28   W: 39.

Phase 5

99.23 Object consisting of two rectangular bone plates riveted together. One end broken, the other end straight with a small notch, and tapered on one side. Five irregularly-spaced small iron rivets join the plates, each of which is decorated along the long sides with double incised lines. Function uncertain; no space between plates for teeth plates of comb, or tang of a blade.   L: 90 W: 15   T: 8. Fig. 84.

154.8 Four bone cylinders of varying sizes, between 26mm and 36mm in length. No pieces definitely join.

165.2 Bone cylinder and offcut from end of long bone.   L: 30 and 20.

229.2 Bone cylinder.   L: 26   W: 31.

Phase 6

135.4 Bone cylinder; roughly cut ends.   L: 21   W:26.

142.21 Bone cylinder.   L: 66   W: 31.

Unstratified

2000.17 Antler peg (?). Short tapering sliver with wide, straight notch cut across one side.   L: 57 W: 16   T: 10.

2000.18 Bone cylinder.   L: 35   W: 37.

REFERENCES

Buckley, A. 1988 Musical instruments from medieval Dublin: a preliminary survey. In E. Hickmann and
    D.W. Hughes (eds), *The archaeology of early music cultures: Third international meeting of the ICTM
    Study Group on Music Archaeology*. Bonn, published as *Orpheus* **51**.
Donaghy, C. 1992 The small finds. Appendix 6 of M. Gowen (ed.), *Development at Christchurch Place –
    archaeology*. Preliminary post-excavation report submitted to the Office of Public Works, unpublished.
Dunlevy, M. 1988 A classification of early Irish combs. *P.R.I.A.* **88C**, 341–422.
Hurley, M.F. 1997a Artefacts of skeletal material. In M.F. Hurley, O.M.B. Scully and S.W.J. McCutcheon
    (eds), *Late Viking age and medieval Waterford: Excavations 1986–1992*, 650–99. Waterford Corporation.
Hurley, M.F. 1997b Artefacts of skeletal material. In R.M. Cleary, M.F. Hurley and E. Shee Twohig (eds),
    Skiddy's castle and Christ Church, Cork: Excavations 1974–77 by D.C. Twohig, 239–73. Cork Corporation.
Megaw, J.V.S. 1990 Bone whistles and related objects. In M. Biddle, *Object and economy in medieval
    Winchester*, vol. ii, 718–723. Winchester Studies 7ii: Artefacts from medieval Winchester. Oxford,
    Clarendon Press.

PART III

Conclusions

CHAPTER XII

Conclusions

This was a typical 'rescue' excavation, taking place in response to the archaeological implications of the construction of the Civic Offices, rather than being a planned excavation driven by particular archaeological research objectives. The excavation was necessitated by the unexpected discovery of intact archaeological deposits, but in view of the obvious damage to these deposits it was not anticipated that the excavation would produce significant new results to add to those already achieved by earlier work at Wood Quay. However, these pessimistic expectations have not been borne out by events. The excavation has, in fact, produced results which can justifiably be described both as significant and as new, even within the restricted context of the history of the development of Dublin's medieval waterfront.

THE EARLY 13TH CENTURY RECLAMATION

Most of the information produced by the excavation is, predictably, related to the 13th century reclamation of the site, which has previously been so well explored by Wallace. Even here, however, the present excavation has helped to sharpen the focus of the known picture of this reclamation process, thanks to a combination of dendrochronological determinations, ceramic evidence and careful analysis of the stratigraphy of the reclamation deposits. It is now clear that this major reclamation project was initiated slightly earlier than was previously thought, around 1200 AD or possibly even shortly before. The main feature of this project was the construction of a number of large wooden revetments, which according to dendrochronological determinations obtained in the present excavation was done by 1201 AD at the latest. Moreover, constructional details indicate that the main revetment (F166) was laid down from east to west, suggesting that the remainder of this revetment, excavated by Wallace, was at least no later than F166.

The excavation also produced evidence that the main revetment (F166, Wallace's Revetment 1) was constructed and assembled on-site, using carefully selected oak timbers and the most up-to-date timber-frame building techniques of contemporary English carpentry. The evidence provided by the revetment timbers for the existence of managed mature oak woodlands in the vicinity of 12th/13th century Dublin is one of the most interesting and important results of the excavation. Indeed, the overall analysis of worked wood from the site gives an invaluable insight into what may justifiably be described as the timber industry in medieval Dublin.

Wallace (1981, 114) suggested that his Revetment 1 was preceeded by a slightly earlier embankment (Bank 4) erected c.1200 AD, representing the first reclamation episode north of the city wall. However, it is now suggested that what Wallace described as Bank 4 (F208 in the present excavation) is actually a component part of the main revetment (F166) and contemporary with it. A significant alignment was observed between the 'origin' post shared by the two diverging parts of F208 and the scarf joint between the two easternmost baseplates of revetment F166. This joint in turn marked the junction between the area of complete planking to the base of the revetment and that of partial planking, further west, and also marked the western limit of the cobbled surface (F176) at the top of the revetment. Thus it seems clear that the 'origin' post/scarf joint alignment represents a significant break in the construction of the revetment and the post-and-wattle fence F208. It is hardly coincidental that the north-eastern corner of the later stone building, Structure A, is also placed on this alignment and it could even be argued (although with less certainty) that the eastern end of the late 12th century revetment F164 possibly respects this alignment. This surely bears out Wallace's (1981, 115; 1985, 386) suggestion that the different construction sections evident in the main revetment could reflect landholding divisions (perhaps even formal burgage property divisions) which were respected even in the as yet unreclaimed foreshore, and which remained in use well into the 13th century, at least.

WOOD QUAY: THE PORT OF DUBLIN?

The actual function of this, and other similar revetments has been a subject of some discussion. It is beyond dispute that they were erected to retain the material deposited on the landward side, but there has been some debate about whether they may also have functioned as docksides, against which ships could have berthed. Thus Wallace (1981, 116–17) has argued for the revetments as docksides, while McGrail (1993, 82, 99–100) does not accept this, at least for the early 13th century revetments. The evidence from the present excavation, however, suggests that there is no reason why the revetments could not have functioned as docksides. Such a function is strongly suggested by the presence of internal cobbling (F176) near the top of revetment F166; this clearly appears to be a working surface, which must have been related to activity taking place at the waterfront (Ill. 14). John de Courcy's (1984, 164 and pers. comm.) conclusion that tidal levels on the Liffey in the 13th century were not significantly different from modern levels has allowed some estimate of how revetment F166 related to actual river levels. De Courcy suggests a typical high spring tide level of approximately 2.0m Ordnance Datum (Malin), which is indicated on cross-sectional drawings in this Report. As O'Sullivan has pointed out (see Chapter IV, above) this tidal level suggests that the ships of the form and size as those indicated by the timbers excavated at Wood Quay could have berthed against revetment F166, at least at high tide (see Fig. 41).

Once it is accepted that the revetment was capable of serving as a dockside, it is difficult not to conclude that it actually did function as a dockside, and that this may have been the revetment's primary function. Indeed, it may well be that the revetment was the main dockside of early 13th century Dublin, and that the port of Dublin was located at Wood Quay in this period. When the revetments at Wood Quay were first excavated by Wallace in the 1970s it was generally assumed that similar structures would have existed elsewhere along the riverfront. In recent years, however, it has become evident that Wood Quay is not typical of the medieval waterfront of Dublin as a whole. Despite considerable archaeological investigation, the only similar waterfront revetments to have been found are at Usher's Quay (Swan 1992), where they were on a much smaller scale, and at Arran Quay (Hayden 1991), where they were of a much later date. Apart from this, there is no evidence for comparable revetments elsewhere on the medieval waterfront, whether on Merchant's Quay to the west (Meenan 1991, 1994, Murtagh 1991) or on Essex Quay to the east. At Essex Quay, indeed, there is positive evidence that the early 13th century waterfront was defined by an earthen bank which would certainly have been unsuitable for docking purposes (Simpson 1995).

Why, therefore, were these timber revetments only erected along Wood Quay? The obvious answer is that even in the early 13th century, the port of Dublin was located in the Wood Quay area, as it certainly was a century later (see Chapter II). The revetments may well have been constructed specifically to function as docksides; if retention of reclamation deposits was all that was required, simpler methods such as the bank exposed at Essex Quay would have sufficed. It might be added that the large number of ships' timbers, including several large, articulated sections of hull planking, which have been found on the Wood Quay site (see Chapter VIII above, and McGrail 1993) are clear evidence for the activity of shipping in the immediate vicinity of the site.

LATER RECLAMATION AND THE RIVERSIDE WALL

The stratigraphy of the reclamation deposits confirms Wallace's suggestions that the main reclamation episode was followed by later episodes associated with the construction of other revetments, to the north of the main revetment of *c.*1200 AD. The evidence for these later episodes is very fragmentary, however, and they remain very imperfectly understood. Another point of interest is that, despite the slightly earlier starting date which has emerged, it is also clear that the reclamation process on the Wood Quay site was completed more quickly than was previously thought. A combination of ceramic and documentary evidence indicates that all reclamation work on the site was completed by the middle of the 13th century, and that the new riverside wall on the line of the modern Wood Quay, which was thought to have been of early 14th century date (Wallace 1981, 117) had actually been erected by *c.*1260 AD at the latest. By the second half of the 13th century the entire site was well and truly dry land and had begun to acquire the elements of the urban form which was essentially to survive into the present century.

WINETAVERN ST AND THE PORT OF DUBLIN

Apart from confirming and refining the results of previous excavations, the present excavation also produced entirely new results in a number of areas. Significant differences have emerged between the present site and the areas previously excavated by Wallace, and these appear to be largely due to the present site's proximity to Winetavern St, which must be seen as an extremely important routeway in the late 12th and 13th centuries, providing a vital access between the town and the riverside. As Simpson (1995, 5–6) has pointed out, Winetavern St currently seems to mark a significant boundary in terms of the reclamation of the river frontage. The area to the east of Winetavern St provides evidence for more vigorous and carefully planned reclamation than to the west, where natural silting seems to have been the main engine of reclamation.

In contrast to the remainder of the Wood Quay site, where there is no evidence for reclamation activity outside of the town wall prior to *c.*1200 AD, there was at least one episode of reclamation on the present site in the later 12th century, associated with a wooden revetment (F164) and foreshadowing the more extensive reclamation of *c.*1200 AD. Walsh (1997, 95–8) also found a series of timber structures, interpreted as remains of a jetty or boardwalk dating to the late 12th century, in Winetavern St immediately west of the present excavation.

Indeed, there may have been even earlier reclamation activity, represented by the Phase 1 deposits on the present site. Mitchell (1987, 15) noted an embankment which he related to Wallace's Bank 4, as well as an apparently natural gravel bank topped with wattle mats, both of which were located to the south of the present excavation. As has been noted, in the present writer's opinion Mitchell's identification of Wallace's Bank 4 was mistaken. In the present excavation the continuation of Bank 4 was identified much further to the north, as F208, just south of the main revetment of *c.*1200 AD. The embankment and gravel bank described by Mitchell must actually be earlier than any of the features exposed in the present excavation, with the possible exception of the Phase 1 deposits. These features, all earlier than the main reclamation episode on the present site, suggest that the Winetavern St area may be an exception to the general progression from east to west noted on the Wood Quay site. Reclamation was apparently taking place here at an earlier date than on the eastern part of the site toward Fishamble St.

In the late 12th and early 13th centuries Winetavern St, outside of the town wall, can hardly have existed as such but the documented presence of the King's Gate in the town wall at this point indicates that there was already a routeway of some importance on the site of the later street. This is confirmed by the evidence recovered by Walsh (1997, 95–103) for activity on the site of Winetavern St (outside the town wall) in the late 12th and early 13th centuries. Although the nature of this activity is not fully understood, it must surely provide the background to the late 12th century reclamation episode revealed in the present excavation.

In turn, the importance of the route that was to become Winetavern St may well be due to the role of the Wood Quay river frontage as a docking area – probably the principal dock of the town. Walsh (1997, 99–103) discovered a large revetment, probably of late 12th or early 13th century date running along the line of the future Winetavern St. She interpreted it as the eastern face of a projecting pier or jetty, with a possible inlet or harbour to the east (ibid., 105–06; Simpson 1995, 6). Such an inlet, directly outside the King's Gate, may well have functioned as a dock and this function could have been extended along the Wood Quay river front. The discovery in the present excavation of an apparent western termination to the main revetment (revetments F246/F1055) may argue against Walsh's (1997, 103) suggestion that the revetment which she excavated in Winetavern St formed 'part of the same integral unit' as the Wood Quay revetment. Nevertheless, it is very likely that both are closely related and formed part of the same overall reclamation/ dockside scheme. F246 and F1055 were constructed on the same north-south alignment as Walsh's revetment in Winetavern St, and they were of similar, apparently unbraced, construction. Walsh (1997, 106) speculated about the existence of a 'parallel revetment … on the east side of Winetavern St', serving as the eastern edge of the inlet retained on the west by Walsh's revetment. It is possible that the F246/F1055 revetment unit is precisely this parallel revetment.

One of the most striking features in the morphology of early medieval Dublin is the well-known 'kink' in the 12th century town wall at Wood Quay. Roughly midway between Fishamble St and Winetavern St the wall, running roughly westwards from Fishamble St, turned abruptly to a south-westerly course for a distance of slightly over 20 metres, before resuming a roughly westerly course across Winetavern St. It is clear that in following this unusual course the town wall was merely reflecting the line of the earlier earthen defences of the town, which featured a similar deviation to the south-west at this point. In turn, it is likely that the earthen banks of the 10th and 11th centuries were following the natural shoreline of the river, and that a small pool or embayment existed at this point. Mitchell (1987, 8, 14) argued that in the Winetavern St area the river extended right to the base of the 12th-century town wall, at least at spring high tides. Such a natural embayment may well have been an attractive landing point for boats and ships, even in the 10th century, and it is not unreasonable to suggest that this may in time have developed into a more formal port or harbour. The presence of Winetavern St and the King's Gate, and the developments outside the King's Gate in the late 12th and early 13th centuries may all have been directly related to this earlier natural harbour.

LATER 13TH CENTURY OCCUPATION

Considering the extent of damage to the later deposits, the site yielded a surprising amount of information on the earliest actual occupation of the site in the aftermath of the reclamation process, which can be dated to the later 13th century. In particular, the large stone building, Structure A, represented by its massive foundations (Pls VII–VIII) appears to be of 13th century date and as such is without parallel on other parts of the Wood Quay site. This was obviously a very substantial building, to judge from its foundation requirements, and presumably an important one. In view of the known historical evidence that Dublin's earliest Tholsel or Guildhall was located in this approximate position in the 13th century, it is very tempting to suggest that

Structure A actually represents the foundations of the Tholsel. This, of course cannot be demonstrated conclusively, but it must remain a distinct possibility.

Regardless of whether this is actually the Tholsel, the archaeological evidence for substantial stone buildings being built on Winetavern St in the 13th century, together with the historical evidence for the Tholsel in this location, again highlights the importance of Winetavern St. Clearly the 12th century activity on the site of the future street carried through into the 13th century and by the later part of that century Winetavern St was well established outside of the 12th century town wall and was a favoured location for high-status buildings.

REFERENCES

Bennett, I. (ed.) 1991 *Excavations 1990: Summary accounts of archaeological excavations in Ireland.* Dublin. Organisation of Irish Archaeologists/ Wordwell.

De Courcy, J. 1984 Medieval banks of the Liffey estuary. In J. Bradley (ed.), *Viking Dublin exposed: The Wood Quay saga*, 164–66. Dublin. O'Brien Press.

Hayden, A. 1991 9–12 Arran Quay, Dublin. In Bennett 1991, 27–8.

McGrail, S. 1993 *Medieval boat and ship timbers from Dublin.* Medieval Dublin Excavations 1962–81, Ser. B, vol. 3. Dublin. Royal Irish Academy.

Meenan, R. 1991 20–23 Merchant's Quay, Dublin. In Bennett 1991, 31.

Meenan, R. 1994 16–17 Cook St, Dublin. In I. Bennett (ed.), *Excavations 1993: Summary accounts of archaeological excavations in Ireland*, 18–19. Dublin. Organisation of Irish Archaeologists/Wordwell.

Murtagh, D. 1991 15–19 Merchant's Quay, Dublin. In Bennett 1991, 31.

Simpson, L. 1995 *Excavations at Essex St West, Dublin.* Dublin. Temple Bar Properties.

Swan, D. L. 1992 6–8 Usher's Quay, Dublin. In I. Bennett (ed.), *Excavations 1991: Summary accounts of archaeological excavations in Ireland,* 15. Dublin. Organisation of Irish Archaeologists/Wordwell.

Wallace, P.F. 1981 Dublin's waterfront at Wood Quay, 900–1317. In Milne and Hobley 1981, 108–118.

Wallace, P.F. 1982 Carpentry in Ireland AD 900–1300 – the Wood Quay evidence. In S. McGrail (ed.), *Woodworking techniques before AD 1500*, 263–299. Oxford. B.A.R. British Series 129.

Walsh, C. 1997 *Archaeological excavations at Patrick, Nicholas and Winetavern Sts, Dublin.* Dingle. Brandon Books/Dublin Corporation.

Bibliography

Allan, J.P. 1983 The importation of pottery to southern England *c*.1200–1500. In Davey and Hodges 1983, 193–208.

Allan, J.P. 1984 *Medieval and post-medieval finds from Exeter 1971–80*. Exeter Archaeological Reports **3**.

Barton, K.J. 1963a The medieval pottery of the Saintonge. *Arch. J.* **120**, 201–14.

Barton, K.J. 1963b A medieval pottery kiln at Ham Green, Bristol. *Trans. Bristol & Gloucs. Arch. Soc.* **82**, 95–126.

Barton, K.J. 1965 Medieval pottery at Rouen. *Arch. J.* **122**, 73–85.

Bennett, I. (ed.) 1991 *Excavations 1990: Summary accounts of archaeological excavations in Ireland. Dublin*. Organisation of Irish Archaeologists / Wordwell.

Barber, J. 1984 Medieval wooden bowls. In D. Breeze (ed.), *Studies in Scottish antiquity presented to Stewart Cruden*, 125–47. Edinburgh. Donald.

Berry, H.F. 1890–91 The water supply of ancient Dublin. *J.R.S.A.I.* **21**, 557–73.

Biddle, M. and Smith, D. 1990 Mortars. In M. Biddle, *Object and economy in medieval Winchester*, vol. ii, 890–908. Winchester Studies 7ii: Artefacts from medieval Winchester. Oxford, Clarendon Press.

Bonde, N. and Crumlin-Pedersen, O. 1990 The dating of wreck 2 from Skuldelev, Denmark. *NewsWARP* **7**, 3–6. Exeter. Wetland Archaeology Research Project.

Brooks, E. St John (ed.) 1936 *Register of the hospital of St John the Baptist, Dublin*. Dublin. Irish Manuscripts Commission.

Buckley, A. 1988 Musical instruments from medieval Dublin: a preliminary survey. In E. Hickmann and D.W. Hughes (eds), *The archaeology of early music cultures: Third international meeting of the ICTM Study Group on Music Archaeology*. Bonn, published as *Orpheus* **51**.

Butler, V.G. 1984 *Cattle in thirteenth century Dublin: an osteological examination of its remains*. M.A. thesis submitted to the Department of Archaeology, University College Dublin, unpublished.

Christensen, A.-E. 1985 Boat finds from Bryggen. *Bryggen Papers* **1**, 47–280. Oslo University Press.

Christensen, A.-E. 1986 Tools used in shipbuilding in ancient and more modern times. In Crumlin-Pedersen and Vinner 1986, 150–9.

Clark, J. (ed.) 1995 *The medieval horse and its equipment c.1150–1450*. Museum of London, Medieval finds from excavations in London: 5. H.M.S.O.

Clarke, M.V. 1941 *Register of the priory of … Tristernagh*. Dublin. Irish Manuscripts Commission.

Crumlin-Pedersen, O. 1986a Aspects of Viking age shipbuilding. *Journal of Danish Archaeology* **5**, 209–28.

Crumlin-Pedersen, O. 1986b Aspects of wood technology in medieval shipbuilding. In Crumlin-Pedersen and Vinner 1986, 138–49.

Crumlin-Pedersen, O. and Vinner, M. (eds) 1986 *Sailing into the past*. Roskilde. The Viking Ship Museum.

Currie, C. 1990 Gazetteer of archaic roofs in Herefordshire and Worcestershire churches. *Vernacular Architecture* **21**, 18–23.

Curtis, E. 1934 Rental of the manor of Lisronagh, 1333, and notes on 'betagh' tenure in medieval Ireland. *P.R.I.A.* **43C**, 41–76.

Darrah R. 1982 Working unseasoned oak. In McGrail 1982, 219–30.

Davidson, B.K. 1972 Castle Neroche: an abandoned Norman fortress in south Somerset. *Proceedings of the Somerset Archaeological Society* **116**, 16–58.

De Courcy, J. 1984 Medieval banks of the Liffey estuary. In J. Bradley (ed.), *Viking Dublin exposed: The Wood Quay saga*, 164–6. Dublin. O'Brien Press.

Devoy, R. 1983 Late Quaternary shorelines in Ireland: an assessment of their implications for isostatic movement and relative sea-level changes. In Smith, D.E. and Dawson, A.G. (eds), *Shorelines and Isostasy*, 227–54. Institute of British Geographers Special Publication no. 16. London. Academic Press.

Devoy, R. 1990 Controls on coastal and sea-level changes and the application of archaeological-historical records to understanding recent patterns of sea-level movement. In S. McGrail (ed), *Maritime Celts, Frisians and Saxons*, 17–27. Council for British Archaeology Research Report **71**. Nottingham.

Devoy, R. 1991 *Sea level changes and Ireland.* Enfo Briefing Sheet 27, Dublin. The Environmental Information Service.

Donaghy, C. 1992 The small finds. Appendix 6 of M. Gowen (ed.), *Development at Christchurch Place – archaeology.* Preliminary post-excavation report submitted to the Office of Public Works, unpublished.

Dunlevy, M. A classification of early Irish combs. *P.R.I.A.* **88C**, 341–422.

Dunning, G.C. 1975 A ridge-tile crest from Lyveden, with notes on ridge-tiles with knife-cut crests in England and Wales. *Journal of the Northampton Museum and Art Gallery* **12**, 97–103.

Eames, E.S., and Fanning, T. 1988 *Irish medieval tiles.* Dublin. Royal Irish Academy Monographs in Archaeology 2.

Fulford, M.G., Rippon, S., Allen, J.R.L. and Hillam, J. 1992 The medieval quay at Woolaston Grange. *Trans. Bristol & Gloucs Arch. Soc.* **110**, 101–27.

Gahan, A. and McCutcheon, C. 1997 Medieval pottery. In M.F. Hurley, O.M.B. Scully and S.W.J. McCutcheon (eds), *Late Viking age and medieval Waterford: Excavations 1986–1992*, 285–336. Waterford. Waterford Corporation.

Gahan, A., McCutcheon, C. and Twohig, D.C. 1997 Medieval pottery. In R.M. Cleary, M.F. Hurley and E. Shee Twohig (eds), *Skiddy's castle and Christ Church, Cork: Excavations 1974–77 by D.C. Twohig*, 108–29. Cork. Cork Corporation.

Gale, S.J. and Hoare, P.G. 1991 *Quaternary sediments.* Belhaven Press.

Gilbert, J.T. 1854–59 *A history of the city of Dublin*, 3 vols. Dublin. McGlashan and Gill.

Gilbert, J.T. (ed.) 1889 *Calendar of ancient records of Dublin*, vol. i. Dublin. Joseph Dollard.

Goodburn, D. 1991 Waterlogged wood and timber as archives of ancient landscapes. In J. Coles and D. Goodburn (eds.), *Wet site excavation and survey*, 51–3. Exeter. Wetland Archaeology Research Project.

Goodburn, D. 1992 Woods and woodland: carpenters and carpentry. In Milne 1992, 106–30.

Goodburn, D. 1994 Trees underground: new insights into trees and woodmanship in south-east England *c.*AD 800–1300. *Bot. Jnl. Scotland* **46**, 658–62.

Harvey, J 1972 *Conservation of buildings.* London. J. Baker.

Hayden, A. 1991 9–12 Arran Quay, Dublin. In Bennett 1991, 27–8.

Hewett, C.A. 1980 *English historic carpentry.* London. Philimore.

Hurley, M. 1982 Wooden artefacts from the excavation of the medieval city of Cork. In Mc Grail 1982, 301–12.

Hurley, M.F. 1997a Artefacts of skeletal material. In M.F. Hurley, O.M.B. Scully and S.W.J. McCutcheon (eds), *Late Viking age and medieval Waterford: Excavations 1986–1992*, 650–99. Waterford Corporation.